SHORT STORIES TO ENJOY WITH WINE

VOLUME ONE

STEPHEN J. KRISTOF

Short Stories to Enjoy with Wine; Volume 1
© 2023, Stephen J. Kristof

All rights reserved. Published by Press Here Publishing. No part of this publication may be reproduced, distributed, or transmitted in any form or by any means, including photocopying, recording, or other electronic or mechanical methods, without the prior written permission of the author or publisher, except in the case of brief quotations embodied in a book review and certain other noncommercial uses permitted by copyright law.

This is a work of fiction. Names, characters, organizations, places, situations, events, incidents and stories are either products of the author's imagination or are used fictitiously. Any resemblance to actual persons, living or dead, or to actual events, incidents or situations is purely coincidental.

(This book is a collection of short stories written by the same author. This is the first volume in a series of books sharing the common title: Short Stories to Enjoy with Wine.)

VOLUME ONE; First Edition: April 2023

ISBN:
978-1-7387757-2-9 (Paperback)
978-1-7387757-3-6 (Hardcover)
978-1-7387757-4-3 (eBook)

Photo of wine glass on back cover by Michal Jarmoluk
Cover design by Stephen Kristof

Benjamin Franklin was right about many things. However, since this is not a political book, let's focus on one of the most irrefutable of his many quoted truths:

"Wine is constant proof that God loves us and loves to see us happy."

For my Wife and Daughter

Denise, thank you for supporting my various career adventures and enduring the stresses they occasionally produced during more than three decades of our marriage. I can only imagine how important wine must have been for you during those years as much-needed therapeutic relief.

Kara, thank you for putting-up with the dad jokes, and with my suffocating style of love and parenting for over two and a half decades of being my amazing daughter. Your enjoyment of the occasional glass of wine has been well-earned.

CONTENTS

PREFACE; **Author's Thoughts**	vii
TORRONTÉS; **Warm Memories of Baseball**	1
CAB. SAUVIGNON; **King of the Neighborhood**	19
CHARDONNAY; **A Familiar Face**	33
CHEAP BOXED WINE; **Disturbing Her Peace**	53
MERLOT; **The Mysterious Visitor**	71
TOURIGA NACIONAL; **The Long Wait**	93
TEMPRANILLO; **Double Vision**	127
PINOT GRIGIO; **Training the New Boss**	155
ZINFANDEL; **Settling for More**	169
PINOTAGE; **Shifting Character**	181
RIESLING; **The Sweet Spot**	219
SHIRAZ; **Identical Twins**	241
AMARONE; **Loving Deeply**	267
SANGIOVESE; **Believing in Someone**	277
SAUVIGNON BLANC; **She Said, He Said**	293
CABERNET FRANC; **Easily Overlooked**	327
PINOT NOIR; **A Distinguished Gentleman**	347

AUTHOR'S THOUGHTS...
WINE AND LITERATURE?

When I shared my next book idea with family, friends and acquaintances, most of them said, "Oooh! I *like* that idea!"

Many of them said that by pairing wine with this book, it would transform a guilty pleasure into a legitimate and even praiseworthy endeavor. *"Hmm," I thought, "that wasn't exactly what I had in mind!"*

I'm not entirely sure I buy that particular rationale. In fact, I don't think that enjoying wine needs *any* justification or excuse, as long as one avoids excess. Wine is, as Benjamin Franklin said, proof that God loves us and loves to see us happy!

As far as the literature aspect is concerned, the one thing I heard most often when I floated the idea for this book, was that the short story is the ultimate reading material to hold in one's hand as one cradles a glass of wine in the other. Short stories don't require the commitment it takes to read a standard novel; something that many find challenging, given our busy lives.

So, if you're the kind of person who enjoys drinking a glass or two of wine while digging into some juicy fiction, then it's really about *enjoying* the pleasurable experience that only the combination of wine and literature can deliver! (If you'd rather read, minus the wine and enjoy the vino after, that works too!)

The bottom line is that if you find wine interesting and enjoy drinking it, you'll like this book. If you like reading wide-ranging literature that doesn't take a huge commitment, you'll like this book. However, if both of those ideas check your boxes, you'll LOVE this book!

Now, understand, as the author of these short stories, I must admit that no wine passed through my lips while writing them. I simply don't have the constitution to maintain the clarity or endurance of thought that's required to write even *one* of these stories while enjoying *any* amount of wine. Heck, I personally couldn't even finish a single coherent paragraph while inebriated. I guess I'm a bit of a lightweight in that regard.

It's an interesting thought, I guess, to play the role of a celebrated and quirky writer who spins compelling yarns while getting sloshed. I have no idea how long that would last without the old liver giving out. Nonetheless, history is overflowing with chronically drunk writers who managed, somehow mysteriously, to turn-out collections of beautifully written and historically significant novels.

But, clearly, I'm not *that* writer! While I really like the feelings of clarity and sobriety, and need them to write, I *do* enjoy a glass of wine with dinner or while reading in the evening! Writing is one thing, but reading is quite another. I've found that a glass of wine can truly enhance the experience.

The short stories in this book are an even better match with good wine, because they are sometimes a bit exotic and deliciously unpredictable; sort of like a chef's entrée of the day!

Here's a suggestion. Go pour a glass of your favorite wine—really, any wine you have on hand will actually do—and start reading. Fantasy, steamy romance, mystery, heartwarming nostalgia, inspiration and uplifting tales await. Enjoy!

TORRONTÉS
WARM MEMORIES OF BASEBALL

Get ready for a profoundly heart-warming short story, but first, here's a little background on this story's Wine Mascot. If you enjoy white wine and are looking to expand your repertoire of South American "vino blanco" options, why not try Torrontes? It's a wine grape varietal that, although unfamiliar to most white wine palates outside of Argentina, has enough going for it to become far more popular.

The first and most important thing to know about Torrontes is something that hits you the moment you lift a glass of it to your nose...and then to your lips. It's like smelling and drinking fresh flowers. This floral profile might even seem quite intense the very first time you sip Torrontes. Mind you, it's not like someone tipped a basket of flowers over your head, but It *can* be quite surprising!

There are a few other white wine varietals that sometimes express a floral character. Muscat is one of them; it's an entirely different and mainly European grape varietal, but its floral nose and flavor aren't as noticeable as is usually found in Torrontes. Some producers of this underrated white wine are even able to extract a tantalizing jasmine essence from their grapes.

You would be hard pressed to find a Torrontes wine made anywhere other than Argentina. In fact, it's often difficult to find a single Argentinian example of it in most North American wine outlets. But it's definitely worth the search! *(Keep in mind that there is a lesser-known Spanish wine grape with the same name of Torrontes, but it is not the same varietal as the Argentinian one profiled here.)*

As it becomes more well-known globally, this unique and delicate wine is beginning to experience some traction in popularity. Along with its aforementioned floral notes, a well-made Torrontes wine also offers peach and, sometimes, lemon peel flavors. Although it's crisp and delicate, the wine has enough character to pair well with sharply flavored entrées.

Perhaps it's a coincidence that Amanda, the main character in our next short story, was recently in Mendoza, Argentina, where she tasted and consumed many different Torrontes wines, along with more than her share of legendary Argentinian beef steaks.

Amanda had recently returned from a business trip in Mendoza to her home in the sleepy and picturesque village of West Haverstraw, New York. While abroad in South America, she met with her new clients; a small group of business men and women who owned one of the country's largest wine production companies. They had recently acquired an old winery property in the Mendoza region and had plans to upgrade the entire facility, bringing the operation and its buildings up to modern day standards; that's where Amanda fits into the picture.

Many years earlier, Amanda followed in her father's footsteps and became an engineer. Just like him, she founded her own professional consultancy firm. But unlike his firm that served regional clients, Amanda's had a global reach. Due to her exceptional vision and talent, her client list was truly international. It was common for her to hop the globe from one fancy cosmopolitan job to the next, often not returning home for weeks on end.

Short Stories to Enjoy with Wine, Vol 1.

While on her latest trip, Amanda spent several meetings with her new client group. She also participated in tours of the newly acquired winery, as well as many other prominent wineries that the company had recently modernized. She studied existing structures and options for new construction, and took time to experience local culture, history and culinary offerings.

Back home, Amanda had already started her CAD drawings, trying out different options for the massive main winery building, and its separate production and bottling facility. She really wanted to make a splash, as this was her first winery job. She knew that a lot more of this type of work was hers for the taking; as long as this first one was as aesthetically spectacular and seamlessly functional as her imagination, talent and hard work could take her.

Feeling like her brain was about to fry, Amanda took a much-needed break and went through the mud room between the back landing and the garage. She knew that she needed to dig into plans for the winery's upscale restaurant and tasting bar, but first, had to clear her mind. Her garage—well, actually, her dad's garage—was her refuge. Just like her dad, Amanda loved hanging-out there, tinkering with one of her two cars or working on some sort of small hands-on project. It gave her a sense of peace and grounding that few other activities could match. This was partly because she always felt like her dad was with her whenever she was there.

It was a Saturday afternoon and the Yankees were playing a matinee home game against the Orioles. Amanda was looking forward to listening to the game while she putzed around. She walked over to her dad's AM transistor radio on the shelf next to a wall where tools hung from hooks on a pegboard. She mused momentarily about the fact that the outdated radio hadn't moved from that spot since she was a little girl.

Amanda pinched the volume button on the side of the radio with her forefinger and thumb, then turned it clockwise, as she had done hundreds, if not, thousands of times before. It clicked, crackled for a second, then came to life. The announcer's enthusiastic voice sounded tinny and flat as it blared through the tiny speaker. She realized she had missed almost the entire game.

"Bottom of the ninth, bases are loaded. Baltimore has the lead. The New York Yankees are behind by two, but are staring straight down the barrel of a win if their next batter can clinch the deal. Velaz steps up to the plate. Yankee's fans here at the stadium are EEElectric! The cheering is overwhelming...I don't know how he can focus...but focus, he must!"

Just as the batter was getting ready to take his first swing, the radio started making a whining sound and the channel began to wander, as would sometimes happen with those old devices. Amanda recalled the same thing happening when she was a child and her dad would listen to Yankees games while he worked on his own projects in that same garage.

The radio lost the baseball broadcast entirely and another neighboring radio station drifted in its place. Murphy's law was in charge! Instead of hearing what was arguably the most important play of the game, the intruding station was playing a rap song that was far from Amanda's personal choice of music. Despite being alone in that garage, Amanda shouted angrily, "Oh, give me a break! What timing!"

She sprung toward the radio to tune-in the original station, in the process, stepping on a wrench that slid—along with her entire body—across the oily cement floor. Amanda and her skateboard-style wrench came to a most ungracious and painful stop, crashing into an upright metal toolchest. The toolchest shuddered a bit and shrugged it off. Amanda, on the other hand, took the brunt of the collision and crumpled to the floor. In the process, she bounced her head off the car's front bumper.

A bit bloodied with bruises on the way, she was shaken-up, but, thank goodness, not seriously hurt. Although she didn't make it to the radio, the tremor from Amanda's collision somehow bumped the radio just enough to knock its tuner back to the ballgame. It was just in time to hear...

"Steer-rike thr--eee and he's out! Awww! They blew it! The New York Yankees had the game handed to them on a silver platter and they just handed it back to the Orioles. Such disappointment for the team and for their fans." The radio announcer went on, painting a vivid picture of the storm of empty beer cups, hotdog wrappers and other debris that were raining onto the field.

"Dammit! Go and destroy my body just in time to hear that pathetic loss?!" Amanda was talking as if someone else were in the garage listening to her. She had a habit of doing that. None of her friends or coworkers thought it was strange; it was just her.

She hobbled back to the old wood and leather office chair; a chair that was strangely out of place in the garage. Because it had been in the garage forever, though, it seemed to belong. That chair wore its original upholstery proudly, even though it, like the radio, was dreadfully outdated. Its green leather was worn to a tatter in some places, yet was still glossy and supple in others. At some point a very long time ago, her dad had screwed oversized industrial castors to the bottom of each of the chair's legs, so that he could easily glide from the desk to the toolchest and back.

When she was younger, Amanda loved running toward the old chair and jumping on it at breakneck speed, which resulted in the most fantastic ride, careening across the garage floor, spinning around and streaking like greased lightning! It was a source of sheer delight, except for the times Amanda slammed against the inside of the garage door or into the tool chest. But even when she did, she shook it off and jumped back on. For her, it was her own no-limit, no-ticket amusement park ride!

Amanda sat on the chair but was too sore and too grown-up to ride it. She thought about all the times in her youth when she rode the chair endlessly, but feeling so physically sore from her collision a few minutes earlier, she was no longer enamored with the idea. She pulled herself up to the old office desk. It had become a junk-collecting shelf for a bunch of unconnected items that she couldn't bring herself to throw away, but which she also had no place to store. She looked at the desk and felt a bit guilty about the mess.

While she may have perceived the emotion as guilt, it was actually displaced grief. After a few minutes, that grief bubbled through to her consciousness. She thought about her dad and how terribly she missed him. She was only eighteen years old when Bill died. She had barely finished high school and was looking forward to spending an entire summer with him before she moved away for college.

Bill lived and worked for the summer; it was the only season that really mattered to him. Although he kept in touch with the office and with key clientele, when those lazy, hazy summer days came around, Bill spent far more time with the kids and his wife, Mary, than he did with work. He took advantage of the fact that summer was a slow time in his profession; that meant squeezing every drop of summer that he could.

Amanda sat at the desk, daydreaming wistfully about camping, fishing, playing baseball, watching baseball and spending days at the beach with her dad. Really, doing *anything* with her dad. She looked around that old garage and had a flashback. There he was, tinkering with his car and asking her to pass him a tool or a towel. A Yankee's game was playing on that same old radio.

Bill was a far better engineer than he was an auto mechanic. He never really accomplished much more than oil changes and brake jobs, and wasn't particularly good at either of those tasks. But he enjoyed the hands-on nature of working on his car, so it was therapeutic for him. That was before the time when anyone considered a pastime to be therapeutic.

Amanda had a terrible time coming to terms with her dad's passing. Being so close to him and still in her teens, she leaned on her mom for as much comfort, reassurance and love as she could squeeze from her. Mary provided just that and did so in droves. However, Amanda only got to enjoy that time with her mom for five more years before she was diagnosed with early-onset dementia. Nine heartbreaking years later, when Amanda was thirty-two, Mary succumbed to the disease.

Mary's initial diagnosis happened at a time in Amanda's life that didn't offer much wiggle room for her to be the devoted daughter that she really wanted to be. Although she had already finished her Bachelor's degree, Amanda was in the thick of her compulsory internship with a large engineering firm just north of Tribeca in New York City. It was exciting and stressful at the same time, but Amanda was filled with doubt and insecurity for most of those four years. At times, she felt like a robot, putting-in time until she could write her board exams; all the while knowing that the mom she knew and loved was slipping further away with each passing day.

Mary's brother, Robert, filled-in the gaps left by Amanda's absence as much as possible, despite the obligations of his own demanding career. Being four years older than she, he was more established in his vocation, which meant that he was more available.

Fortunately, Bill's life insurance policy provided a generous safety net that made Mary's round-the-clock care possible. Although she continued to decline, she was at least able to live out her final years in the comfort of her own home.

During that time, Amanda tried to visit and support her mom, but she was pulled in so many directions. After finishing her internship, Amanda worked for a much smaller but far more prominent New York City engineering firm where she made quite a name for herself. Not long after that, Amanda hung out her shingle and launched her own prosperous practice.

A few years into managing her business, Amanda was ready to build her dream home, but was stuck on where exactly to build it. She also had no time to devote to what would be an intensive search for suitable property in what was an already overpriced market. The whole idea would have to wait.

When Mary's journey came to an end, Amanda and Robert shared responsibilities as co-executors of Mary's estate. Her biggest asset was her house, so the two children had to make some decisions. After quite a bit of soul-searching, Amanda decided that she wanted to spend some time living at her old home while she sorted-out some things. She paid Robert half of the property's appraised value, but added an additional one-hundred-thousand dollars to that sum, wanting to make sure that Robert got more than his fair share of the inheritance. He begrudgingly accepted the extra funds simply to stop Amanda's incessant insistence that he accept the money.

Deep in her soul, Amanda was not ready to let go of her childhood home. Her upscale condo in Manhattan's Upper West Side had a magnificent view, all the amenities she had ever wanted in a home and was a mere twenty-minute walk up Amsterdam Avenue to her office. Yet, the excitement that she once felt living in the heart of the city had become frenetic and taxing.

She felt relief and immeasurable comfort moving back to West Haverstraw. However, after a few months commuting between the small town and New York City, heavy traffic and excessive time on the road began to wear on her.

The more she thought about it, what initially seemed like a crackpot idea started to sound like quite a sane solution. Amanda moved her firm to an office building in Haverstraw and gave her employees the option of commuting, moving or working remotely.

Life had to make sense to Amanda. Especially when it didn't, if that makes any sense. Some people have no problem plodding along and ignoring the cacophony of disjointed fragments that sometimes come from all directions; fragments that call into question our very existence. For them, life doesn't need to make sense. They just do what they have to—what they *need* to—and they move on without putting much thought into it.

Not Amanda. Those fragments absolutely had to fit together. Like a 3-D jigsaw puzzle, the different pieces of her life had to have a top, a bottom, bounding sides, a beginning, an end and an overall meaning; otherwise, it was chaos for her. This is a window into why Amanda was drawn to her chosen profession. Engineers tend to share a preoccupation with order, precision, connectivity and bounded creativity. And safety. Don't forget the safety!

For Amanda, calmness came from being back in her childhood home. She could control things like order, precision and so-on. More importantly, it felt to her like the safest place in the world at that particular point in her journey of life.

As she sat on that old leather rolling chair in the garage, Amanda watched as her father tinkered with the car. He spun around and faced her, handing her a tool and asking for another. Whether it was what she *wanted* to see or it was a surfacing fragment of her memory didn't matter. He looked so real, so handsome, so reassuring. He smiled at her; his eyes were so bright and his smile filled her with warmth.

Her beautiful vision was interrupted by the depth of her emotion; she was overwhelmed. She became aware, for the first time, that she had never really gotten over her dad's death. She was a trooper when it came to going through the motions, but was only living her life partially; robotically. She hadn't fully allowed herself to experience a full range of emotions for the longest time.

She felt crushed and exhausted, and suddenly realized that she had felt this way for many years. Pushing forward, glossing-over losses and disappointments repeatedly by ignoring them, never allowing herself to be happy with her own accomplishments or to feel the joy of her relationships; it had become her blueprint for life. She had simply replaced it all with work.

At such a young age, Amanda had already achieved a degree of success in her career that most people could only imagine. It was remarkable enough that, at just thirty-two, she was the owner of a prestigious New York-based engineering firm with high-profile international clientele. Being recognized as one of the world's top professionals among her peers was even more mind-blowing.

However, while others admired her hard work and prestige—many actually idolized her—she wouldn't allow herself to derive any pleasure from it. Far from being humble, she just wasn't prepared to be joyful.

In a sense she was right. She had learned way back in high school that if all one focuses on is chasing the dream or the end result, the satisfaction is merely fleeting. She had gone through years during which all that mattered was winning top marks in her exams and classes. Her dad helped her to see that the journey is even more important than the destination. He helped her understand that the emotional reward of winning lasts for a mere fraction of the time it took to get there and then it's gone; gone until the short-lived reward that's waiting at the end of the next big challenge.

The problem was, as an adult who was well into her magnificent career, she wasn't enjoying the journey either. Sitting in her dad's old garage, searching her heart for some shred of reassurance, she realized that it wasn't just her career. She wasn't enjoying her journey of life either.

Amanda wasn't sure exactly how long she sat at the desk in the garage, thinking about life, but it didn't matter. She couldn't stop thinking about her dad and how much he meant to her. She loved and missed her mom very deeply, but at this particular moment, it was all about her dad.

She had a nagging feeling that he was trying to tell her something. She fiddled around and rearranged the various items on the desk. She made a little bit of room by throwing away a few things that she finally admitted to herself were useless and then continued to move the other stuff from side-to-side. As she repeatedly repositioned the items, she realized she must have looked a bit like a street-corner con-artist shuffling metal cups on a wooden box. The result was the same; moving the items on the desk was nothing more than slight-of-hand distraction.

Amanda's eyes welled-up and she prayed for clarity. Prayer was something she hadn't done in a very long time. She remembered how her dad would give her advice without being preachy. A teardrop trickled onto the desk as she recalled the way he would metaphorically tie wise bits of life advice to rather unlikely things such as threading a worm onto a hook or pulling a bike chain back onto the sprockets.

Where was he, now that she needed him and his words of wisdom so profoundly? It was so unfair, she thought! She needed him when her mom got sick and when she struggled to achieve her career dream. She had to do it all by herself and began to curse whatever or whoever took him from her.

She felt short-changed; not only because he was gone for so long, but also because of the way she had chosen to prevent herself from feeling things for so many years. This only made her question other decisions she had made. The trickle of Amanda's tears became a torrent as she grappled with her thoughts, memories and emotions.

Amanda reached to grab a tissue from the middle drawer on the right side of the desk. Naturally, she stored a box of tissues there because her dad always kept one in the same place. She grabbed the box and, in her emotional state, dropped it onto the floor.

Like a row of dominoes, one event led to another. The box tumbled just out of reach, so she contorted her body to retrieve it.

Looking somewhat like a human pretzel, she managed to get it, but then smacked her knee against the bottom of the open drawer. That, in turn, caused the drawer to slide completely out of its track and crash to the floor.

Amanda rolled the chair backward and grabbed the drawer with both hands. She was about to slide it back into its guides when she noticed that a small envelope was stuck in a tiny slit between the bottom of the drawer and its wooden back piece. She pinched the envelope and plucked it out of its resting place.

The envelope looked like it had been there for ages. It was covered in years of dust and pencil shavings that had escaped the drawer above it. She took a deep breath and blew it all away.

Her breath caused the dust to whoosh, forming a little plume of whirling speckles that glimmered in the shaft of light coming through the garage window. As much as she wanted to open the envelope, she found herself momentarily captivated by the beauty of the twinkling dust. She marveled at its magical appearance; it looked as though someone had thrust a handful of fairy dust into the air around her.

The sealed side of the envelope faced her. Amanda turned it over to reveal three characters hand-written in pen. It was, unmistakably, her dad's writing; an attractive, precise and measured style of penmanship. The letters "A G P" appeared to her as if they were glowing. They were her own initials; Amanda Grace Parker.

In that moment, she wasn't thinking about the coincidental timing of finding the letter or about how greatly she had just been missing his advice. She just wanted to find out what the envelope held; it was, after all, something that her dad had prepared especially for her.

Amanda took a snap-off knife from the top drawer and slid its sharp edge in-between the envelope's two sides to create a new opening. She was extra careful to avoid damaging whatever was inside.

She gently blew into the slit and peeked inside. She pulled out a piece of cottony paper and unfolded it, revealing a note from her dad.

> *"Dear Amanda, I don't know when you'll read this letter or if you'll even find it, but I realized something today which compelled me to write it.*
>
> *As I sit at this old desk in our garage, looking at the various tools and fixtures, I can't help but see you in here with me, helping with my inept attempts at car repair, spinning in the old green chair or just hanging out with me! I can't begin to tell you how much it warms my heart to see you in my memories, always by my side as we go about our summer adventures.*
>
> *With Bobby being older than you, his life has changed, as it should, and he's not been as available as he once was. Bobby knows that I love him beyond words, and we have a very close and rewarding father-son relationship.*
>
> *But, Amanda, you and I have always had a different sort of connection that is so very special in its own way! I've always known that you cherish our time together regardless of what we're doing; even if it's nothing in particular. I hope you realize that the feeling is absolutely mutual! The time we've spent together over the years is one of the most valuable gifts in my life!*
>
> *As I write this, you are fourteen years old; hardly into your teenage years and just beginning to dream about what your future may hold. Perhaps you will find this letter before you even decide on a career. Or, maybe, you've happened upon it*

years after you're well along your path. Who and what will you eventually become? Will I be there to watch you grow into the beautiful, intelligent and caring woman that I know you will be?

It's impossible for any of us to know what the future holds, but what occurred to me today is that some of us never get the chance to say the things that could be very helpful to the people who mean the most to us. How many people lose their parents well before they could be of immeasurable help years down the road; when they have to weather one of life's storms and could really use that help?

In that vein, I don't know what my own future holds. While I pray that I'm here for you for many decades to come, there are no guarantees. This has been nagging me today; what if you really need me at some point, but I'm no longer there for you?

I don't know why, but I have a feeling that this old desk will stay with our family for many years to come. I know that it looks like it's ready to haul away, but did you know that my grandpa's dad passed it along to him and he passed it on to me? Apparently, it's been in our family for many generations...at some point it was actually in a proper office!

Well, I've purposely tucked this letter at the back of the tissue drawer. It's kind of like insurance, in case a day comes that if I'm not able to comfort, guide and prop you up when you most need me. If this comes to pass, I hope you will find this letter when you're emotionally burdened and reach for a tissue to dry your eyes."

Amanda took a deep breath and tried to digest the enormity of the letter. When she reached for a tissue before finding the envelope, her tears were bitter and troubled. After reading the first part of her dad's letter, she was crying even more profusely, but her tears had mellowed and were comforting. In the past, no matter how much she tried, whenever she thought about him, Amanda was unable to hear her dad's voice. However, this time, as she read his letter, she could hear him talking to her! She grabbed another tissue and continued reading.

"So, Amanda, if something's bothering you, maybe I can still help. Just off the top of my head, here are a few truths that have carried me through more than my fair share of trouble! First, always remember that life is only a passage.

Whatever is troubling you, put it in perspective. We're here for a short time. Each of us has been given different talents and the end goal, ultimately, is to use those talents to make a positive difference in other people's lives. Troubles come and go, but our lives are much more than them!

Second, whatever your struggle is, focus on your faith. I'm not an overly religious person, but I hope I've been a role model of faith for you. I've learned that during the toughest times, everyone's faith is shaken; it's happened to me many times. Don't get bogged down by that. It's not your fault! If you feel like your faith is gone, invite it back into your life. Neglecting prayer starves faith. Prayer feeds faith!

Third, if you realize you've made mistakes in your life, even really big ones, join the crowd! I've always told you that callouses grow character. Well, that extends to making mistakes! Making mistakes and learning from them makes us better people. They allow us to grow and it's never too late to make changes. God already forgave you, so don't waste time punishing yourself. If your personal map pointed you in the wrong direction, re-draw that map and follow it with the deep passion I've seen in your spirit!

Fourth and most important, love yourself! I know you so well, Amanda; you are an exceptionally beautiful person, inside and out! You deserve the love of others and of yourself! Accept yourself for who you are; a perfectly imperfect person who is magnificently lovable!

Amanda, life may not always go your way or the way you expected, but that's normal. It would be quite strange otherwise! Put things in perspective, lean on God, re-draw your map every once in a while, and love who you are!

I hope, Amanda, that you can hear my voice as you read my words. I will always want the very best for you, whether you're twelve or ninety-two! There will be times when life is far from easy, but I hope that my advice is at least somewhat helpful as you navigate those difficult times.

I pray that you will be able to feel my warm embrace right now and any other time you need it. I'm sending my love and my hugs with all my might, sweetheart, to be held in trust for you whenever you need to feel my presence.

Brighter days are ahead, my sweet girl!

Oh, and one more thing...Go Yankee's!!

Love Always,
Dad
XOXO"

The letter left her feeling incredibly bittersweet. No matter how hard she tried, she couldn't ebb the flow of her tears. But she *did* feel her dad's presence. His warm bearhug was every bit as real and as present as every other sensation in her body!

Amanda's dad was once more in the garage working on his car. In a way, it was like she saw him earlier. This time, though, it was different. He was there. It was no longer merely a fabrication of her memory. He turned to look at her and smiled ever so tenderly and then slowly vanished.

"Hope"

The word popped into Amanda's head. Her heart was suddenly overflowing with hope. Her life no longer felt shallow and meaningless. By avoiding emotions and ignoring the journey, Amanda had created a void in her spirit. That void was, in an instant, overflowing with love. She somehow knew that any emptiness that remained was merely waiting for her to fill as she started living life fully once again. Amanda also sensed the warmth and light of faith re-entering her heart.

She decided to renew her priorities and redraw her map. The first thing on her list was to place a phone call to her brother. Just to say "Hi," and just to reminisce and talk about dad.

"Hey Bobby, how are you? I was just sitting here at Dad's old desk. I was thinking about the two of us and those amazing summers we spent together..."

Stephen J. Kristof

Cabernet Sauvignon
King of the Neighborhood

Cabernet Sauvignon is often referred to as the king of red wines. As a grape, it has nobility and pedigree. It's hard to argue otherwise. It is one of the most famous, sophisticated and age-worthy varietals in the wine-making world. In fact, many of the most expensive red wines presently and throughout history boast Cabernet Sauvignon as the principal or singular grape variety.

From first-growth French chateaux producing historically significant Bordeaux to esteemed new world wineries in California's Napa Valley and almost everywhere else in the winemaking world, Cabernet Sauvignon often plays an indisputably regal role. The varietal has a broad range of flavors and aromas, but it is almost always known for deep dark fruit flavors, full body and firm tannins. It is also known for its ability to give wine ageing potential.

Cabernet Sauvignon plays a pivotal, even, regal role in the in the world of wine. Some people also play a pivotal role in their own particular setting; a role that, whether they realize it or not, has a royal aura.

The summer of 1968 was a terrible one for French Bordeaux. The dismal growing season, combined with too much rain in

August ruined the Cabernet Sauvignon crop. Not good for wine fans. On the other hand, the summer of '68 was a good thing for fans of the Detroit Tigers, because it led to the Tigers winning the World Series. But for Brody, a nine-year-old boy growing up near Detroit, neither one of those things was as important as the summer itself.

Summer had just begun. It was officially only two days old, meaning that Brody had an entire two months to explore, play, fish, do pick-up sports, blow up small things with firecrackers, daydream and do whatever else nine-year-old boys did back then in the summer.

It was Monday morning, around nine o'clock. No sleeping-in at Brody's house. Mom made sure that the kids were, as she said, "Up and at 'em," early in the morning, so as not to waste the day. Truth be told, she also wanted to get the kids out of the house as soon as possible so that she could go about her own routine unencumbered.

Spending the day inside was just not an option, unless of course, the weather was too wet or dangerous to be outside. Living your summer outdoors for a little kid in the late sixties wasn't so bad. In fact, it was an awesome way to grow up.

As far as the Detroit thing, the race riots that occurred in the summer of 1967 put a scare into the region; a scare that reverberated throughout the nation and lasted for years. However, Brody lived in a town that somebody on a stage once referred to as South Detroit. Now, outside of some mysterious lyrical world, South Detroit does not actually exist on any map.

However, several suburbs and small cities in southern Michigan, and even some Canadian border cities really *do* exist south of Detroit. Brody hailed from one of those towns. It was close enough to Detroit to put parents on edge, but far enough away from the city to prevent them from disallowing their kids to play outside.

Mainly, Brody grew up in a time when kids got to be kids. After all, kids not only *got* to be kids, they also *learned* to be kids. On their own. And with friends. And with minor enemies. But the key was that they learned how to be alone and to like it; how to be their own person. They also learned how to get along with others and to like that too.

It's actually too bad that many of today's *"adults"* never learned both of these things.

There wasn't much going on in Brody's average middle-class neighborhood at eight in the morning. As he sat on his front porch steps watching nothing happening, his eye caught a lonely firefly walking with difficulty beside him. He thought it must have been a leftover from the night before. Brody gently picked-up the bug and rolled it over in the palm of his hand. Its bum wasn't glowing anymore and it wasn't very responsive. He attributed its sluggishness to a lack of sleep.

Brody reasoned that the firefly worked overtime the night before trying to light-up the yard and flew around well past its bedtime. In his vivid imagination, Brody could actually see the bug falling asleep on the porch, while all of his friends flew home to wherever it is that fireflies sleep at night.

He carried the bug, ever so carefully, to a comfy little patch of mulch hidden under a shrub in the front landscape. Brody placed it on the soft mulch and then ran inside.

"Mom, can you please get me a piece of toilet paper?"

"Sure Brody! May I ask what you're planning to do with it?"

"Ah, it's just for a firefly. It didn't make it home last night, so I'm making a temporary bed for it."

Brody's mom, Elizabeth, promptly tore-off a single sheet of toilet tissue and brought it to her son with a smile. "Here you go. I hope that firefly appreciates how much you're helping it!"

"Yah, I'll take care of that little guy."

Brody flew down the front porch steps as if he had a super power. He was relieved to find that the bug decided to wait for him. He tore a smaller square out of the tissue and used it to cover the bug like a blanket. Brody liked his own bedsheets to be tucked under his mattress, which made him feel safe and secure as he slept. He figured that his little friend would like the same thing.

He searched for the perfect tiny chunks of gravel and stone, and found nine of them. He used them to secure the tissue on three sides, leaving the top open for the firefly's head to peek out.

Brody had already completed the first of many little adventures that he would have through the day and it was only ten after nine.

Fp, fp, fp, fp, fp, fp... The rhythmic sound caught Brody's ear. Whatever was making the sound became louder and faster as it got closer. A few seconds later, it sort of sounded like a motorcycle. Jeffery Stewart raced by on his new ten-speed bike. Fp, fp, fp, fp, fp, fp... Brody wondered how his bicycle was making that sound.

Jeffery had been in Brody's class that year and he wasn't Brody's first choice to play with. He lived with his grandparents just down the street from Brody, but he was new to the city. Word in the neighborhood was that Jeffery's parents had split-up at the end of the previous summer and each of them relocated to different states that were about as far from one another as possible.

Jeffery, their only child, ended-up living with his mom's parents, who were more than willing to raise the boy. Unfortunately, they were also far too old to be doing this once again in their lives; particularly with a boy who was proving to be as much work as Jeffery was.

Rumors grew as the school year progressed, likely fueled by the mystery of Jeffrey's relocation and, more so, by the cruel imagination of some children. Brody had heard that Jeffery's dad killed his mom and then escaped on a boat to China, where he continued to hide while tending to rice paddies. Brody never really believed the rumor and avoided broaching the subject of Jeffery's parents when he was with him, but he often wondered what the real story was.

Jeffery circled around on his bike, proceeding up Brody's driveway. As his bike slowed-down, the sound changed from a motorcycle to a slow flapping noise. Brody ran over to see what it was. Clearly, this was a very important moment! It was the beginning of a trend. Within days, every boy and girl in the neighborhood would be pinning baseball cards, hockey cards or playing cards to their bicycle frames to make this sound as the cards flapped against the spokes.

Kids started doing this in back in the 1950s, but the practice went through cycles and continued to resurface from time-to-time in different areas as something new again. After bragging about his new bike and his even newer invention, Jeffery popped a wheelie as he took off down the street.

Yes, he did tell Brody that the card trick was his own personal invention. Brody knew him too well to believe that nonsense.

Brody raced into his house and went straight to his bedroom closet. He pulled-out an old wooden cigar box from the top shelf. The box had warnings on it written in marker, along with the words, "Private - Brody's Property" and crude illustrations of skulls and crossbones.

He placed the cigar box on his bedspread. It still had the pungent scent of cedar that mingled with the sweet, woody bouquet of unlit cigars, which intensified when it was opened. Brody lifted the top, revealing an eclectic collection of flattened pennies from the railroad tracks, baseball cards, ladyfinger firecrackers, a bigger-than-your-mouth gumball, a fake mustache, a few large cats-eye marbles and genuine x-ray glasses. There was also a working miniature spy camera loaded with real tiny film that he ordered from an ad in the back pages of a kid's cartoon magazine.

He pulled out a random baseball card which happened to feature Mickey Lolich. It was at the top of the cigar box, because he got it a few days earlier in a pack of gum. Years later, Brody would regret using that particular card. Lolich played a pivotal part in winning the world series that year, so the card would fetch a tidy sum if sold. Unfortunately, a tattered, half-ripped, spoke eaten card wouldn't be worth listing.

"Mom, can you get me a clothespin?"

"Actually, you can get it, honey. There are some older ones in a bucket in the garage. I use them when I hang-up laundry in the backyard, so don't take any more than one or two."

"Thanks Mom! I'm taking my bike out. I'll see you later."

"Okay Brody. Have fun and be safe. Remember to stay in the boundaries."

Brody's boundaries were pretty liberal; especially compared to today's helicopter-style parenting. Brody had to stay within an area bounded by eight blocks to the east or west and four blocks to the north or south. Even though the punishment or consequence of breaking that boundary was never discussed, Brody never did venture beyond that boundary. Then again, why would he? Virtually everyone and anything he would like to see or do was inside the boundary.

In the blink of an eye, Brody had clipped the Lolich card to the bicycle's frame on the fork that held the front tire in place. He took it for a spin in front of his house and determined that, while it sounded cool, it didn't sound anything like a motorcycle.

Brody played with the positioning of the card and, after about ten minutes, got exactly the sound he wanted. Now that the bike sounded like a motorcycle when he went fast, he was ready to belt it out on every road and alley within his boundary.

By noon, Brody had hung-out with four different friends from his own school and two other friends who went to the other school in his neighbourhood; the Catholic school. Nothing had been planned, but that was the fun of it. Brody simply rode around and wherever he saw a friend, he simply joined them and did "stuff" for a while, before getting back on his bike and going elsewhere.

Three of his friends wanted to get their own bicycles to make motorcycle sounds, so Brody helped each of them with the task. Unlike Jeffery, Brody didn't take credit for inventing the new sensation, but he also made a point of not mentioning that he got the idea from Jeffery.

After a busy morning helping with spoke cards, playing hide-and-go-seek, having a two-person football scrimmage and playing kick-ball, Brody decided to go to Tommy's house. Tommy wasn't Brody's best friend, but was one of his good friends. In actuality, Brody didn't regard any of his friends as a "best friend," but he had a lot of close friends in the neighborhood. Some of those friends believed that they and Brody were best friends; a notion to which Brody was oblivious.

You see, Brody never felt the need to have a singular best friend. He had so many friends that it never occurred to him that he was expected to have some sort of unique or special relationship with just one of them. He didn't feel that as an expectation and, interestingly, it worked out well for him.

As a kid, Brody had already established that he was his own person. He wasn't a loner, but he had no problem spending hours on his own, finding something captivating to do and being in charge of his own time.

To his many friends, Brody was seen as a leader. He could always get something interesting going, even when his friends couldn't find anything at all to do. He was really good at bringing others together for a group sport or activity. He would also often step-in when there was an argument and before long, whatever the argument was about was history.

In short, Brody was admired by his friends, who generally regarded him with a sense of nobility. There was just something special about him that nobody could ever put a finger on, but it was definitely there. He had something unique; something that defined him as being singular.

Brody never sensed any of this. When it came down to it, he didn't have a care about what anyone else thought about him. He didn't see himself as anyone special or unique; he was just himself.

On the way to Tommy's house, Brody rode past a few girls from his class, who were playing with something on a beach blanket on the front lawn. The girls sang out with loud, sugary voices in unison, "Hiiii Brodyyy!"

Although he hadn't a clue, the girls were very much members of Brody's fan club. He stopped, leaned his bike on the grass and walked over to see what they were doing. Trying hard not to insult their choice of toys, he simply said, "Hi Kim. Hi Cheryl. Cool! Barbies and troll dolls. What are you doing anyway?"

The girls were so smitten they didn't hear a word. They just giggled and made silly faces, which didn't make any sense to Brody. He got back on his bicycle and as he drove away, yelled above the card clatter, "Bye girls! See ya later."

Brody didn't care much for girls yet. He was past the cootie stage, but he realized that girls weren't interested in the same things as he was and, to be honest, there was always a more interesting guy to hang around with.

When he finally got to Tommy's house, he knocked on the closed wood frame side door and hollered at the top of his lungs, "TOMMMMYYY! IS TOMMY HOME? CAN TOMMY COME OUT TO PLAY?"

Brody always thought that Tommy's family, the Campbell's, were nice people. Tommy's mom and dad were a lot like Brody's parents, and their family seemed to get along well, just like his own.

The Campbell's were very much like Brody's; they were genuine, compassionate, decent people who didn't try to seem like people they weren't.

The door opened with a squeak. Tommy's mom greeted Brody with a warm smile. She was genuinely happy to see him and loved that he and her son were friends.

Patti Campbell was a stay-at-home mom, just like most of Brody's friends' moms. She looked far younger than her thirty-one years. Her short pixie haircut played a part in her youthful appearance, as did the fact that she never wore makeup.

She said, with her typically bouncy and uplifting voice, "Brody, so good so see you!"

"Hi, Mrs. Campbell. Can Tommy come out and play?"

"Tommy's up in his bedroom. He fell into the creek in the park and came home covered in stinky mud! Can you believe that?"

"Oh, I can believe it, Mrs. Campbell...and I say, Yuck!" he replied.

"Yes, yuck is right. Anyway, he just took a shower and is changing. He'll be down in a few minutes. Why don't you come inside and wait for him?"

"Sure! Thanks, Mrs. Campbell."

As Brody entered the home, he immediately smelled the familiar aroma of homemade macaroni and cheese. Like Pavlov's dog's conditioned response to a bell, the sharp whiff of baked cheddar cheese and buttered breadcrumbs made his stomach rumble.

But there was something else that didn't quite fit. Brody couldn't quite make it out; it almost smelled to him a bit like the Lake Erie shore, where he'd sometimes spend an afternoon trying to catch a perch or sunfish.

"Brody, I've just made macaroni and cheese and fish sticks for lunch. Are you hungry? You can eat lunch with Tommy when he comes down, if you'd like."

"Fish sticks?" Brody thought. "Ohhh, that must be that other smell. Grrross! But I like the mac and cheese part." Of course, he would never verbalize such rude thoughts. Despite what he thought about the fish, he was a well-mannered young man.

After considering it for a bit, he blurted out, "Umm, yes. Thank you, Mrs. Campbell." Brody smiled; his head bobbed in agreement.

He added, "I've never had fish sticks before! I don't know if I'll like 'em, but I'll try 'em. Either way, I like mac and cheese for sure."

Brody's parents taught him things like respect for elders, being polite, proper etiquette and so-on. He didn't want to sound impolite, but he also wanted to make sure that Tommy's mom wasn't offended in the event that the fish was not to his liking.

Brody found out that he did, indeed, like fish. Well, to be more accurate, he found out that he liked greasy, overly battered, minced, something-like-fish sticks. Despite being a picky eater at home, where his mom routinely treated the family to five-star gourmet meals, Brody devoured everything on his plate.

Ironically, although Tommy usually had a healthy appetite, he spit out a tiny flake of the fish stick after merely touching it to his tongue and only picked at the mac and cheese.

With lunch out of the way, Brody and Tommy hopped on their bikes and rode to the corner convenience store, where they each purchased a small but fully loaded paper bag of mixed candies for the incredibly affordable price of thirty-five cents. Their next stop was the creek that ran through the park. Tommy wanted to show Brody where he fell in earlier that morning.

Somebody had constructed a makeshift bridge over the creek by nailing some scrap construction lumber to a few saplings that were, regrettably, uprooted well before they had a chance to grow into trees. It wasn't sturdy enough to hold a skinny nine-year-old boy, let alone two of them. Nevertheless, the two boys were determined to give it another try.

The wobbly wooden bridge, if you could call it a bridge, had crashed onto one of the dry sides of the creek when Tommy unceremoniously fell into the water. They mustered all of their nine-year-old strength and managed to pull the span up to level ground. From there, they twisted and levered this unruly jumble of wood and, in the process, discovered how a fulcrum works.

Once they got the bridge back into place, they couldn't wait to try it out! Now, keep in mind that there was a proper, professionally installed metal bridge with a solid wood plank deck about a hundred yards down the creek. However, it's very hard for any nine-year-old boy to resist the temptation of trying out a homemade bridge rather than using the obviously safer span!

Somewhat miraculously, Brody and Tommy made it over the water without falling in or injuring themselves in any way. Even if they had fallen in, it wasn't a long drop at all. Maybe about three feet at the deepest part. But the creek was disgusting. It consisted less of water and more of a putrid mix of slimy mud, green algae and garbage. Oh, and the occasional mudpuppy as swell; a scary looking salamander that seemed entirely out of place near Detroit.

Tommy waited until after Brody crossed the bridge, being that his confidence took a little hit earlier that day. Once Brody cleared it, Tommy nervously took his turn.

With his arms straightened and raised at his sides, Tommy took tiny exaggerated tip-toe steps and wobbled as he did so. Brody looked back at him from the other side. His eyes grew wide and a huge smirk unfurled across his face; he laughed uncontrollably. In

Brody's mind, Tommy looked like an awkward cartoon flamingo pretending to be a ballerina!

As Tommy's right foot touched the ground, the makeshift bridge tipped, fell into the creek and broke into pieces. Tommy pushed forward with all his might and, this time, avoided tumbling in.

If Brody were to have a best friend, Tommy would have been the obvious option. The two of them always got along together like lifelong friends, but Brody just wasn't wired that way. As far as Tommy was concerned, Brody *was* his best friend. As for Brody, he just didn't overthink it.

Brody possessed three characteristics that exceeded his years. The first one was his integrity. Brody's integrity existed partially through osmosis based on his parents' excellent parenting, but it was also an inborn characteristic. Sort of like the way he never betrayed his parents' trust on the boundary issue; it would simply never occur to Brody to be dishonest or disobedient. It wasn't in his genetic makeup.

The second older-than-he trait that Brody possessed was his sense of humility. It was partly responsible for his ability to lead others; the fact that he didn't feel any more special or favored than anyone else, ironically, made others feel that he was, in fact, special and singular.

Thirdly, Brody was far older than his chronological age in terms of his self-assuredness. As a result, he was able to more fully experience and enjoy the intensity of every moment of his young life. He wasn't distracted with trying to impress others; their opinion of him was completely irrelevant. He was a very little man, of course, but he was his own little man!

As for his very full day of playing, exploring and doing nine-year-old stuff, it was coming to a close. Another unwritten rule that Brody always observed was to be home no later than five, clean-up and be ready for dinner at five thirty, as usual.

As he drove his bicycle past all of his friends' houses on his way home, Brody imagined he was driving a huge motorcycle, spewing noise and exhaust everywhere along its path. It was his kingdom to rule and he loved that feeling more than anything. *It was freedom*; perhaps a greater and more authentic sense of freedom than he would ever feel as an adult navigating his world.

Frankly, Brody *was* the King of the Neighborhood.

Stephen J. Kristof

CHARDONNAY
A FAMILIAR FACE

Highly adaptable, enthusiastically embraced and pleasing on the palate; three characteristics that aptly describe white wines made from a grape varietal that almost every adult has at least heard of. It's true; Chardonnay is so ubiquitous in the realm of white wine, that even teetotalers and wine-haters alike are familiar with it.

But, for many of today's uninformed wine snobs, the mere mention of Chardonnay provokes ridicule. Their usual sentiment goes something like, "You're still drinking Chardonnay? That's so eighties and nineties!"

Truthfully, though, those decades *were* host to what was known as "Chardonnay Mania." Unlike today's Chardonnay-based wines, many of the mass-appeal offerings from that era were cloyingly sweet, excessively oaky clones of one another. Fortunately, styles have changed and winemakers stepped up to the plate to produce more modern, yet, mature versions of Chardonnay that have distinction and layers of complexity.

So, no, the varietal has not gone away. Far from it; Chardonnay remains one of the most, if not *the* most, famous and popular varietals in the world! In addition to wines that are simply labeled "Chardonnay," it's also the principal grape in other famous wines, such as Montrachet, Chablis and even Champagne.

Chardonnay can't be pigeonholed into one particular taste, bouquet or style. Multiple factors influence this varietal's outcome in the glass. Whether or not it was aged in oak barrels, variations in growing climate and altitude, the presence of certain minerals in the soil and, of course, varied winemaking techniques; these things mingle to inspire delicious, but, distinctive wines.

As much as the finest Chardonnays are distinct from one another, certain *people* are also quite singular in their unique appearance. They stand-out in a crowd and even after meeting or seeing them just once, it's easy to recognize them long after.

On the opposite end of the spectrum, far more people have a vague and unremarkable physical appearance. Even after being in their presence on several occasions, they blend in with the crowd and are not very memorable.

Think about it in terms of people you know. Some of them have faces and bodies that look like a lot like everyone else. It's not that they're attractive or unsightly; they're just...*average*. You likely also know people, far fewer of them, of course, who couldn't blend in if their lives depended on it!

Elaine Smith was more like one of those distinctive Chardonnays; she had a very singular appearance. So much so, that she had never been mistaken for anyone else. Throughout her life, she would often hear others say that she looked familiar. Usually, they had only seen her once or twice—maybe merely in a crowd—but her visage nevertheless became indelibly printed on their brains.

Yes, Elaine had the Romanee-Conti Montrachet Grand Cru of faces. That particular ultra-distinctive Chardonnay is hard to find and single bottles of it cost multiple thousands of dollars.

Having a distinctive and memorable appearance can go either way. It runs the gamut from grotesque—to interesting—to downright magnificent! Elaine was, in fact, magnificently gorgeous. At forty-six years-old, she was every bit as beautiful as she was at twenty-six. She didn't see herself that way; genuinely stunning people who don't need to put much work into their appearance are rarely aware of their beauty. However, she *really was* stunning.

She had a delicate, well-proportioned frame and was taller than average, with long, toned, satiny legs. Her radiant auburn hair had blonde highlights with large wavy curls that dropped just below her softly-chiseled shoulders. Her hair looked fun and bouncy with casual attire, but magically transformed to look elegant and glamorous when she wore an evening gown. Elaine's perfectly symmetrical facial features had an alluring exotic appearance.

Elaine was a bit of a shape-shifter. Not in terms of her face; her facial appearance was one-of-a-kind. But her overall appearance could swing between that of an intimidating, yet, spectacularly well-put-together business executive to that of a carefree blue jeans and plaid shirt cowgirl; she could pull-off both looks with ease.

As one of the nation's top architects specializing in interior design, Elaine was very much in demand and could easily charge whatever fee she wanted. And let's just say that she did *very* well. She had expensive tastes and equally expensive habits, and feeding them required a healthy cash flow.

In terms of family, Elaine had no children and only a few distant relatives. Her parents had passed away years ago in a tragic accident while vacationing in Mexico. Bob and Cheryl Smith took an excursion from the resort where they were staying. Their bus flipped over and tumbled violently down a cliff. Only six people, including the bus driver, survived; twenty-four passengers perished. It took a day for the Mexican authorities to positively identify the victims, but they were able to suppress news of the accident from the media because of the remote location of the crash.

Being the next of kin contact, Elaine received a telephone call from a government official who gave her the tragic news. The man lacked any sense of empathy and seemed more interested in obtaining a credit card number from her to cover the expenses of repatriating her parents' bodies.

As difficult as it usually is to find closure after such a tragedy, Elaine somehow rallied the strength to move forward, and she did so with remarkable independence and positivity. She always had a firm grasp on the concept that it's pointless to expend precious time or energy on things over which people have no control. She also understood that when it came to things that she *could* control, there was a very simple relationship between her decisions and her efforts, and the outcomes.

While a lot of her friends secretly criticized Elaine's decision not to marry and create a family, she knew what they thought and didn't give a crap. This was *her* life, she thought, and she wasn't about to let anyone else's values, preferences or judgments influence her own decisions. She really *was* happy with her life; both the personal and professional sides of it.

Elaine had what she considered a perfect love life. In reality, there was no actual love involved, but she did have a very satisfying sex life. She had never been able to maintain a relationship with a man for much longer than a year. No matter how compatible she and her current guy were, how much they were into each other or even how great the sex was, she eventually became bored and was ready to move on.

Travis was her latest beau. They had been dating casually for about two months, after which things really heated-up and became more serious. Travis was a thoracic surgeon who worked at one of the Boston area's top heart hospitals. They met at an out-of-town convention in Orlando; Elaine was attending an architectural convention, while Travis was at a cardiac care convention. Both were being held in different ballrooms at the same massive resort hotel.

Elaine had left her session to go freshen-up in her room. Travis had the same idea and, as fate would have it, they met as they both queued at the elevator. She instinctively looked at his wedding ring finger and was happy to see that there was nothing there, nor was there any indication of a ring having been there recently. They were instantly attracted to each other and talked briefly about their respective conventions. The elevator stopped at Travis' floor, but Elaine got out with him to continue their chat in the hallway, even though she was staying on a higher floor.

She tried her best not to be too obvious, but she couldn't help but take him all in; her eyes lingered far longer than they should have as she did a measured once-over. He, too, had a remarkably singular appearance. There was no argument that he possessed certain quintessential cheesecake elements, but his visage had far more to offer than just that.

Elaine thought Travis looked around her own age, but she couldn't be too sure. Something about him told her that he was a bit older than that; perhaps he was in his early fifties, she thought. Maybe it was his persuasive confidence or his salt-and-pepper hair? Regardless, his good looks and overall presence drew her in and she didn't want to leave.

Elaine asked him what it was like to be a surgeon. As Travis fumbled with an answer that was neither too methodological nor overly academic, her mind wandered; she didn't hear a word of what he said. She noticed a slight shadow that revealed a six-pack under his designer shirt and wondered how often he visited the gym? She also questioned how a surgeon could have such a ruggedly masculine look? His appearance was unlike what she had associated with that of a surgeon.

Having endured convention sessions all day long, Travis' strong jawline was by this time speckled with an alluring five o'clock shadow, which only added to Elaine's wandering mind. Her thoughts turned to a more romantic venue, as she envisioned Travis removing his expensive shirt and embracing her with his strong arms. At that precise moment, Travis reached out and cupped her shoulder with his right hand. It lasted for just a moment, but she could feel his strength and it sent shivers down her spine. He was in charge. His self-assurance was, in itself, tremendously attractive.

Her smokey hazel eyes and his deep blue eyes met and, at once, she felt embarrassed. She wondered if she had revealed too much of her very intimate thoughts through the intensity of her gaze?

Just before Travis removed his hand from her shoulder, he told her that it was wonderful meeting her and that he hoped they would see some more of each other before the weekend was over. He left it at that. The disappointment she felt was palpable. She very much expected and wanted him to ask for her cell number—or her hotel room number. She stood there, uncomfortably not knowing what to say or do. Did she misread his interest in her? Was it one-sided?

She smiled softly and said, simply, "I hope we do see each other again! I look forward to that."

He didn't take the bait; didn't ask for a contact.

In life, there's no such thing as a coincidence. The same is true for love. Elaine was reminded of this when, on the way back to her session, her elevator stopped at Travis' floor. As he entered the booth, they both laughed about the happenstance, but this time, neither one could ignore their feelings. That initial spark had now grown into a flame. Before the elevator reached their convention space floor, they decided to ditch their respective sessions and do something more fun and, possibly, intimate. It wasn't spoken, but was understood.

It was a comfortable and balmy evening. An exotic floral-scented breeze welcomed the couple as they stepped outside and made their way toward the poolside bar. Elaine and Travis had been cooped-up in their respective conventions for most of the day, so getting outside was the perfect antidote to counter the physical sluggishness that had been dogging both of them.

Elaine took a deep breath and felt refreshed. With Travis now by her side, she also experienced a sense of excitement and anticipation. She couldn't help but think about what the rest of the evening may have in store.

Anthony, the pool bartender, had silky brown skin, a generous smile and a deep sing-song voice. He loved getting to know about his patrons and was always eager to lend an ear, give gently-veiled advice or tell a cute anecdote that was actually far wiser than it sounded. He was so good at his job that, with tips, he earned more than the hotel manager.

Although he had never met Elaine or Travis before, Anthony's smile revealed that he somehow seemed to know before they even sat down, that they would end up spending the night together. He would be correct.

As they got to know each other, they talked about their work, their interests and a bit of their history. Somehow, Elaine wasn't surprised at all to learn that Travis also lived and worked in Boston. Travis appeared to be very surprised and equally happy when Elaine told him that she lived there as well. That particular revelation made Travis far more interested in Elaine, as if a switch had been flipped.

After downing their third shot of top-shelf tequila, Anthony asked if they would like another. Travis thanked him, signed his tab and dropped a fifty-dollar tip on the bar. Anthony smiled broadly and wished them a good evening.

The tequila may have influenced their amorous intentions or merely hastened the inevitable. They had barely closed the door to Elaine's room when Travis reached out with his right hand and gently cradled the side of her face. He drew her closer to him, but rather than going in for a kiss, his lips met the side of her face and he whispered in her ear, "I want you so badly, but I want to make sure that you want me the same way."

Travis' chivalry only aroused Elaine further. Her eyes met his and she said with a whisper, "Yes."

Despite the intensity of their shared passion, they took things slowly, savoring every moment, every touch. As their lips met, they both felt a harmony set forth; their bodies and their minds were fully melded and in-sync.

They slowly and gently undressed each other, delighted in what each one saw. Each touch, every caress, created a tingle that lingered even after a hand or finger moved on. Eventually shifting to the bed, Travis began to massage Elaine with confident, yet yielding palms. Elaine received massages on a regular basis, but this was nothing like any she had ever had. This one was magical; every stroke of Travis' warm hands felt virtually orgasmic and she shuddered in response.

She was so under his spell that Elaine hadn't noticed when Travis's hands gave way to his tongue. He licked her glistening skin with confident mastery. The touch of his tongue made her super-sensitive wherever it grazed and nibbled. Travis worshipped Elaine's body for what seemed like hours.

They made love with an insatiable hunger. It was exhilarating; everything about it was perfect. His moves, her moves; the way they moved together. While they were in the throes of passion, Elaine couldn't help think about how much their intermingling felt like a well-rehearsed symphony. Everything felt new, original, unscripted; yet none of it came as a surprise.

After sharing the most intense moments of their lovemaking, the couple lingered in the bed, their bodies both tingling and somewhat numb at the same time. They spooned, with Travis' larger frame enveloping Elaine's, his arms wrapped around her torso. His warm, muscular body felt safe to her as his nestling mirrored her own fetal position.

She could feel Travis' still firm manhood press against her inner buttocks. Even though they were both physically spent, the sensation excited her and made her crave even more. Each time he shifted his body or moved even slightly, Elaine pulled him toward her even more tightly, not wanting him to let go of her.

A lot of things went through Elaine's mind during that afterglow. She had had plenty of one-night stands, but realized this was not at all that sort of thing. Something about this encounter told Elaine that this was very different; that it was the start of an enduring and extraordinary relationship. At least, she hoped that was the case.

There was something about Travis that Elaine couldn't pin-down, but he seemed so familiar. "This is too easy," she thought. The physical and emotional novelty of being with a new lover was thrilling, but somehow, also felt nostalgic, as if she had been with him before. Of course—she hadn't.

Apparently, Travis also experienced the same sensation of déjà vu. He told Elaine that, although he'd never so much as seen her before that day, the depth of conversation that they shared earlier and the familiarity of their intimacy convinced him that he somehow knew her before even meeting her.

Elaine and Travis spent most of the remainder of the weekend together rather than returning to anything other than the most important sessions of their respective conventions. Although they initially had different return flights home to Boston, Travis changed his ticket so that he could fly home with Elaine.

Six months had passed since their first encounter and their relationship had only grown stronger. Elaine's friends and coworkers actually believed that this was the one. *That was a first.*

More often than not, Elaine stayed overnight at Travis' home or he stayed at hers. Elaine's happy-go-lucky disposition, the affectionate way she talked about Travis and the amount of time they spent together suggested to everyone around her that something *was* different about their relationship.

Thanksgiving arrived on November twenty-forth, and Elaine and Travis decided to celebrate by flying to Paris for an extended weekend. They arrived at Charles du Gaulle Airport on Friday morning after a mostly sleep-filled evening flight from Boston. They had booked a door-to-door transfer service in advance and had the driver drop them off at their hotel, where they stored their luggage temporarily until they could check-in later that day.

They say that springtime is the best time to visit Paris, but autumn has its own charm too! Elaine and Travis were blessed with beautiful weather for their entire stay. With sunny skies and daytime temperatures in the high fifties, the weather was ideal for exploring the city by foot, wearing nothing more than a light jacket. The warmth they experienced as they strolled hand in hand, their warm bodies cuddled up against one other, was greater than what the pleasant weather could provide.

They walked and walked until their feet ached, exploring some of the less touristy nooks and crannies that Paris has to offer. It had been an unusually warm autumn so far and, as a result, many of the trees had still not dropped their colorful leaves.

The irresistibly smoky smell of chestnuts roasting over charcoal on a street vendor's cart mingled with the enticing sweet aroma of freshly baked croissants at nearby bakeries. A concerto of scents wafted through the air, just like the live street music that also mingled around the corners and along the streets. Echoed notes could be heard from an old musician playing an accordion somewhere in the distance; the sound was classically Parisienne. As the couple turned a corner, different music became louder and took its place.

This time it was a young jazz musician plucking away on a huge double bass. As he worked the bass, occasionally spinning and swaying it to and fro, he accompanied the notes by humming and buzzing in harmony. His warbling sounded very much like American scat singing; Elaine said it sounded similar to an old 1950s record that her dad used to play.

Elaine and Travis agreed that the incredible ambience was very much like the signature cliché feel of a romantic movie. They were the star couple of that movie.

All senses were stimulated and were working overtime! The sights, sounds, smells and sensations were enough to make the hardest of hearts melt! However, Elaine wasn't the type of woman to get weak at the ankles and let herself be swept away by romance. She could be passionate, for sure, but that was different. The idea of romance, to her, came along with the notion of commitment and having one's future locked-down permanently. *That*, was definitely not for her.

Time, though, has a way of changing some things. Her six months with Travis seemed to soften her fear of commitment. Even she was aware of this change. She wouldn't admit to softening her position, but caught herself thinking about marriage on more than a couple of occasions.

After returning to their hotel to check-in, they grabbed their stowed luggage and went up to their room. It was a luxurious suite with an absolutely spectacular view of the city. One of the oldest hotels in Paris, the property had been welcoming guests for over 170 years. Elaine could actually sense the history and mentioned to Travis that she felt more comfortable there than she had ever felt staying at any other hotel property.

They took a shower, Elaine first, followed by Travis, followed by Elaine again when she joined him. A bit of jet lag and physical exhaustion from walking around the city wasn't enough to curb their desire. After drying off, Travis picked-up Elaine and brought her to the bed. He placed her so gently on the bed, it was as if he was handling a delicate work of art.

Travis' skilled tongue explored every inch of Elaine's body. He was methodical, artistic and unhurried. Her body shivered with each swirl and her anticipation became unbearable. Their bodies entangled and heaved, pulsating with pleasure. The familiarity that they initially experienced on their first 'date' in Orlando was still alive. So were the feelings of novelty and excitement.

Afterward, Elaine lay on the bed, taking in the picturesque sights that the window had to offer. Travis sat in a comfortable armchair and sipped a coffee that he had just made with the in-room coffeemaker. He had draped a towel on the chair and sat, naked, on the towel.

Elaine found herself spending more time looking at him than at the stunning architecture outside. She stealthily reached for the hotel notepad and pen on the nightstand, and quietly began sketching his form. Although she used modern 3D design software to create visualizations for her architectural clientele, she still loved to sketch by hand. She moved the pen sideways to depict shadows that revealed Travis' muscular physique and chiseled jawline.

Travis caught a glimpse of Elaine drawing him and he objected, jokingly, to being objectified. He smiled mischievously and said, "I see you drawing...what am I? Just another strapping studmuffin to add to your collection?"

"I couldn't resist!" she replied. "But, no, you aren't just a studmuffin...you're *my* studmuffin! You'll just have to get used to that!"

Travis swung around and said, "Well, *you're* naked too. Maybe I should start drawing a picture of you on the bed?

Elaine laughed and replied, "I've seen your artwork. Please don't insult my lovely body by trying to draw it!"

Elaine then showed Travis her sketch. He uttered a simple "hmm," but his facial expression revealed how pleased he was with her drawing. She couldn't decide whether he was more pleased with her artwork or with the way he looked? Either way, she was happy.

"You know, you look more like a magazine model than a surgeon," Elaine said. "I wonder if your patients ever picture you being naked?"

"Only the depraved ones," he answered with a smile.

She thought again about how she felt she shared a history with Travis; something she couldn't manage to explain. She then wondered if there was a way to freeze this moment forever in time. Besides the sketch she had just drawn, she tried to take a picture in her mind and wondered if she'd be able to recall everything as she saw and experienced it at the time?

Would she be able to remember and feel its fullness; the contentment, the delight, the desire, the intimacy? She wondered if an intentionally crafted memory could possibly contain all of those very personal elements?

Elaine and Travis both fell asleep, she in the bed and he in the chair. After a few hours, they awoke, hungry and ready for dinner. They had every intention of dining at one of the hundreds of excellent restaurants in the city, but the day proved a bit too much for them and they decided, instead, to dine at one of the hotel's two in-house restaurants.

The restaurant they chose was the more formal of the two and, as it turned out, was, indeed, an excellent choice. It wasn't your standard hotel fare; far from it, this hotel's restaurant was one of the top 20 options in the city, which also boasted a very well-known and celebrated chef.

The décor was very traditional and, although everything was in perfect condition, looked like it hadn't been updated for a hundred years. That wasn't far from the truth. On the walls hung many original oil paintings. Some of them were worth a fortune; knowing their value, Elaine was surprised that they weren't secured by glass cases.

Elaine took-in all of the design and décor elements, locking them away in her mind for fusion with contemporary ideas, potentially for an upcoming project.

Their dinner began with champagne, with which they toasted their whirlwind Thanksgiving weekend. Their appetizer came quickly; Escargots drizzled in Black Truffle Butter. After finishing what they agreed were the best escargots they had ever had, the waiter quickly brought a second small plate, Sea Bass Ceviche with White Asparagus. The plating was so beautiful and artistic, Elaine had to take a picture of it.

Travis, fully fluent in French, asked the waiter, "Monsieur, c'est une soirée spéciale pour nous deux. Pourriez-vous ralentir un peu le service?" The waiter seemed displeased that a dinner guest would be so rude as to ask him to slow-down his service. Perhaps Travis' American accent had more to do with the waiter's predisposition to secretly brand him as boorish.

Nevertheless, the waiter *did* put the brakes on service and padded the time between courses. While waiting for their main entrée, Elaine and Travis put a healthy dent in their bottle of Chablis; the Chardonnay-based white wine tasted every bit as decadent as it was expensive. In-between sips, they talked, laughed, gazed deeply into each other's eyes and held hands across the table. It was truly magical!

So immersed were they in the moment, that they became startled when they both realized their waiter was standing next to them with their entrée plates. Elaine ordered the Lamb Confit with Marrow Bone Toasts, while Travis had the Charolais Filet Mignon with Prawns, decorated with tiny Stuffed Morels.

After enjoying their three enchanting courses, there was hardly room for dessert. Even though the food portions were meagre compared to American standards, Elaine and Travis were more than satisfied. Still, Travis ordered a sumptuous dessert from the menu, which had the following description, "Cacao Péruvien Rare avec Sauce Framboises Fraîches, arrosé de Gâteau au Fromage Traditionnel." Elaine had no idea what to expect.

When it arrived, the dessert turned out to be a rich baked cheesecake drizzled with a fresh raspberry and rare Peruvian cocoa sauce. A dessert of this caliber isn't meant to be 'eaten,' but rather, *adored*. They took their time savoring each tiny forkful!

The entire meal was over the top. They ended with a toast, Travis raising his glass and saying, "What a perfect end to a perfect day with my favorite person in the world!"

Well, perhaps the sentiment was a tad premature; the day had not yet come to an end. Just before leaving the restaurant, Elaine excused herself to visit the ladies' room. As she walked through the dimly-lit corridor, she noticed a series of framed photographs flanking the walls on both sides. There were dozens of them, each depicting different people who, it seemed, worked for the hotel and restaurant over a period of time that spanned multiple decades.

Some of the pictures were almost as old as the property itself, while others were more recent. There seemed to be no order or design to the arrangement, as though a manager tasked the project to a bellhop or cook who had no artistic training.

Mysterious faded black and white Daguerreotypes from the mid-1800s exposed on silver-plated copper sheets hung beside enlarged color prints from the 1960s and 1990s. The only common thread shared by all of these photographs was that they depicted hotel employees who held a variety of positions.

A label with a typed description had been hastily fastened to the wall underneath each picture. Many of the labels were askew and some had strike-throughs with corrections written in pen. They included the names of the individuals depicted in the photos and, in some cases, their positions of employment. Group photos identified an employee's first initial only, followed by their surname.

Fascinated by the history, Elaine lost track of time. Travis sipped what remained of his wine, waiting patiently for Elaine. When she finally returned, Travis knew something had changed. Something was wrong.

Elaine was pale and short of breath. She looked distressed. "Travis, is this real or am I dreaming?"

"Slow down Elaine. What are you talking about? *Of course* this is real. What's going on?"

Elaine was all over the place. She seemed very confused. Her voice was shaking. She said, "I'm sorry, I'm just...I don't know what to think. Maybe it's just a coincidence, but..."

"Okay, sweetheart, please take a breath and calm down. Now, tell me what's going on. I'm...I'm concerned about you."

"Travis, I can't explain it. You have to see it." Elaine stood up and took Travis by the hand. She led him down the hallway toward the lavatories and pointed-out the pictures on the walls, explaining how they depict various employees going back over 150 years.

Travis was concerned. He had never seen Elaine act like this. She was so anxious and flustered that it scared him. As a physician, he began to consider various medical conditions that could manifest in ways similar to how she was behaving.

Elaine stopped in front of a large picture of a group of hotel and restaurant employees taken in the fall of 1921, three years after the end of World War I.

In addition to the label that identified all of the individual employees shown in the picture, there was a second label off to the right, that was printed in both French and English. It indicated that the picture had been taken just six months after the hotel and restaurant had finally reopened to guests following a temporary closure during and after the war. It said that the property had sustained significant damage from the war. During the subsequent three-year period, the property had undergone significant redesign and repair. This was the first full staff picture taken after the property was, once again, fully operational.

The employees were arranged in pyramid fashion, with the hotel and restaurant manager, along with other bigwigs seated in the short front row. Everyone else in the photo was standing behind this row of executives. All of the rows moving toward the back were arranged according to employees with diminished influence and responsibility. The back row was the longest row, occupied by chambermaids and laundry workers. Every employee wore their respective uniform, except for staff in the first two front rows, who were dressed in formal business wear.

Elaine raised her hand and pointed her finger toward a few people standing in the first row behind the seated bigwigs. Her hand was shaking. They were impossible to miss. How was this possible? Elaine and Travis were staring at…***themselves***.

Initially, Travis wasn't very surprised by what he saw, simply because he had seen so many Photoshopped and deep faked pictures that it was nothing new to him. However, he was visibly shaken when it finally sunk in that this picture was real, was truly from 1921 and was not a joke or a trick.

Elaine's singular appearance was impossible to overlook. Travis said, his voice trembling, "You know, I've never met anyone or even seen anyone who looks like you and, now, finally here she is, but it's a century ago. I don't get it. This is *you*."

He moved closer to the photograph and squinted. Travis turned toward Elaine and then back again to the picture. He said, alarmed, "My God! She even has the same tiny beauty mark that you have above your left lip."

"I know. And look at the man standing next to me. He's the spitting image of you. Same eyes...nose...mouth...same chiseled jawline. It's you!"

Travis switched his gaze from Elaine's twin to his own. Examining the man more closely, he said, "I'm stunned. This guy has the same dimples I got from my great grandfather! How's it possible that, not just one of us, but both of us have twins in a one-hundred-year-old picture?"

"Exactly. It's not just a coincidence, Travis. I don't understand it or what it means, but this is huge."

Elaine kept talking but Travis didn't hear another word. He was focused on the label under the picture. Each person in the front two rows had their name and individual position title inscribed, while others behind them simply had a group title, such as "Employés de Cuisine" and "Employés l de Entretien." Travis' body-double was identified as "Médecin de l'Hôtel, Dr. T. Comtois."

Elaine's counterpart was identified as, "Directeur de la Reconcevoir de l'hôtel, E. Beaudoin."

Elaine had glanced at the label before getting Trevor, but disregarded it, not understanding French. Trevor pointed to the label and asked, "Elaine, did you read this?"

Before she could answer, he translated slowly, "Hotel Doctor, T. Comtois."

Elaine's eyes grew wide as Travis' words sunk in. His double was *also* a doctor and his first name started with T.

Travis continued, saying, "Manager of Hotel Redesign, E. Beaudoin. Do you get it? He was a doctor and she was an architect!"

Silence permeated the corridor as the gravity of what they had just discovered struck them. Elaine bent forward and placed her hands on her thighs, as though she had just been struck across her abdomen with a baseball bat. Travis simply stepped back and used the wall behind him for support.

It wasn't until that very moment that Elaine and Travis noticed something they hadn't previously seen in the picture. How could they have missed it? The hotel doctor's left hand was resting on the wooden chair in front of him; the chair in which the hotel manager was seated. The manager of hotel redesign, Elaine's counterpart, rested her right hand on the doctor's hand.

They were a couple. Perhaps it was a visual cue for the few in-the-loop employees back then; perhaps a message to someone a hundred years in the future? Either way, it was evident that T. Comtois and E. Beaudoin were together.

This was a lot to digest. So many unanswered questions. Why them? Why see the picture now? What were the odds that they would choose Paris or even that particular hotel for their Thanksgiving weekend getaway? What were the chances, with all of the hundreds of restaurants to choose from, that they would select *that* restaurant and, thereby, venture into the dimly lit hallway with the historical employee pictures?

So much coincidence, it could never be ignored nor forgotten. What message was the universe trying to convey to Elaine and Travis? Could they have been early time travelers who somehow lost their memories as a side-effect of the travel? Was God, Himself, trying to tell them something? Or, were they just letting their imaginations run wild toward the exaggerated and irrational?

No, it wasn't exaggerated. Anyone with eyes could easily affirm the remarkable—make that *identical*—likenesses. The resemblance and the details were far too overwhelming to be ignored. It would be foolish *not* to recognize them. It would be shameful not to believe in and respect the truth that the picture revealed.

Elaine and Travis walked hand-in-hand, quietly, beautifully, through the hotel lobby toward the grand staircase that led to their second-floor guestroom. As the couple approached the staircase, time began to slow down and continued to slow further until they climbed half way up that staircase. At that moment, with the imposing antique chandelier hanging above them, it happened; time paused.

Time plainly came to a standstill for every witness present in that hotel lobby. Time became entirely irrelevant and, instead, true magic reigned.

It was profound; everyone there experienced the magic. Waves of warm energy flowed around the lobby, feeling like random currents of warm, silky water that gently wrap around one's body while bathing in the ocean. Everything shimmered, colors were exaggerated and lush, every sound reverberated as if part of a chorus, and the couple literally glowed with love; all of this frozen in a moment while they were ascending the imposing staircase.

It was the scene—the experience—of a lifetime and one that the privileged few who saw it will never forget. Danielle, a local struggling artist was one of those witnesses. She experienced an aura that foretold of the magic just as Elaine and Travis entered the lobby. She grabbed her phone from her back pocket and took a picture. She had already envisioned her own interpretation of the scene in the form of an oil painting.

In the months to come, Danielle painted the moment and it eventually became the most famous of all of her paintings; the one that put her on the map as a legitimate and globally-recognized artist. Danielle was able to capture a tiny bit of that magic for all to appreciate.

As for Elaine and Travis, there was never any doubt that the magic would last as long as they remained a couple, for they had *always* been a couple.

CHEAP BOXED WINE
DISTURBING HER PEACE

Drip, drip, drip, drip. The rhythmic sound was initially mesmerizing. She tried unsuccessfully to fight sleep while reading the latest release in a series of mystery novels. The series had recently become her current literary addiction.

The dripping noise became entangled with the sentence she was reading, both elements reverberating and soothing her into a dream-like state. A choir of tree frogs provided the refrain for her nighttime symphony. A large wine goblet sat precariously at the edge of the side table; its missing contents also played a role in helping her to nod off.

It was an early night, to be sure. The clock on her night table read 8:03 p.m. and Isabella was already asleep. It had been a beautiful night and she felt more relaxed than she had in months. Some folks say that August in Savannah is a miserably hot, humid and, well, disgusting time of the year. Northerners with thick blood and low heat tolerance describe it that way.

Isabella was no stranger to the heat, nor to the thick, swampy mugginess that accompanied it. In fact, she loved the feeling. She tried, to no avail, to explain to her friends and colleagues back home in Ohio, how the steamy atmosphere felt soothing on her skin and was comforting to her soul. She described how the botanical fragrance of the dew-covered flora mingled her consciousness with nature. They would never understand how it buoyed her mood and soothed her innermost feelings, bringing tranquility to her very being.

Isabella's "get away from it all" home on Talahi Island was where she felt most alive, grounded and human. Growing-up on Drayton Street, directly across from Forsyth Park in Savannah's Victorian neighborhood meant that she'd always be a southern girl at heart. Decades later, she bought her own vacation home not too far from where she spent her childhood. This adult home away from home wasn't very pricey or luxurious, but it was special enough to her.

Real estate professionals always say that "location, location, location" is the fundamental consideration when buying property. In that sense, Isabella struck a home run, because Talahi Island was the ideal location for her second home. It was a mere ten-minute drive west into Savannah or east to the beaches on Tybee Island.

The interior of her house had been completely gutted and updated by the previous owner, who also restored the exterior to its former historical grandeur. Well, to be honest, there never really was any "grandeur" to the old house. It looked like a fresher version of a very old cottage. There weren't many of these historical structures left on Talahi Island, because in recent times, most of them were eventually replaced by larger, more modern and far more expensive homes. Nevertheless, Isabella loved her getaway.

The house was on a half-acre parcel of land. Her yard was speckled with palmettos and other sub-tropical foliage. There was a beautiful old paw-paw tree that still produced the tasty rare fruit, a patch of banana "trees" and several stately 200-year-old live oaks draped with swags of Spanish moss. On the front lawn, twin palm trees growing from a central trunk were flanked by a gorgeous magnolia tree on the right. The magnolia was also dripping with Spanish moss, but the last of its custard-fragranced spring blossoms had dropped several months ago.

Isabella loved nothing more than relaxing on her rattan daybed style long chair in the back room. The room looked a bit like a screened-in porch, but was a structural room with 15 windows that provided a magnificent view in three directions. When the window sashes were raised, it was like being in the middle of her yard, yet with the protection of her home. Whether she was reading or going through casework on her tablet, it was her very favorite place in the world.

They had been silent for a while, but randomly, a tree frog began to chirp just outside a window. Then another and then even more joined in from somewhere in the distance. The same choir of tree frogs that had lulled her to sleep an hour ago now stirred her out of a deep sleep. She was groggy and had no idea how much time had gone by since she nodded-off. Before long, she once again heard the dripping sound coming from the kitchen.

Although its rhythm, like the tree frogs, was sleep-inducing an hour ago, she began to focus on it. Like a clock ticking, the dripping was tolerable at first, but then started to become annoying. Not annoying enough, however, to motivate her to get off the daybed and tighten the kitchen tap.

Fifteen minutes later, Isabella realized that she wasn't going to get any more sleep until she took care of the leaky tap. She also figured that she should make sure the house was locked and get to sleep in her actual bed.

Despite turning the kitchen faucet tightly, the dripping sound persisted. She looked around, wondering where the sound was coming from.

A few seconds later, Isabella stepped in a puddle on the kitchen floor; evidence of a leaky faucet. However, she quickly realized that the red liquid wicking-up her white socks wasn't tap water. Briefly, she panicked, thinking that she was bleeding. Then she found the leak. It was, indeed, a failing tap, but not the kind she expected to find. The cheap boxed wine on the kitchen counter had been leaking out of the rubber valve for hours.

Although she was alone, Isabella yelled, "Damn," as though she had an audience.

When she picked it up to move it, she realized that the brand-new box of wine she had opened just hours ago was now nearly empty. She was more upset about the wasted wine than she was about the mess and said, "Ohh, this is sub-par!"

Isabella appreciated fine wine, and even though money wasn't an issue, she had a strong frugal streak. This was about the only characteristic she borrowed from her late mother, Agnes, who didn't exactly earn the "Mother of the Year" award. She figured that boxed wine was good enough for a basic house plonk.

After squeezing several sponges of wine down the drain and cleaning-up the rest of the mess, she thought about whether to return to the back room or just go to bed. It was still early; just past nine, but she didn't feel her second wind, so going to sleep seemed like the most prudent thing to do.

She headed for her bedroom, looking forward to what promised to be another lazy, hazy, sticky, sweltering day. She thought about making it a beach day, but wasn't about to commit to anything because she didn't have to. That was the best part of retreating to her Talahi Island home; schedules, commitments and expectations were pretty much non-existent.

Isabella tried reading a bit more of her book by the dim orange glow cast from her duck light on the nightstand. The light fixture didn't really fit in with her upscale coastal décor. In fact, the old duck light would best be described as kitsch, with its porcelain mallard duck sitting on a wooden base, a brass post sticking out of its back to support the lampshade.

It's not that the duck light held any particular sentimental value or represented anything that was special to her. Years ago, she had been driving through rural Tennessee, somewhere outside Chattanooga, when she pulled over to check-out a yard sale. That, in itself, was totally out of character, as she had never done that before and has never attended a yard sale since. But something drew her to that particular yard sale; she saw what it was as soon as she got out of her car. She couldn't explain why, but she had to have it. Being frugal, she also loved that the lady selling it only wanted a buck for it. Sold!

As she read a little more, Isabella's eyes grew heavy and before she knew it, she was in a deep sleep. Getting away from it all on Talahi island also meant getting away from annoying wake-up alarms. As an eminent litigation attorney in Columbus, she had enough alarms and appointment reminders throughout the day, so when she was on "retreat" in greater Savannah it was an alarm-free zone!

Alarm or not, Isabella was roused from a deep sleep. It was morning, but still before sunrise. She heard a commotion outside. It sounded like a man and woman arguing loudly. She thought it was unusual; the island had a rather small population and a laid-back feel. Strangers didn't often venture far off the main road into residential areas. Beyond that, Isabella knew her neighbors' voices, but she didn't recognize the ones arguing outside. At this point, she was more curious than concerned. She tapped her phone and saw that it was 5:34 a.m.

Isabella walked to the living room and peeked through one of the two large windows facing the front yard. She was unnerved at the sight of a couple standing in her driveway. They were having what appeared to be a very heated argument. They stood in front of what appeared to be a very expensive sports car, which was parked diagonally across the driveway. Not being a car nut, she couldn't tell whether it was a Lambo, Porsche or Ferrari, but she knew it wasn't a garden-variety car and was certain that the vehicle was very expensive. Isabella figured that they pulled-off the road abruptly.

Isabella had developed sharp observation skills over her several years practicing law; something she relied upon, both in and out of the courtroom. She quickly assessed the situation. She had a boatload of experience examining what occurs in an unusual situation. She had seen how the slightest movement in one direction or the other can result in a person being on the outside or inside of an incident. She knew that when someone ends-up on the inside, it can easily have a life-altering impact.

Isabella thought, "I'm sure as hell going to stay on the outside of this ruckus, whatever it is!"

However, the fact that this couple was on her property meant that she was already involved, albeit on a cursory level. She watched as the two shouted at each other and swapped minor physical shoves and slaps. Isabella opened the window sheers a bit wider to get a better view as she tried to discern who the aggressor was. She quickly came to the conclusion that both of them seemed to be equally antagonistic.

Most people would have called the police immediately. However, Isabella had personal experience defending cases in which an innocent bystander becomes part of the case, *because* they chose to call the police. She also knew that the quarter-million-dollar vehicle sitting in her driveway was an indicator that the argument was likely rooted in power.

She thought, "That kind of money and power has the potential to result in some serious collateral damage for anyone who gets in the way."

This wasn't her first rodeo. Isabella placed her phone sideways on the window frame and began recording the fight. The file could be valuable, she thought, in the event that she somehow got wrapped-up in this. Like most of her neighbors, Isabella had multiple security cameras around her home and property, but she felt that it wouldn't hurt to see things from another angle.

Five more minutes went by and the couple were no closer to reconciling. Far from it; the physical violence had escalated. Whatever they were arguing about seemed to be eclipsed by the deep animosity the couple seemed to have for one another. Isabella couldn't just stand by. She knew that she was witnessing an incident that had some of the hallmarks of cases where one person—or both end up dead.

She grabbed her phone, stopped recording and dialed 911. She moved away from the window, but was close enough to still see what was happening.

Ironically, although Isabella had heard 911 recordings played in the courtroom on several occasions, she had never personally dialed 911 herself. The operator said, on script, "Nine, one, one. Police, fire, ambulance. This line is being recorded. What's your emergency?"

Isabella said, "My name is Isabella Vittori. I live at 534 Ibis Crescent on Talahi Island. There's a couple fighting on my front lawn. Their expensive yellow sports car is parked across my driveway; it looks like they pulled-off the road suddenly."

"Do you know or recognize the couple," the operator asked?

"I've never seen either one of them before…or their car," answered Isabella.

"Do you see any weapons?"

Isabella said, "I don't see any guns, but that doesn't mean there isn't one."

"Is anyone holding anything that could be used as a weapon?"

"No. They are both holding their phones, but I don't see anything else in their hands."

The operator asked, "Is anyone physically injured or bleeding?"

"Not that I can see," said Isabella, "but they are shoving and pushing and slapping each other, and they're shouting loud enough that I can hear every word from inside my house."

"Is there anyone else present or just the couple?"

"Just the couple. I don't see anyone else."

"What are their genders and approximate ages?"

"Male and female. He looks well into his sixties, and she doesn't look any older than forty-five." Isabella added, "Although maybe she's had a lot of work done, judging from the expensive car..."

The operator interrupted, asking curtly, "Please describe their appearance. Height, weight, clothing, facial hair, any identifying marks. Please start with the male party."

Isabella pulled the sheers away just a few inches so that she could get a better look. She gave her report, saying, "Like I said, he looks to be around sixty-five, salt and pepper hair, clean-shaven... ummm...on the tall side—just over six feet I'd say, a hundred and eighty pounds, muscular frame, dressed in yellow boat shorts and an oversized white linen shirt."

The operator jumped in, saying, "and the female party?"

"Mid-forties I guess, her hair is dirty blonde, straight, shoulder-length...she's very pretty, thin, petite, maybe 110 pounds. She's wearing blue capri pants and a white top."

"How long have they been on your property?"

"I don't know exactly. I woke up about ten minutes ago...they woke me up actually. So, at least ten minutes."

"I'm going to dispatch an officer right now, but I'm not going anywhere. Please stay on the line."

Isabella kept thinking how strange it felt to be participating in this conversation, rather than listening to it as an exhibit in the courtroom. The woman was no longer arguing, She sat on the lawn with her back propped-up against the magnolia. The man hovered over her and continued to berate the woman, but she was looking at her phone and trying hard to ignore him.

The operator suddenly chimed-in again, asking, "You said their vehicle is yellow? Do you know the make or model?"

"It's yellow with black stripes. I really don't know what it is, but it's not your average car. Maybe a Lamborghini or something like that?"

"What about the license plate. Can you read it?"

"The car is kind of sideways, but the rear is within eye-shot." Isabella continued, saying, "I'm going to use the zoom on my phone camera, I think I can make out..."

The operator interrupted her again and said, somewhat dismissively, "That's great."

Isabella pinched and drew her fingers across her phone display to zoom-into the license plate. She was concerned that the couple would notice her, so she contorted her body in such a way as to avoid being seen, although in doing so, she looked extremely awkward.

She said, "South Carolina plate, E, E, no, sorry, that's E, F, umm...S, 7..."

The operator entered the license plate as Isabella dictated the digits and got a hit before she could hear the last three. She said, "You're good. I don't need any more. I've identified the vehicle."

Isabella heard the operator report the vehicle and owner information to the officers who were on their way. Before she was finished, she stopped and said, "Oh, wait..."

It was clear that the operator had seen something on her screen that was significant and unexpected. She didn't divulge what it was to Isabella, but informed her that she was going to put her on hold for a few minutes. Isabella realized that whatever the operator had just learned was not for her ears. She became more curious and more concerned at the same time. Her imagination started to dictate her thoughts.

The operator came back on the line, saying, "I need to support another call that's coming in. Everything should be fine. The officers will be there shortly. Thank you for reporting this." Click.

Just as she was thinking that something didn't sound right about this, her smartphone rang. The display read, "Unknown Number, Langley, VA." Isabella thought there was little chance that the call was unrelated or coincidental.

"Ms. Vittori," the female voice said, "we understand that you placed a call to an emergency line this morning regarding an altercation."

Isabella's eyes widened. She heard her heart pounding in her eardrum. The woman continued, saying, "I would advise you to close your blinds and go to another room. Stay in your house and do not leave. Don't unlock or open any doors until you have heard from me again."

With a million things racing through her head, Isabella asked in a hushed tone, "Who are you?"

Silence.

"What agency are you with?"

Silence

"Am I...am I in immediate danger? Like, what's going on?"

"We are tasked to resolve situations like this one," the caller said. "Listen, Ms. Vittori, I'm awfully sorry, but I cannot say anything further at this point about our involvement, other than assuring you that we are taking care of this incident as we speak and that you will be perfectly safe. Just do as I said and the disturbance will be over soon."

Realizing that the woman omitted more information than she revealed only made Isabella more curious. She said, no longer whispering, "No, *you* listen! I am *clearly* in danger or you wouldn't have told me to basically hide in my own home while you're arranging some sort of police action on my own damned front lawn! Just be honest with me. What's going on and who are you?"

Isabella was vexed. At this point, nothing the caller could say would calm her down or quench her curiosity. Except for one thing and the woman knew exactly what that was.

"Ms. Vittori, I understand that, as a prominent litigator in Columbus, you must have a lot of questions about this; far more than the average homeowner..."

Isabella saw red flags. Deep concern overtook her curiosity. She interrupted the woman, saying, "Excuse me, how do you know my profession and where I work?"

"Ms. Vittori, like I said, we're taking care of all of this. Let me put it this way, with your professional experience, you more than most people should have some insight into when it's prudent to leave things alone. I would suggest that you practice that discernment now."

Isabella was dumbfounded. Her mind raced, trying to think of different government agencies, law enforcement or other parties that might be involved. And then she thought about her own professional practice and how easily someone with real power could mess things up for her.

The caller continued, saying, "I know you have questions, but I simply cannot tell you anything else, other than the fact that I exist courtesy of your tax dollars."

Isabella thought about how important it is to stay on the outside of an incident. She yielded.

"Okay, I get it. Leave it alone. Right? And I never saw the fight or the yellow sportscar. Correct?"

"What yellow sportscar? A fight? I don't know what you're talking about. We do appreciate your cooperation. And remember, that we're here for you." The caller paused, abruptly sounding less robotic and more human. She added, "Um, I really hope that you leave this alone. I probably shouldn't say this, but if you need a bit more convincing, I would suggest that you think about your 1995 case, United States v Shepfield. And then leave it alone for good."

Isabella was defeated. She answered in a hushed tone. "Alright. It is forgotten. I appreciate you taking care of whatever it was."

The agent gave a final caution. She said, "I would strongly recommend that you permanently delete any recording you may have taken of this incident, either on your phone or outdoor cameras."

Even though she didn't understand exactly what was going on, Isabella realized how deep this went. She said, "Yes. Consider it done. Thank you for..."

Click. The caller hung-up. Isabella had a fleeting desire to use an app on her phone that does a deep dive into unknown numbers to reveal hidden information. But she didn't dare do it. She already figured-out which agency called her.

She sat in her kitchen; the window shades were drawn. She tried to listen to what was going on, but other than muffled voices, car doors opening and closing, and the background chatter of walkie-talkies, there was no clue. She also realized that there had been no sirens. Somebody or some people—she wasn't sure—showed-up at her house to have a discussion with the couple, but it didn't sound like a high-risk take-down of any sort.

She replayed what she could remember from the past hour. She thought about how it sounded like the couple stopped their fight almost immediately, as though they recognized whoever arrived at her house. Isabella was on her third cup of coffee. Subdued conversation continued for some time. The early rays of orange-tinged sunlight began to peek around the blinds.

Isabella heard a few cars drive away and looked at the kitchen clock. It read 6:44 a.m. She wondered if whatever it was, was all over? Then she heard three short knocks at her front door.

In the short time it took for her to walk to the front door and open it, whoever knocked was already gone. Or were they watching from afar, Isabella wondered? Either way, the coast was clear. She thought, had she never heard the commotion and slept through it all, she would never have noticed anything amiss.

Isabella went about her day as though nothing out of the ordinary had happened. She decided to go to the beach and started her day with a walk at the edge of the ocean. As she felt the bubbling waves caress her feet, she caught herself thinking, "What if?"

She quickly dismissed the questions. For the time being.

Autumn came early in Ohio and the weather turned unpleasant; it was unusually cold and windy. Isabella liked the look of fall landscapes, but despised the weather. However, she was too attached to her career in Columbus to move south. She realized that she should have made the move several years ago, but she was now wearing velvet handcuffs; she had made partner five years prior, so leaving at this point was financially not viable.

She had spent the last few months researching and working a major civil suit in which her firm represented a plaintiff's claim against a very wealthy "old money" defendant. If she won this case, it would result in one of the largest windfalls in the firm's history.

As she was preparing for the upcoming courtroom litigation, Isabella happened upon an old case. It was the United States v Shepfield case that the clandestine caller from August had mentioned. She had completely forgotten about the case and, frankly, was a bit frightened to open the accordion folder.

Despite her best judgment, Isabella just couldn't resist her curiosity and started to leaf through the pages. The case was fought very early in her career; she was co-counsel and had forgotten much of what it involved. She refamiliarized herself with the basics; the government was trying to recover funds from an extremely wealthy young client who had become instantly rich selling high-tech solutions that had extremely important military applications. As it turned-out, the government lost the case due to its own lack of due diligence and some other things that weren't exactly kosher.

As she replayed bits and pieces of the actual trial, Isabella suddenly remembered an important detail that didn't exist in the filings or case notes in front of her. She recalled how the defendant confided in the lead counsel that he was a secret "contractor" for the government prior to selling the tech solutions. This was code for spy. Outside of the courtroom, the client said in confidence that there were a lot of very questionable dealings on both sides.

The very origin of the high-tech solutions-for-sale was debatable. Kick-backs and pay-for-play arrangements to players in various "no such agencies" had been paid. The government's lead counsel seemed to recognize as she got further into the case, that the dirt was so far-reaching, pursuing recovery of funds any further could potentially expose significant larceny and other criminal activity by civil servants at the very top of more than a few agencies.

Isabella considered digging deeper into the Shepfield case files, but her better judgment prevailed. "Let sleeping dogs lie," she thought.

Another two weeks passed and Isabella had just finished her closing arguments in the "old money" civil case that had consumed her for most of the fall. A few days later, the jury reached a verdict that was extremely favorable for her client, the plaintiff. The commission plus fees generated a hefty $21 million chunk of revenue for the firm.

Isabella was exhausted from this case and it showed physically. She couldn't wait to go on retreat again in Savannah. She felt that she really earned the 3-week respite that she was about to start enjoying.

Somewhere in the middle of the diagonal trek from Columbus to I-77, Isabella pulled over to get some gas and a snack. She glanced at her now antique leather messenger bag on the empty passenger seat and thought warmly about her dad, who had purchased it for her when she started her law career. It was old, shiny in some spots and frayed in others, and had seen a lot of courtrooms and a lot of action over the years.

The bag would always be special to her. She packed her laptop and some personal papers into that bag in the morning before she left for Savannah.

Isabella stowed it temporarily in the hidden compartment in her trunk. She tucked it under the felt cover and repositioned the computer inside to make the bag fit in the snug space. As she backed away, she noticed that a post-it note was stuck to the back of her hand. It was an old case note with various things scribbled on both sides.

She gasped as she read the name "Shepfield" on the note. "What a coincidence," she thought.

Isabella was frozen with trepidation as she read a sentence that she had written about her client nearly 30 years prior. "Client just bought his first yellow sportscar. Obscenely expensive."

She pictured the thirty-five-year-old client from that case. He had an unusual appearance; not at all unattractive, just unusual, but in an alluring way. Isabella mentally added thirty years to his appearance. It was him. The man who showed-up on her property back in August; the man who was fighting with the woman.

The revelation produced more questions than answers. Why her? Was it just a coincidence that, of all the places he could have stopped, Shepfield just happened to stop on *her* property? What would have happened had she never called the police? She helped him retain his ill-gotten money, so why did he appear in her life again?

She couldn't even imagine the answers to these questions. She was right about one thing, though. When a lot of money and power are involved, collateral damage can occur to people who get in its way. She decided, once more, to leave it alone.

It didn't take Isabella long to realize that, ultimately, leaving Shepfield out of her thoughts and out her life was the right decision.

Isabella enjoyed her three weeks of bliss on Talahi Island, much of it in her back room with the windows open. She felt recharged and at peace. After closing everything and locking-up, she hopped in her vehicle and headed north to Wilmington, North Carolina, to spend Christmas with family. Although she grew-up in Savannah, none of her surviving relatives still lived there.

She took a pit-stop at a plaza with a gas station and diner just south of the North Carolina state line. After losing a fight with a rather unsatisfying and stale sandwich, Isabella grabbed a few snacks and a cold cola from the gas station store. At the counter, she fumbled with her purse while asking the cashier to add sixty dollars' worth of gasoline to her bill.

As she tapped her credit card on the payment device, she noticed a local newspaper from South Carolina in the rack next to the counter. The headline caught her eye. It read, "Local Real Estate Tycoon and Wife Found Dead on Boat."

It sounded like a fascinating story; especially for a lawyer. She bought the newspaper and returned to her vehicle with her purchases. Her estimate was surprisingly accurate. She was barely able to fit sixty dollars' worth of gas into the tank, which brought the gauge to the top of the full line.

Just before she pulled ahead, Isabella glanced at the front-page article and read the first few sentences before getting on the road again. The couple were found dead on their luxury eighty-foot yacht, which was anchored about two miles off-shore. Apparently, there were no signs of struggle or physical injury, except for a single gunshot to each of the boaters' foreheads. The article identified the dead boaters as Burrell and Aria Shepfield.

Isabella tossed the paper onto the back seat, paused and flipped her visor to reveal the mirror. She retrieved a tube of lipstick from her purse and, looking into the mirror, reapplied it to her lips before getting back on the highway. She felt, somehow, wiser. She didn't give it another thought, put her vehicle in gear and headed up to Wilmington. It was Christmas Eve.

By five-thirty in the evening, Isabella had enough Christmas and family to last a few years. She didn't particularly care for turkey, although she politely took several reused margarine containers of it that her aunt had forced upon her. After a succession of uncomfortably long goodbyes from relatives that she hardly remembered and those who she had never met, Isabella hopped in her car and drove to a local inn where she spent the night.

The next morning, she started the last leg of her return trip to Columbus. The winter sun had just set when she finally arrived back home. Since she owned both homes and each one had everything she needed, she enjoyed the luxury of traveling light. She grabbed her old bag and a few other items including the newspaper, and went inside.

Before she left for her trip down south, Isabella had left some kindling and newspaper in her woodburning fireplace. She touched a lighter to the paper and within minutes had a crackling fire to welcome her home.

A box of cheap red wine was sitting on the kitchen counter. The box had been waiting for her return and kept its promise of preserving its contents while she was away. Isabella was happy to see that this one's spigot worked properly and hadn't leaked even a single drop during her extended absence, unlike the one that had left a mess in her Talahi Island home.

She drew a glass of wine and sat by the fire, sipping the wine as she began to open the stack of mail that had grown in her absence. Not surprisingly, most of it was junk mail. The fifth envelope was not. It was personally addressed to Isabelle. The return address was a residential street in an obscure town in South Carolina; the affluence of homeowners there was a well-guarded secret. The sender was identified only by the initials of "B.A.S."

Isabella didn't catch it at first. This was surprising, considering what she had just experienced and the fact that she was such an intelligent and observant individual. Nevertheless, she opened the hand-written letter and began to read it.

> *"Dear Ms. Vittori, you probably don't remember me, but my name is Burrell Shepfield and you were co-counsel quite a long time ago for a case involving me and the government. What I have to tell you is extremely important and timely. If any freak accident or violent episode should take me and my wife's life, there's something you need to know..."*

Isabella took the letter and envelope, and calmly placed them on top of the newspaper that she had picked-up during her gas and lunch stop in South Carolina. She rolled-up the newspaper the same way delivery boys used to. She tossed it into the fireplace and smiled as she watched the flames dance around the roll and begin to consume it, page-by-page.

Unexpected visitors occasionally show up in our lives. They all carry baggage, but sometimes their baggage is just too dangerous to allow into our homes or into our lives.

Merlot
The Mysterious Visitor

Merlot is Merlot, right? Wrong. Not even close. That myth is easily debunked during blind tastings of Merlot wines. You see, well-made Merlots can be as different as night and day!

Now, that's not to say that a basic, homogenous, bland style of Merlot doesn't exist; it exists in droves! However, that plonk is not the type of Merlot wine we're talking about.

There are countless styles of Merlot throughout the wine-producing world. For instance, it's not merely that French Merlot differs from California Merlot, but different producers in the same region can also create wines that convey unique characteristics and flavors.

Perhaps a common denominator shared by various Merlot wines is that they tend to be robust and smooth. Robust and smooth are two terms that aptly describe the unexpected visitor to the Miller's home one late afternoon nearly five decades ago, when their two children were still young.

Sarah was eight and Jacob had just turned ten. In fact, it was Jacob's birthday; July 1, 1974. Yes, it was the ideal day for any ten-year-old's birthday; the first Monday of the first full week of summer vacation. Jacob was so excited about what the next two months would bring. He was also relieved about not having to deal with school, teachers, homework and being bored out of his skull for that same stretch.

Most of Jacob's friends started getting restless after only a few days away from school. Unlike them, Jacob was quite adept at occupying himself and he rarely got bored. That is, except when he was at school. Yet, when *he* was in charge—meaning school was out—that was a different story. Whether it was during Christmas break, spring break or summer vacation, Jacob loved to wake early, keeping himself busy and engaged until his mom forced him to go to bed.

While he absolutely loved spending time with his little sister, Sarah wasn't into the things that were really fascinating to Jacob, such as hunting for bugs or building "projects," as he called them. Sarah was a girl, Jacob thought, and quite appropriately she was into girly things. He loved her dearly and was the best big brother Sarah could have had. She idolized him and rightly so; Jacob didn't mind spending an hour or two with her, playing with her dolls and letting her style his hair. However, there was a limit!

In terms of school, Jacob was less patient. It's not that he was a bad student. Quite the opposite, he was any teacher's dream; he listened attentively, got straight A's consistently and rarely, if ever, needed a corrective caution. However, he was bored stiff. Although he was starting sixth grade in September, he would have been far more challenged and engaged with an eighth-grade curriculum.

Regardless, summer had just begun and Jacob was at his best. He could do whatever he wanted and he had a lot of plans to fulfill and daydreams to dream. Even when he appeared to be doing nothing, the gears were turning and his mind was at work!

Life was different in the 1970s. Kids could be kids and that meant that they could make their own days as dull or as thrilling as they wanted. Many of them also had this interesting skill that, these days, seems to have disappeared. It's called imagination.

If you grew up back then, it's unlikely that you were allowed to sit inside all day looking at a screen. Instead, you probably remember your parent telling you to, "Go outside and play!"

If the weather wasn't outright dangerous, children were generally expected to be outside during most of the daylight hours. And those daylight hours weren't excessively regimented with sports, camps and organized activities the way there are today. The bottom line is that summer vacation was really different for kids back then. Children learned valuable skills and gained important perspectives as they explored, discovered, played pick-up sports, invented new games, played entire neighborhood contests of hide and seek, or merely lay silently in a field of tall grass while seeing things in the clouds.

Jacob loved the fact that the beginning of his favorite time of the year started with his birthday. Mary, his mom, allowed Jacob and Sarah to choose what they wanted for dinner on their birthdays. Robert, Jacob's dad, didn't really care what was for dinner, just as long as it was ready and waiting for him when he got home from work. He wasn't what you would call *'comfortable'* in the kitchen.

As with his last two birthdays, Jacob again requested a taco dinner, which was quite exotic for a Midwest family in the early 1970s. He got the idea from an episode of the Partridge Family, in which Danny requested tacos for his birthday dinner. After dinner, Mary and Robert were planning to pull out the Game of Life board game, following which they had planned to watch TV and allow the kids to have ice cream and coke floats along with potato chips.

Gunsmoke was airing that night, but the kids didn't really care for westerns, so instead, they opted to watch the ball game between the Kansas City Royals and the Chicago White Sox. Jacob wasn't much of a baseball fan, but his dad was a diehard Royals supporter, so he was at least looking forward to sitting next to him and cheering along. Sarah didn't really care what she watched, because she got to stay up late, and have her float and chips.

Around four o'clock, just as Mary was beginning to prepare dinner, the doorbell rang. Jacob had just taken a shower, having gotten filthy playing outside all day. He heard the doorbell and wondered who it could be? Jacob's grandparents had already come over with some gifts for a pre-birthday visit the day before.

Robert wouldn't be home from his job as an insurance broker until just after five, so when Mary opened the door to see who it was, she was surprised to see Robert home early, but with a stranger; a man who looked to be well into his eighties with grey hair and a broad, warm smile.

Mary said, "Hello," almost as a question, her eyes darting glances between Robert and the stranger.

As she examined the old man, looking confused and trying to figure out who he was, Robert said, "Honey...Mary, I want to introduce you to someone I met this afternoon. I'm sorry I didn't call in advance, but this is Leonard and he has asked to meet with our family today. He has something important to share with each of us."

Jacob opened the bathroom door just wide enough to listen to the conversation. He heard his mom grasping for words. He couldn't figure out whether she was annoyed or confused. Perhaps a mixture of both. Mary said, "Oh, um, you remember it's Jacob's birthday. I, I'm...sorry, I don't want to sound rude, but this is just unexpected."

Jacob continued to eavesdrop. At this point, he was standing in the middle of the hallway in his underwear, his hair dripping wet. He heard his dad trying to explain, saying, "Mary, I know this is unexpected, but I really want you to hear what Leonard has to say. It's even more important today, on Jacob's birthday, because..."

Leonard interrupted Robert, saying, "...because having met your husband, a true family man with loads of compassion in his heart, I want to meet the rest of his family who, no doubt, also have abundant beauty radiating from their souls!"

Leonard's voice was full and round. It enveloped the foyer and somehow softened Mary's apprehension.

Sarah heard the commotion and came out of her bedroom. She was about to tip-toe down the hall to the top of the stairway to get a peek at what was happening downstairs. She didn't expect to see her skinny little brother standing almost naked in the hallway, his body twisted toward the stairway while dripping and creating a pool of water all over the floor. She quickly shut her door and went back to playing with her brightly painted wooden characters that were known for their magical ability to wobble without falling down.

Jacob didn't know what to think. He didn't understand what the visitor was saying, but his curiosity was piqued. "Who *is* this guy? His voice has such a deep and interesting sound...I wonder if he *looks* the way he *sounds*?"

As much as he was looking forward to the birthday tacos, ice cream floats, chips and TV, Jacob didn't care that his special evening might be interrupted. He was mesmerized by the visitor's voice; it was like a magnet and he couldn't wait to meet him.

Jacob went to his room and got dressed. He sensed that it would be best for him to wait until he was called down, so he started making some new geometric designs on paper with his rotating marker machine. It was a gift from Christmas that he played with constantly during Christmas break. It went back in the box after the holiday and this was the first time he had touched it since then.

Robert brought Leonard to the living room. Leonard politely accepted Mary's gracious offer of coffee and pastries. Robert invited him to make himself at home while he helped Mary in the kitchen.

Jacob's parents had a muted, but serious, conversation while preparing things. Mary admitted that she sensed Leonard was a good person, but asked Robert why he would even consider bringing a stranger to their home without warning and, especially, on Jacob's birthday of all days. Robert tried to explain that Leonard's charm must have overtaken his senses.

He paused, turning his head toward the floor for a bit and then looked at Mary. His demeanor became more serious.

"It's more than that, Mary. I don't know exactly who Leonard is or where he came from, but I am strangely drawn to him in a way I can't possibly explain."

Mary asked him to try, but Robert said, "I don't understand it, but there's something else. He told me things about our family—things that we've told nobody else—things that, somehow, he knew."

Mary said, nervously, "What on earth did he say?"

"He knew that when Jacob was born, he had polydactylism, his extra little toe. He knew that we had decided to have it removed just before his first birthday," said Robert.

Mary became flustered and said, "How does he know that? Only his doctor and the surgeon knew. We didn't even tell family."

Robert had to hush her so that Leonard didn't hear. "Shhh. Honey, I know it sounds creepy, but I somehow feel okay with it. He said other things that nobody except you and I could know, because we're the only ones who've talked about them."

Mary asked, "Other things? Like what?"

"You are the only person I have every discussed my plans with about making a play for the McKinley insurance brokerage in the next few years. You know, before Ed begins to consider retirement," said Robert.

Mary dismissed it, saying, "Robert, there are only four independent insurance brokerages in our city. Ed's is the largest and ours is second. I think someone could easily guess our intention."

Robert said, "True enough, but he also knows about how we intend to pay for it."

"The gold bars? He can't possibly know about that," said Mary.

Robert said, "Yes. Not only that, he gave me all of the details. Leonard confirmed that we have 25 twenty-ounce bars in the hidden safe downstairs. He even told me the combination."

Mary appeared pale and shaken. "Nobody knows any of this except us. I mean, well, us and your late mom. Listen, as much as I somehow trust this complete stranger, this is getting very personal and possibly even a bit scary," said Mary.

Robert's dad passed away in his thirties when Robert was a young teenager. Five years after Mary and Robert got married, his mom was diagnosed with early onset Alzheimer's. During the first few years after that diagnosis, while she still possessed the faculties to do so, she quietly converted the family's significant assets into gold bars and parked them with Robert. It was an under-the-radar move that effectively avoided bereavement taxes.

Robert did his best to assuage Mary's fears. "Listen, Mary, I don't feel threatened by the guy. Let's face it, instead of telling us what he knows, he could have already just gone ahead and taken everything from us. The only reason he *did* tell me any of this was because I asked him to prove that he's not some sort of crackpot."

Robert continued, "He even knows where the gold came from, but I'm not concerned. I really don't think he has any ill will toward us or our kids."

Mary appeared to calm down, but had so many questions. She asked, "So what exactly does he want to share with us that's so important. And why on Jacob's birthday?"

"First of all, he says that he knows and cares for our little Jacob like he's his own son," explained Robert. He said that he knows something—a simple thing—that could alter the outcome of Jacob's life tremendously. He feels a responsibility to share his knowledge...he said...as much as any parent would."

"A lot of this doesn't make sense, Robert," cautioned Mary. Her voice started to sound shaky and nervous. "Like, how does he know all of this about us and feel like he's so close to Jacob, when we've never even met him before?"

"Apparently, we *have* met him before," said Robert. "He told me that he looks different now, older, but he assured me that we have spoken in the past."

Mary said, "I have no recollection at all of ever meeting him, and I think I would remember!"

"Me too," said Robert. "I don't remember meeting him, but I have this gnawing feeling that we *have* met him before. I just can't place it."

Leonard sat quietly in the living room while Mary and Robert were talking about him. He leafed through the current issue of Time Magazine that was on the coffee table. Its cover featured caricatures of the main Cold War characters Richard Nixon and Leonid Brezhnev meeting each other. Bits and pieces of hushed conversation from the kitchen were audible, but Leonard didn't seem concerned.

Mary emerged from the kitchen, holding a tray with three porcelain coffee cups on matching saucers, a creamer, a sugar bowl, three teaspoons and napkins. Everything was arranged with perfect symmetry.

Robert followed, holding an ornate silver coffee urn. As he poured the coffee into the cups, Mary said, "So Leonard, Robert has told me some of the fascinating things the two of you talked about earlier. I'm intrigued and, to be honest, a bit nervous. Please tell me what *really* brings you to our home this afternoon?"

Leonard smiled warmly and said, "Mary, I have gifts and good news for everyone in your family! Very good news. I'm going to tell each of you some truths that I know will warm your hearts, along with some advice that is sure to allow your lives to blossom as beautifully and as fully as possible. I also have some advice for Jacob that is a very simple thing for a ten-year-old boy to follow, but can pay off with abundance throughout his life."

His flowery way of speaking was as captivating as he was. Mary and Robert were squinting at Leonard, because the late afternoon summer sun was shining through the sheers that covered a picture window behind him. The blinding shaft of light made Leonard appear as a shadowy figure, which only added to his mysterious nature.

Mary asked, "For some reason, I really do trust you, Leonard. My brain is very skeptical, but my heart says believe. Yet, I have to admit, I'm a bit concerned about what you want to tell my son. Please share that with us before you tell him. I think as his parents, we deserve that and ultimately have that responsibility."

Leonard said, "Of course! I'm not hiding anything. I'm going to explain to Jacob how to stay on the right path...how to make sure that he's careful with his future relationships and chooses well."

Robert said, "That sounds like pretty basic and good advice.

"You do realize that in the most positive way possible, I am very protective of little Jacob," said Leonard. "Like you, I want the best for him. It may be hard to conceive, but in a way, the emotional impact of his decisions in life will touch my heart as well."

"How do you know him," Mary asked. Her quizzical expression suddenly revealed lines in her forehead that were previously hidden.

"I realize this sounds insincere, but I really can't explain that, Mary. Not yet, anyway. But I know *all* of you. You just don't know who I am. Not yet, anyway." Leonard kept smiling warmly as he gave his cryptic response.

Okay, well, Jacob just took a shower," said Mary. "What a mess he was! He came in covered head-to-toe in mud."

"What little boys get into!" said Leonard.

"Yes, if it's not mud, it's frog slime or something of the sort," said Mary. "Well, it sounds like he may be done his shower. I'll call him down in a bit."

Leonard took a sip and drained what was left of his coffee. He had already eaten four of Mary's delicious cookies and four slices of banana bread. He reached for another cookie and then hesitated. He stopped himself, saying, "Too much of a good thing."

Mary said, "Oh, no, please help yourself and have as much as you want. It's the best compliment you can pay to a pastry chef!"

"Thank you, and, yes, I will," said Leonard. He poured some more coffee from the silver urn and then reached for a cookie. Taking a bite, he smiled and said, "I've had these same cookies and this banana bread before. This is a very special treat for me! Thank you!"

Leonard took another bite and paused. He looked deep in thought. The silence sliced through the small talk, creating a chasm that was too wide to ignore. He filled the void by asking a question. "What would you think if I told you that a few decades down the road, Jacob will eventually own and manage Robert's insurance business?"

"Well, I'd say that it's a strong likelihood. At least it's something that Robert and I are hoping will happen," said Mary. "I mean, we don't want to push him into it, but if it's something that Jacob wants as a career, we think it will be a tremendous gift. And that goes for Sarah as well, if she chooses that path."

Leonard nodded and said, "Jacob *will* take on your business and the rest is truly up to him. It may go either way. Sarah will pursue her own passion, which will be teaching. They will both touch many lives in many positive ways."

Robert liked what he just heard and was satisfied to leave it at that. Mary was more inquisitive and decided to poke at the elephant in the room. She asked the obvious, saying, "You're saying this as though it will actually happen! Are you suggesting that you can see into the future? How do you even know *anything* about our children? I'm sorry, I don't mean to be rude, but..."

Leonard interrupted Mary with assurance. "You're not being rude at all, Mary! Believe me, I'd be far pricklier if our positions were reversed."

He lowered his generous voice to his best impression of a whisper, although his 'whisper' still had greater resonance than most people's regular conversational timbre. It was a stunning, yet, ambiguous revelation. "I'm related to Jacob in a way that I simply can't explain. I'm not a great uncle or some cousin that you've never met, but I've always been there in the background, watching him grow. In a way I can speak for Jacob. I'm related by a construct we call time, which is, I understand, extremely confusing. I'm not an angel, but it might help to think of me as his guardian angel.

Mary and Robert looked stunned. They were both at a loss for words and appeared not to know what to do with this information; information that they didn't even understand.

Leonard continued with his spiel, purposely preventing Jacob's parents from thinking too deeply about what he had just revealed. "I know that it's Jacob's tenth birthday today and I want to give him a very important and special gift. In fact, I have gifts for all of you."

Unbeknownst to the adults, Jacob had just come downstairs and was about spy on the living room from a distance to get a peek at the visitor. As he tip-toed into the dining room, he slid on some of the bathwater that he had earlier shed near the top of the stairs. The water found its way onto the dining room floor just below the loft-style hallway above.

The adults turned their heads toward Jacob in unison and chuckled as soon as it was evident that he was not hurt. He was terribly embarrassed, but his curiosity won the battle, so he picked himself up and continued. As Jacob entered the living room, he sensed an immediate attraction to the old man, despite the fact that both of his parents were obviously very confused and somewhat distraught. He jumped up and plopped himself onto the long sofa along the wall where nobody else was seated.

Robert introduced Jacob to Leonard, saying, "Here's our little man of the day! Jacob, I want to introduce you to Mr. Leonard. He's a very nice man who has come to wish you a happy birthday today."

Jacob didn't understand why, but really liked the man's appearance, with his square jaw, brilliant white teeth, broad smile and the liveliest eyes he had ever seen. His booming, round voice was like music to Jacob and he felt an immediate connection with the man.

Even though Jacob was taught to be polite, he couldn't help blurt out, "Do I know you?"

Leonard laughed heartily and said, "Now Jacob, don't you worry. You don't know me yet, but you will. The important thing is that I know you. I know you very well; ever better than you know yourself. And I want to give you a very special birthday gift today!"

Jacob didn't know what to think, but he was suddenly focused on the idea of a gift. He had been a bit fixated on the fact that he never did get the new five-speed spider bicycle with the banana seat for Christmas. Jacob wondered if the stranger had left the bike waiting for him on the front porch?

Leonard leaned in toward Jacob and said in a very serious tone, "Jacob, you are ten years old today. I am going to tell you a secret that won't seem like much of a big deal right now, but if you trust me and do what I say, you will thank yourself for it, for a very big part of your life. Trust me. Trust yourself."

A few years ahead of himself, intellectually, Jacob knew enough to realize that what Leonard was about to tell him just might be more valuable than any bicycle. He stammered, saying, "Wha...what is it?"

"At some point this year, you will have a very important decision to make. No ten-year-old should face this situation, nor should they have to make such a decision. But you will..."

Jacob nodded, saying nothing and listening with the greatest attentiveness a ten-year-old could muster.

Leonard continued, "A new boy will show up in your life. His name is Charles and his family name starts with a T, but you'll know him as Charlie. Now, listen, I'm not able to explain how or why, but you have to believe me, Jacob, when I say that I know you better than you could imagine and I don't want anything bad to happen to you now or in the future. Now, this is the important part..."

Jacob listened with laser-sharp focus and was starting to feel nervous and a bit frightened.

Leonard's eyes grew wider, then narrowed as he looked down at Jacob.

"As much as Charlie is a nice boy, and as much as you will want to play with him and become his new friend, you MUST avoid playing with him," Leonard warned.

This didn't make sense to Jacob. He was smart and was raised to value integrity. What Leonard was suggesting simply sounded rude. It went against what his parents and teachers had taught him about being inclusive and welcoming.

As he was contemplating this "gift," Sarah bounced into the room. However, nobody acknowledged her. She had been taught not to interrupt adults, so she remained silent, but quietly helped herself to some cookies and banana bread.

Leonard said, continuing to lock eyes with Jacob, "I know this doesn't make sense to you right now and it may even seem impolite, Jacob, but this is one of the most important gifts you'll ever receive. Don't be mean to him, be courteous, but do not play with or become friends with Charlie. Ever. Do you understand what I'm asking you, Jacob?

Jacob was confused, but he believed the old man and decided to take his advice. Jacob said, "Yes sir. I understand."

Leonard asked, "Do you have any questions for me?"

Jacob said, frowning, "I have a lot of questions, sir, but I'm afraid to ask…but…but…I promise, I will *not* make friends with this Charlie kid."

"I'm very, very glad to hear that Jacob," said Leonard. As far as your questions, don't be afraid; go ahead and ask. I'll try my best to give you honest answers."

Jacob asked, without missing a beat, "What do I say if this new Charlie guy wants to play or hang-out with me? Can I tell him that you said no way?"

Leonard cautioned, "Jacob, you must not talk about me. You do not need to give a reason. This is good advice in general, young man! A lot of people go through life feeling like they have to give reasons for all of their decisions, but it's not always necessary and sometimes can make things worse."

"What about when I'm talking with my parents," asked Jacob? Don't I need to tell them my reasons for things?

Leonard said, "Everything I have said excludes your parents."

Jacob thought about what he just said, but didn't understand the meaning of the word "exclude." Leonard could read this on his face, so he rephrased his directive, saying, "Always tell your parents *everything* and don't leave anything out! My advice was specifically for Charlie and for other people you may deal with down the road who have no reason or right to know what's behind your own decisions."

Jacob thought about what he had just heard for about five seconds, but it was still too complicated for him to understand. He lost interest and, instead, blurted out, "Who you are? It's so easy to talk with you. Like, it just feels like I've known you for a long time, even though I've never seen you before. It doesn't make sense."

"Yes, it makes a lot of sense," said Leonard. "I have known you for longer than your ten years, even though you've never seen me."

Jacob asked, "Are you my guardian angel?"

Mary's jaw dropped. She knew that her son was smart for his age, but this level of insight appeared to surprise her.

Leonard appeared equally surprised, saying, "You're a very smart young man to ask that question, but no, I'm not your guardian angel or anyone else's for that matter. But, in a way, it's very much *like* that. I've watched you grow up. I know this is hard to understand, but I promise you that, one day, you'll see me again and you will remember our meeting today. Then it will make sense. You'll just have to trust me; trust yourself."

Mary noted that it was the second time Leonard used that phrase. She asserted that it was beyond her son's comprehension. "Leonard, you've said that twice, for Jacob to trust you and to trust himself. I don't understand how you expect him to trust you *and* to trust himself. *I* don't even understand what that means and *he's* only ten, for goodness' sake!"

Leonard said, "Some things make no sense at all and, then suddenly, one day they do. And some of those things turn out to be such significant turning-points in our lives that we refuse to acknowledge how critical our decisions are, because doing so reveals how fragile life really is."

Mary partially understood what Leonard meant, but was a bit puzzled. "I think I get what you're saying, but this is all so strange and…I don't know…it's just hard to reconcile all of this with…I just…don't even really know you, but…"

Leonard interjected. His voice was filled with truth and compassion. "Mary, I understand. I wish I could tell you more, I honestly do, but I am more appreciative than you could know that you trusted in me enough to invite me into your loving home on such an occasion as your son's birthday. The fact that you've allowed me to talk with Jacob and with your family speaks to your character. You are truly a beautiful human being, and your faith in God and in what is good is astounding."

"Well, you're welcome, but it's just basic hospitality! And thank you for your kind compliments, Leonard. You know, I don't understand it, but from the moment you walked through our door, I was somehow drawn to you in ways I can't articulate. I have no idea *why* I should, but I *do* trust you and I can't get over the connection I feel."

Leonard pursed his lips, as though he was trying to explain the inexplicable. "Mary, Robert, Jacob and little Sarah, please understand that I feel the same connection with all of you, but…in a different way. You see, for me, there are these intense feelings of elation and contentment, yet I'm wistful at the same time." Leonard intentionally chose words that would resonate with Jacob's parents, rather than with he and his sister.

He continued with his flowery speech, saying, "Time...is a funny thing. This short time I've spent with you on this single day in 1974 fills my heart with immense joy that somehow transcends time."

Jacob watched keenly and tried to listen-in as Leonard huddled with his mom, with his dad and with Sarah, all individually, before he left. While he couldn't hear what the visitor told each of them, it was apparent that what he shared was extremely important. However, Jacob was at least able to discern from their facial expressions that whatever Leonard said brought each of them deep comfort and delight.

Leonard said his goodbyes and left before dinner was served. Jacob felt a void in his gut when Leonard left; the same sense of loss that everyone in the Miller family felt that late afternoon. Yet, somehow their collective feeling of loss was dwarfed by the peace and encouragement that Leonard's visit did to buoy their spirit.

Like grains of sand tumbling through the middle of an hourglass, seventy-seven years flew by before anyone noticed. The Miller family never did see Leonard again. In the decades that followed, Robert and Mary had long forgotten about the mysterious man's visit. It was as if it had never happened. Perhaps it never did. Even Jacob and Sarah had no recollection of the meeting.

July 1, 2051 arrived without much fanfare. During that span of time, Robert and Mary had gotten very old and lived their last days, and eventually, Jacob and Sarah also grew old with their own families. They had gathered to celebrate Jacob's eighty-seventh birthday. Regrettably, Jacob's money well had dried-up decades before and, accordingly, his budget dictated a modest affair.

Sarah, then eighty-five, attended her brother's party along with several grandkids, nieces and nephews. Sarah's husband, Brandon, was there too. Jacob was solo, because his wife had passed away three years prior to the party.

After dinner, Jacob warmly thanked everyone in attendance for their love and support. Jacob reached into the inside pocket of his suitcoat and pulled-out a quarter-folded wad of papers, upon which he had scribbled a speech. He cleared his throat; the room hushed in response.

Jacob began by toasting his late wife, Jessica, speaking eloquently about their fifty-six beautiful years together and how she played such an important role in raising their children. He lamented the fact that she had developed a heart condition that was brought about by the stress of losing their family business. He also shared what he had learned about life by enduring the heartbreaking failure of his insurance business in his early forties and about the difficult road that led to that loss.

He talked about the people who had been positive influences in his life, but remained silent about those who had led him astray; specifically, Charlie, who had wormed his way into the family business and destroyed it like a cancer.

Family and friends tried their best to make his party a celebration, but Jacob's deep regret and his lingering grief from the loss of his wife hung over the evening like a persistent fog. About an hour before the party came to its end, Jacob blew out the candles on his birthday cake. Like a Hail Mary pass, Jacob parlayed the magic of an old man's birthday wish into the biggest play of his life.

His wish came true.

After the last party guest left his home, Jacob poured a glass of Merlot from an open bottle. He toasted himself and his eighty-seven years before hitting the sack. It was the deepest and most therapeutic sleep he had gotten in several years.

In the morning, Jacob slowly pulled himself to the edge of the bed and rose slowly so as to avoid becoming light-headed. He made his way to the bathroom. His reflection caught his eye as he splashed some water onto his face.

Jacob was pleasantly shocked to see that many of the wrinkles on his face had disappeared; the deepest ones were diminished and revealed character rather than the tired appearance of bitterness and sorrow that he saw just before he went to bed the night before.

IT WAS AT THAT PRECISE MOMENT that Jacob recognized Leonard's visage staring back at him. He suddenly remembered his family's meeting with Leonard so many years ago. As Leonard promised, he did indeed come to recognize who the man was and everything finally made sense.

Jacob looked around and realized that the bathroom he was standing in was the same beautiful ensuite bath that was part of his dream house; the home that he was forced to sell over forty years before, when his insurance business failed. Somehow, Jacob found himself wedged between what he thought was his existence and an alternate new reality that was rapidly replacing the former one.

He rushed back into the bedroom; it was the same spacious bedroom from his *previous* house. Jacob went to bed in his insufficient and shabby 'last resort' home and awoke in his previous dream home. Jacob nearly fainted when he saw Jessica sleeping peacefully in what was just a few moments earlier, a lonely and vacant spot beside his.

He scrambled across the bed with the elasticity of a teenager and hovered over Jessica. He took in all of her beauty and marveled at the miracle that had just taken place. He could feel his grief of her loss evaporate as the reality of her living, breathing self took its place, just as the brilliance of a sunrise bathes a previously gloomy landscape with soothing, beautiful light. Jacob's world was once again vibrant and colorful.

Jessica awoke and looked startled to see Jacob's face just inches above hers. She said, "Look at you! You've got that look in your eye! But why are you staring at me like you haven't seen me in years?"

Jacob said, "It's hard to explain, but it feels as if I *haven't* seen you in years. I love you more than you could ever imagine. This is the happiest moment of my life!"

Jacob's tears of joy bounced off Jessica's cheeks and dribbled onto her pillow. Looking bewildered, she said, "Honey, that's beautiful to hear, but I've got to admit, I've never felt so confused in my life. Am I okay? It's like everything is blank and I'm just remembering this bad dream where we had this life of struggle and sadness."

"But it was just a dream, right? You realize that?" asked Jacob.

"It's all coming back. My memories are…kind of like…filling-in," Jessica said, smiling. "I love you, Jacob."

As Jacob began to familiarized himself with his new eighty-seven-year-old self, his head abruptly filled with multiple memories that touched-off an intense emotional rush. It was as though he were experiencing them all at once. It was the most powerful feeling that he had ever felt; one filled simultaneously with love, fulfillment, pain, challenges and exhilaration!

At the same time Jacob began to question the authenticity of certain other memories, such as his lifelong, yet troubled and tumultuous friendship with Charlie. Within minutes, any recollection of Charlie and the negative collateral damage that he wrought, faded away fully and permanently.

As all of this was happening, Jacob became aware of a sort of shroud or curtain that had been obscuring his consciousness. At once, it tore apart to reveal sidebar memories, seeing his life through Leonard's eyes. While he had new recollections of his own life, which had been significantly different from what he had actually lived, he also had memories of seeing his younger self from Leonard's perspective as a baby, a young man, and throughout the rest of his life.

This was a lot for anyone to digest, let alone an old man. However, Jacob was aware that it was *he* who ignited this flame. He remembered his birthday wish from the night before. He then heard his own deep, round, soothing voice in his inner ear. ***"Trust me and trust in yourself."***

Jacob trusted as instructed. He recalled snubbing young Charlie's attempts to form a friendship. It made little sense to his young boy perception of what was right and wrong, but he trusted in what the old man Leonard had advised and, somehow, trusted in himself to do the same.

The magic of an old man's birthday wish is not universally fulfilled. However, under the most perfect circumstances, it can be granted. The result can be powerful enough to cross time itself, changing actions and consequences.

By the way, Merlot grapes are nowhere near as powerful as an old man's birthday wish, but they can open our minds to accept as plausible, what may have once seemed impossible.

Stephen J. Kristof

TOURIGA NACIONAL
THE LONG WAIT

Port wines depend on it; many other delicious red wines from Portugal's Douro and Dao wine regions also rely on it. Of course, we're talking about the noble Touriga Nacional grape! Like many wine grapes, this particular varietal is sometimes vinified into single varietal wines. However, for most Portuguese red vinos, Touriga Nacional is a very important component of a complex blend, along with other red and black grapes.

Being so essential, one would expect many more hectares of Portugal's granite soil to be reserved for Touriga Nacional grape vines. Although it was Portugal's predominately planted wine grape at one time, it takes up less of a footprint today. In the late 1800s, the Phylloxera insect devastated most of those early vines. Today, it is still grown successfully, but has taken a back seat to clones that are more disease resistant and productive.

Nevertheless, Touriga Nacional is a benchmark grape that produces red wines that are some of the darkest, densest and richly-bodied anywhere in the world. It is said to be as important to Portugal as Cabernet Sauvignon is to France. How does it taste? This very special grape produces wines that have brooding dark fruit and plum flavors along with delightful violet-type fragrances.

Such a heavy, dark wine demands a similarly dark story. Accordingly, you're about to read a dark story, **but be warned!**

This might not be the best choice if you're looking for a happy and peaceful bedtime story!

Unlike the enchanting effect that a Touriga Nacional wine has on the taste and olfactory senses, the forthcoming dark yarn is bitter and austere. But, as in life, delight and appreciation of the good times is only possible when punctuated by times which are, well, not so good.

Jiminy, as he was known to his 'boys' in the crew, was a low-level gang-based badass. His idol was a fictional character, Tony Soprano, which would be amusing if it weren't for the fact that Jiminy actually believed him to be a real-life person. A mob-boss wannabe, Jiminy had an inferiority complex that held him back from attaining such 'success' despite committing countless offensively violent acts and possessing a dangerously narcissistic personality. His given name was James. His father left town shortly after learning that his on-again, off-again girlfriend was pregnant.

James' mom began calling him Jimmy shortly after his birth. The nickname stuck until he was sixteen, when a fellow gangmate with a penchant for animated movies started calling him Jiminy. At thirty-four, he was still known by that diminutive moniker. It's just one of those things; career criminals almost always become a magnet for nicknames, regardless of how silly or childish they may seem.

Jiminy was on the short side, but was physically fit and unexpectedly handsome, despite the menacing scars on his face. One thick scar went diagonally across his right eyebrow, splitting it in two. The blade from that particular encounter just narrowly missed his eye. Another scar looked like a thin V-shaped checkmark with visible stitch marks; that one adorned Jiminy's upper right cheek.

Those facial scars were the result of two different knife fights, but he had yet another one that ran parallel under nearly the entire length of his lower lip. The incident that created that lip scar also resulted in a vertical six-inch scar near the mid-right side of his abdomen. The injuries that led to those scars almost took his life.

Jiminy blasted through a glass door while trying to get away from a robbery that had gone very badly. Police were waiting for him on the street side of that door. Jiminy was rushed to the local hospital; his bottom lip was hanging by a thread and blood was gushing from a deep wound in his abdomen. A long shard of glass from the door had plunged through his gut and sliced-off part of his liver. He stayed at the hospital in protective custody for nearly a week before being taken directly to jail.

Jiminy was quite familiar with incarceration and with the justice system in general. He had a rap sheet five pages long and had served over ten short-term stints in county lock-up. He had also begun a five-year stint in state prison for armed robbery causing injury, but was released before his first month was up. He felt like he had won the lottery when his conviction was unexpectedly reversed. During a local media interview, a juror in the trial carelessly disclosed his familial relationship to the victim; something he denied in the juror selection phase. The judge in that case granted a request for mistrial and the district attorney dropped the case.

Personal safety is a primary concern for anyone in jail; particularly for someone as short and slender as Jiminy. Not to worry; Jiminy's bantam frame concealed a powerful left hook that took many by surprise. Watching him fight was upsetting, if not entirely frightening. He could explode into a dizzying flurry of fists, knees and feet, bouncing and spinning, punching and kicking so swiftly that he was just a blur.

At thirty-four, most of his former schoolmates had established themselves in progressive career situations, had become parents, had invested wisely for their futures, and lived in attractive homes in safe and well-kept neighborhoods. By contrast, Jiminy had no real tangible or deposited assets to his name and lived in a dirty basement apartment rental that was too cramped even for just one person.

However, Jiminy did have a career and he had just earned a promotion. Jiminy was recruited a year earlier to join a new, loosely-knit gang run by a local thug who was far more powerful, far more clever and far more successful than Jiminy was or would ever become. Nonetheless, Jiminy was quite proud of himself, because he had just been boosted to a "Capo" position in the thug's gang.

This thug had built quite a little empire for himself in Jiminy's hometown. Whether townsfolk had ever met him in person or had only heard of his fabled existence didn't matter. Few knew his real name, but his odd nickname was somewhat legendary. He was known by the amusing moniker, "Teeth," due to his extraordinarily handsome choppers. *(Not, by the way, a very common attribute amongst folks living and working in Teeth's particular layer of society.)*

Jiminy looked up to Teeth; he saw himself as the guy's protégé. His ultimate goal in life was to replace Teeth. It was an objective which had nothing to do with the fact that many of Jiminy's interactions with other people resulted in them having to replace their own teeth.

Ah, but we digress. Yes, Jiminy saw himself eventually stealing, earning advancement to or killing his way to Teeth's throne. Thank goodness that at least he had a life plan.

So, who exactly was Teeth? Head of a disjoined crew of flunkies, among which Jiminy was an associate, Teeth had earned a reputation as the town's go-to guy for a variety of enterprising services such as loansharking, illicit drugs, theft and prostitution. The usual and customary stuff for these types of guys. Oh, yes, he also provided rented muscle for clients who got themselves into situations that required physical intimidation or worse; clients who either did not have such muscle themselves or who saw the need to have it done by someone else from a safe distance.

Deep down, Jiminy had a sense that Teeth saw him as the weak, insecure dolt that he really was, but he couldn't bear to deal with it on a conscious level. Instead, he chose to harbor the illusion that he would eventually be the next 'big' thing in charge of the local crime scene. In reality, Teeth found an easy mark in Jiminy. To Teeth, Jiminy represented a cheap, highly disposable and obedient lapdog.

Teeth could count on Jiminy to accomplish a variety of highly illegal and disruptive acts. Best yet for Teeth, Jiminy silently settled for a financial cut that was far less than his compadres received. His fellow lowlifes earned much more for doing far less dangerous and illegitimate things than did Jiminy. It was so unfair, considering that Jiminy did those very dangerous and illegal things with exceptional effort and dedication! In terms of his work ethic, Jiminy was a model employee.

It was just past six-thirty in the evening and Jiminy was getting ready for the night shift. He wasn't sure what Teeth had in store for him, but he was told to meet him at the warehouse after seven o'clock. It was something bigger than usual, but Teeth couldn't tell him anything more than that. Teeth told him to make plans not to go home after the night's job was complete. Instead, he was instructed to hang-out at the warehouse for a few days.

Jiminy stuffed a backpack with extra clothing, toiletries, beer, three cans of cocktail sausages, and several bags of chips and salty snacks. His delusion of being health-conscious was satisfied by the few bottles of high-end spring water he also packed. He had enough stuff, he thought, to keep himself going for a few days away, lying low after finishing whatever the big job turned out to be. Jiminy put his right hand on the handle of the exterior door that led from his basement apartment to a set of rickety old stairs up the side of the house.

As he turned the handle, Jiminy heard knocking from the interior door at the top of the staircase. There was only one person who ever knocked on that door. It was his landlord, DeeDee. She was the sixty-eight-year-old owner of the house who lived upstairs. For the most part, DeeDee's remarkably active libido remained unquenched, although she tried her best to advertise.

Oh, and she really did know how to advertise! She was old enough to know better, but her closet was full of blouses with plunging necklines that exposed far too much. Neighbors loved watching her strut down the sidewalk, wearing pink hot pants and matching sparkly high heels. Seeing her climb into her deep pink 1972 Cadillac Coupe DeVille while wearing that outfit, was beyond entertainment!

DeeDee didn't care what anyone thought; she was as thick skinned as a Rhinoceros. Her protective armor plate was matched by an abrasiveness toward others that felt like steel wool rubbing against tender skin. However, she could instantly turn-on the charm, duping any stranger into easily believing that she was a sweet and delicate flower...with a provocative naughty streak.

DeeDee lived entirely for herself and had long given-up on earning her golden pennies in heaven; something the nuns tried to teach her as a young child attending Catechism Sunday School. Having Jiminy as a tenant, a much younger, vigorous and muscular man, presented a temptation that DeeDee found too much to suppress. Jiminy's scars and rough masculinity only got DeeDee's engine revving faster.

Jiminy was genuinely afraid of DeeDee. Surprising, really, considering his overall fierceness. Her persistent advances made Jiminy uncomfortable. She made it clear that she wanted to knock knees with him, but he was firm, in that it would never happen. Yet, despite their age difference, he didn't trust himself. Here you have this very aggressive man with quite the violent streak—you wouldn't think that kind of guy would feel so defenseless against DeeDee's lustful entreaties.

He didn't like being ogled and treated like a hunk of meat. It made tough guy Jiminy feel vulnerable and defenseless. He was at a loss in terms of how to handle DeeDee. Nevertheless, he was adamant that he wouldn't let it happen. Well, at least he wouldn't let it happen *again*. What? Hmmm...

He was so ashamed of the time that he paid-off his monthly rent with his body, he refused to acknowledge that it ever happened. No worries; DeeDee didn't forget about it and frequently asked Jiminy if he needed some 'help' with the rent.

Hearing DeeDee's urgent knocking at the top of the stairs, Jiminy realized that he had to make a quick and quiet getaway. Teeth needed to see him anyway, so he left a bit earlier to avoid DeeDee. He slipped outside and closed the exterior door ever so quietly. He scooted up the exterior stairwell like an unseen breeze. It was seven o'clock and the sun had just begun to set. Jiminy grabbed his scratched-up old black mountain bike from behind the shed and took to the street.

Even though he was thirty-four, he still rode the same bike that he had when he was sixteen. The bike was his only means of transportation, but was reliable and helped him blend-in to his surroundings. All of Jiminy's 'associates' in Teeth's criminal enterprise had cars or pick-up trucks. Even the ones who were almost half his age had their own wheels. This only fed Jiminy's inferiority complex and bothered him deeply, but it manifested mostly in his sleep. He fed a lie to himself and to others, claiming that he did his best work using the old bike and that a motor vehicle would only complicate things. Nobody believed it; not even Jiminy.

Jiminy used a special route to get from his rental to the back door of a small warehouse near a small private dock. It was Teeth's "headquarters" and nerve center for his illegal empire. He chose to operate from this little obscure dock because it wasn't on anyone's radar and offered the privacy he required.

The town's official commercial port also had a handful of vacant warehouses from which Teeth could have operated, but it was way too visible. Instead, Teeth's kingdom was contained in a long-abandoned, derelict steel barn at a rarely-used dock that most townsfolk had long forgotten about.

He had a unique arrangement with the property owner, who allowed Teeth to use the building clandestinely and as long as he wanted, in exchange for the occasional special favor. Those favors ranged from the provision of prostitutes to roughing-up commercial tenants in his other buildings who were late on rent. The occasional free bag of weed and cocaine also helped seal the deal and kept Teeth in good stead with his "landlord."

Riding his bike over rough patches of gravel and winding through a network of neglected alleys, Jiminy made it to the warehouse in just about five minutes. His special route saved Jiminy's ass on several occasions. It allowed him to avoid city streets and open parking lots where Jiminy could be seen or captured on camera.

He pulled-up to the back door. His front wheel skidded as he turned it sharply to the side. Bits of gravel that had stuck in the grooves of his tires went flying and made an echoey pinging noise as they bounced off the thick steel door. Jiminy leaned his bike on the wall. One of Teeth's security guys was inside and heard Jiminy's noisy arrival. He poked his head out the door and held it open just long enough for Jiminy to slip in.

Inside, the warehouse was predictably sparse and dimly lit. The door opened to a huge empty space with three side-by-side cement block rooms off to the right side. A large table sat in the middle, with a fancy tiffany-style light hanging above it. The fixture seemed out of place. Ten chairs surrounded the table, not one of them matching the other.

A hallway in the back led to a bathroom with a very nasty toilet, sink and shower stall; none of which appeared to have been cleaned in years. Teeth had his own personal bathroom attached to his private office. It was reportedly immaculate. NOBODY except Teeth ever used it, nor would anyone else dare to ask for permission to use his private commode. The disgusting back bathroom was the only option for crew members, most of whom used it only when absolutely necessary. Anyone in their right mind would choose an alternative, given the option.

The back left wall of the warehouse was covered in a patchwork of pegboards with hooks, upon which hung a variety of auto wrecking equipment, break-in tools, and a variety of ropes, chains, electrical cables and strange-looking metal objects.

To the left of the main walk-in entry door was a massive motorized barn door. Teeth could engage the motor to open the giant door simply by pushing the red button above the light switch on his office wall. He also enjoyed tapping an app on his phone to open and close it. Shipments of contraband, stolen vehicles and other illegal items were received through that big door, where they were quickly hidden from public view. When their dishonest schemes went to shit, that same barn door also allowed gang members to swiftly drive their cars and trucks directly into the warehouse, where they were safely veiled from police and, potentially, other curious eyes.

As Jiminy looked around for Teeth, he noticed half of a Lincoln Navigator on the floor with the other half strewn about in pieces. Teeth was nowhere to be seen. He wasn't at the table and, of course, he always stayed clear of the disgusting bathroom at the back. Jiminy figured his boss must be in his office.

His office was one of three floor-to-ceiling cinder block rooms built onto the right inside wall of the warehouse. Shortly after securing the building through his special arrangement with the owner, Teeth hired a couple of very handy and equally corrupt guys to do some pretty aggressive renovations to the place. They started by building those three very secure rooms. The rooms were, basically, vaults. The only way to get into them was through heavy gauge steel doors inside the main warehouse space. Insanely thick deadbolts provided further security.

Basically, nobody was getting in those offices unless Teeth wanted them to. A rival criminal or disloyal member of Teeth's own crew would need extreme determination and a death wish to breach those rooms without his approval.

Beyond Teeth's personal office, the other two rooms served as secure storage areas. Jiminy had been in those rooms only one time. A few months prior, Teeth must have been in need of validation, so he invited Jiminy in to take a look around. That invitation was, essentially, Teeth's way of touting his success and power.

The first storage room was full of a variety of handguns, assault rifles, clips, ammo and knives. Jiminy had once seen C4 explosive putty packs and blasting caps in the room, but he had never personally used the stuff and had no idea how to even handle it.

The second room was a transitionary space for short-term storage of a variety of contraband and spoils. This was where drugs and stolen items sat until they could be safely moved onto the street or into large buyers' hands.

The whole set-up was like Fort Knox. Cameras were mounted above the storage rooms and above Teeth's personal office. Beyond the half-inch thick steel doors and deadbolts, Teeth's office door could also be secured from the *inside*. It had another deadbolt and two heavy steel security bars that slid into brackets; those brackets were bolted to the cement wall on both sides of the door.

Teeth had it all figured out. It was nearly impossible for others to break into his office without a lot of time and special equipment. Explosives would do the trick more quickly, but they would probably destroy everything inside his office, including Teeth's teeth.

In the event that he had to make a quick escape, Teeth had prepared workarounds for that as well. Teeth's office had an exterior door for a quick exit; of course, that door also had serious protection, making it equally difficult to breach from outside the building. He often used that quick exit when he wanted to avoid an unwanted visitor in the warehouse or simply didn't have the patience to deal with the boys in his own crew.

Then there was the money. Dirty cash often needs to sit for a while before it's distributed or laundered. That currency was kept in a safe inside the safe room; the safe room was underground. The old warehouse did not have a basement when Teeth secured it. Although it sounds a bit extreme—like something you'd see in an international spy flick—Teeth actually had his thuggish handymen build a tunnel and safe room. Jiminy had been in the tunnel only once. It was the coolest thing he had ever seen and made him feel as though he were an actor in a high stakes crime movie.

The tunnel was pure genius! It was forty-feet-long, connecting his office to an escape hatch beyond the warehouse. It was modern and clean, complete with lighting and a six-and-a-half-foot ceiling. In case of emergency, whatever that might be, Teeth could access the tunnel through a trap door in his office's personal bathroom. In the middle of the bathroom's tile floor was a huge decorative Italian travertine panel. That slab was actually the tunnel's entrance. It had hidden hinges that allowed it to be swung upward, revealing the tunnel's stairs.

Teeth realized that, at some point, the proverbial shit could hit the fan very badly. He was a good scout. He was prepared for just about any scenario. He decided that he needed a secure hiding place, as well as a secondary getaway option.

Once opened, Teeth could unlock the back exit door from his office, which would make it appear to police or to an intruder as though Teeth had already escaped. Instead, however, he would climb through the opening under that travertine slab, descend the stairs, pull the panel back in place and evade his would-be captors. He had the option of waiting it out in the safe room or using a secret egress away from the warehouse. The safe room had the aforementioned cash safe, food, drink, a computer, Wi-Fi, a toilet, a couch and a bed.

If staying put was a bad idea and Teeth needed to flee, the tunnel led to another trap door in the floor of a small metal storage shed that was adjacent to the warehouse. The escape hatch in the shed floor was concealed slyly under a resin storage cabinet that was designed to swing-out using a lever in the tunnel that opened that hatch. After his escape through the shed portal, Teeth would simply swing the cabinet back into place and no one would be the wiser. The shed was alongside a short canal connected to the dock. Teeth kept an old speedboat moored to the canal's break wall. If needed, it provided a very sneaky escape to open waters.

The whole thing was quite an elaborate and expensive set-up for a small-town criminal. When it came right down to it, though, Teeth was not going down. No way. Never.

He had fostered several connections in town with very influential and powerful people. It's not like he was *above* the law or *was* the law, but Teeth paid-off enough well-positioned people to buy his way out of just about any trouble he might find himself in. The elaborate security in the warehouse, the safe room and the tunnel were just additional means of potentially saving his own ass.

Jiminy had never given much thought to the fact that he and his gangmates enjoyed no such safety or distance from the long reach of the law. The warehouse itself was, ultimately, pretty easy to broach. The three offices and the tunnel were not. It came down to this; although Teeth and his plunder remained fairly safe, the boys in his crew were completely vulnerable to take the fall.

The bribes that judges, law enforcement and municipal government officials had taken didn't extend beyond Teeth to Jiminy or any of his gangmates. Those guys were easy to find, were easy to expose and were, ultimately, sitting ducks.

Yes, Teeth was a shrewd operator. Jiminy was disposable. Remember that.

After entering the warehouse and looking around, Jiminy eyeballed the security guy who motioned for him to go to Teeth's office. He looked at his phone, which read 7:08 p.m. He hoped that Teeth was ready for him. Jiminy knocked on the slightly open door with two short taps. He heard a muffled voice telling him to come in and to shut the door.

There he was. Teeth was wearing a finely tailored silk suit with a stylish dark patterned shirt. He looked like a business man. Well, he did run a business, but just not a legitimate one. Teeth smiled at Jiminy, his perfect choppers gleaming more brightly than usual. He told Jiminy to have a seat and said that he had something extra special for him that evening.

Teeth opened the top left drawer of his desk and took out a bundle of fifty-dollar bills. It was about a half-inch thick. He placed it on the desk and, using his thumb and forefinger, flicked it toward Jiminy. The bundle rolled a few times and then stopped, bumping into Jiminy's left hand. He couldn't take his eyes off the wad. He had handled far more money than this on many occasions, but this was the first time a bundle worth so much was meant just for him.

Teeth snarled, "Time to grow some balls and earn some *real* money, Jiminy."

Jiminy reached for the bundle and slowly raised his eyes to meet Teeth's. He cleared his throat and asked, "So what's this all about?"

"You're my Capo, kid. You deserve more. I've got a special job for you tonight and you're the only one on my crew I can trust with this...are you in?"

Without considering what, specifically, he had to do to earn that money and feeling more flattered than anything, Jiminy shook his head affirmatively, saying, "Yeah, sure. I'm in."

"Keep the five thousand. You do this right, and you get the other five thou."

Jiminy felt important. He was convinced that he had finally made it to the big time. Never mind what he had to do for the cash; it was only up from here. Jiminy's eyes grew wide. He asked, "So what's the job?"

Teeth ignored Jiminy's question. "You screw-up and I take back the first five thou. You lose your balls and have second thoughts, then you've *really* screwed up. Do that and I take something else from you. Something you can't get back. Get it?"

Jiminy had no idea what Teeth was talking about. He just shook his head yes, looking like a deer in headlights.

"Okay, then we're both talking the same language."

Teeth extended his hand. He and Jiminy shook on it. However, Jiminy still didn't know exactly *what* he was agreeing to.

Teeth opened another drawer and pulled out a handkerchief. He wrapped it around his hand and used it to grab a black handgun that was also in the drawer. Teeth dumped the gun into Jiminy's hand without directly handling it. He then picked-up a loaded clip for the gun and gave it to Jiminy in the same manner.

Jiminy took the pistol and clip. It was a beat-up Beretta 92; probably an old police surplus gun that was picked-up on the cheap. He wondered why he was given such an old gun when

Teeth had several perfectly new Glock 19s in lock-up. He also thought it was strange that Teeth was so careful to avoid getting his fingerprints on the gun. He was about to ask, when Teeth chimed in.

"So, there's this broad in Oxchley, you know, over near the wineries. Her husband wants her gone...permanently. He's taking her out to dinner tonight at La Fois Grois for their anniversary. Their reservation's for seven-thirty. He wants it to happen when they're leaving the restaurant. Nice guy, huh?"

"So, you want me to...to...kill her? Like, as in, shoot her dead?" Jiminy's voice was faint and shaky.

He had done more than his share of roughing-up people and even beating some to a pulp. One of his victims ended up in a wheelchair, while another lost an eye, most of his teeth and the use of his right hand. But this was different. Teeth was talking about murder. Jiminy had used guns plenty of times to threaten, harass, and even shoot some feet and kneecaps. But he had never shot someone dead before.

"KILL her? Um, yah," Teeth said sarcastically. He straightened-up in his chair and said forcefully, "I'm starting to have my doubts about you. Listen, if you're not up to the task, I'm sure Bobby would jump at the opportunity."

Jiminy looked at the handgun that he was already cradling in his hands and then glanced at the stack of fifties. He rationalized the job as a test of sorts; a test to determine if he really had the metal to step up to the plate and take his well-deserved place at the table. Still, though, Jiminy gave a momentary thought to the seriousness of what he was about to do. He began thinking about the woman, someone he had never met or seen before, and how she's out enjoying an anniversary dinner with her murderous husband; how she doesn't have a clue that her life's about to end...and about to end so violently.

Only a few seconds went by, but to Jiminy, it felt like hours. Thoughts of his mother interrupted his musing and his eyes welled-up.

Teeth saw that Jiminy was having second thoughts and ramped-up his dialogue to get his boy back on track. "You can't take your bike to this job. There's a black sportscar inside the warehouse by the barn door. To be honest, it's a bit of a shit box, but it still has some guts and will get you there no problem. Don't speed. Don't draw any attention."

Jiminy maintained a driver's license, but without ever actually owning his own vehicle, he was the worst driver in the crew. His concern for the victim was quickly replaced with excitement about the possibility that Teeth was letting him keep the car.

"Do I get to keep the car?"

"I'll get to that. Now listen carefully. Get there no later than 8:40 p.m. Park the car at the back end of the empty lot on the corner of Palmer and Lyster. The lighting's bad there, and it's a fast twenty-second run down the alley to the back of the restaurant. The client is planning to leave the restaurant with wifey at 9:05."

"Okay, so where do I wait for them? How do you want me to do it? Shoot her in the back, I presume?"

Teeth looked shocked. He shouted, "Shoot her in the fucking back? What the hell! Who are you, man? You don't want to make it look like a fucking execution!"

Jiminy said, sheepishly, "No, no...I'm sorry...ah...it's just, I never, um, yah, that wouldn't look good. So how do you want me to do it?"

"You have to make it look like a robbery, but a robbery gone bad. You've got a lot of experience doing robberies, so that part's nothing new to you, right?"

Jiminy shook his head in agreement and said, "Um-hum."

"There's a mailbox on the sidewalk between the restaurant's front door and where the husband's going to park his car. You need to crouch and hide behind that mailbox, so she doesn't see you until it's too late."

Jiminy had been to the restaurant once before when he was a kid and was picturing it in his mind. His mother took him there for his twelfth birthday along with her boyfriend of the month. He remembered how awful the night turned-out, with the creep boyfriend getting drunk, yelling at him and taking a swing at his mother. He wondered why someone didn't exterminate that cockroach back then, the way he was going to kill some woman he'd never met in just a few hours.

"As they walk past the mailbox, you need to jump in front of them, not behind, and point your gun at the couple. Tell them to give you everything they have. Yell at them. Tell them to do it quickly and threaten to shoot them both."

"What about the husband? You want me to take his stuff too?"

"Yes. It's gotta look like a robbery, kid. Get it?"

"Got it."

Teeth handed him a small black zippered nylon bag with a carabiner attached to it. The bag was heavier than he expected. It already had something in it. Teeth had already placed a large rock in the bag.

"What's with the rock in here?"

"I'll get to that. One thing at a time. Step-by-step, Jiminy. Do not remove the rock. *Ever*."

"Okay."

"So, as soon as you get to the restaurant and crouch behind the mailbox, unclip this bag from your belt loop and make sure it's unzipped. When it's time, you tell the guy to put his wallet and ring in this bag. Don't handle anything. Have them do it for you. Don't take your gun or your eyes off them!"

Jiminy's expression grew far more solemn as the seriousness of everything began to sink in. He asked, "Then the woman?"

"Do NOT take her purse. It'll only slow you down as you try to get away. Tell her to get her wallet out of her purse and put it in the bag. Then her rings."

"You're right-handed, correct?"

Jiminy nodded in agreement.

"Okay, so put the gun in your left hand and keep it pointed at the woman. Hand the bag to the woman."

"You want me to give the bag with the loot *to the woman?*" Jiminy was confused.

"Yeah. Tell her to zip the bag. To close it. Then grab it from her and clip the carabiner to your belt loop. Now this is very important...switch the gun back to your right hand. Push it up to the woman's face. Push it under her nose, you know, like right under her nostrils and point it upward. Like this..."

Teeth grabbed the gun from Jiminy's hands. He used Jiminy's face to demonstrate. Jiminy hated the feeling of the barrel pressed up against the bottom of his nose. It was cold and painful. Teeth pressed it harder than he needed to, but he knew that it would be an effective way of teaching Jiminy a very important lesson.

Jiminy felt completely overwhelmed by the sensation; both physically and mentally. It was far more powerful than the mere pain he felt in his nose. He felt paralyzed and helpless. Suddenly, he was struck by the absolute power that the gun gave Teeth. His life was in Teeth's hands. Teeth knew how important it was for Jiminy to learn this.

Teeth removed the gun from Jiminy's face and grabbed a hand towel from a desk drawer. He took out a generic spray bottle from the same drawer and sprayed the entire gun. Jiminy didn't know what was in that bottle, but it smelled to him like a very strong mixture of rubbing alcohol and ammonia. Teeth rubbed the gun with the towel and handed it back to Jiminy without touching it.

"So, while you push that gun up her nostrils, you accuse the woman of hiding something in her purse." Teeth's voice grew louder and angry. "Grab for her purse with your left hand and, as you throw it onto the ground, pull the trigger. Make sure you point the gun straight up her nose. Point it upward toward the back of her skull and when you pull the trigger, try to push it forward at the same time."

Jiminy was confused. He asked, "What do I do with the purse, then?"

"Nothing. The whole purse thing is just to make it look like a robbery gone bad. Just in case there are any witnesses. You've got to make it look like you struggled with the woman and got angry with her."

"Okay. I get it. And that's it? Just run to the car and get the hell back here?"

Teeth looked frustrated and started to bite his lower lip. He said, "Just listen to me. You're not done yet. While the husband pretends to be freaking out over his wife, you make your getaway. Run down that same alley toward the car and drive away in the opposite direction down Lyster Street. Do NOT come back here!"

"Where am I going?"

Teeth answered sarcastically, saying, "To hell." He flashed an uncomfortable smile with those perfect teeth, paused a moment and continued.

Jiminy's heart was racing and he started to feel light-headed. He said to himself, "Pull yourself together, man."

"You need to drive slowly. Don't spin your tires and scream out of the lot like it's some fucking TV show. Just get in the car as quickly as you can, close the door quietly and drive away like an old lady. Got it?"

"Yup."

"Turn right on Hillsview Street and take it all the way up to Pick Valley Road. Follow Pick Valley down to the lake. Half way there, there's a curve in the road, where the creek gets really close to the road. It's pretty deserted along that road most of the time. Stop the car in the road."

"Pull off onto the shoulder, though, right?"

"NO! Just keep the car in your lane and put it in park. If you pull over, the cops will see the tracks on the shoulder later on and they'll likely drag the bottom and find the gun. Quickly get out of the car and throw the gun into the middle of that creek."

"Understood. Then what?"

"Keep driving on Pick Valley until you get to the small lake. There's a parking lot there with a little dirt path that leads to an old boat launch. The place should be deserted at this time of year. There's a flashlight in the glove compartment. Take it with you. It'll be pitch dark out there. Are you following all of this?"

"Yes. Pick Valley, stop at curve near the creek. Keep in lane and toss gun. Proceed to the lake. Take the dirt path to the old boat launch. Flashlight. Got it."

"Now, once you get to the launch, kill the flashlight. There's a skinny old dock next to the boat launch. Walk out to the very end of that dock. Again, keep your flashlight off! Sometimes there's some kids out there drinking or making out...you don't want them to see you. Unclip the carabiner and throw that bag of loot as far out into the lake as you can. Get yourself back to the car and take a right on Pine Drive. Keep going for about ten minutes to the big box store just before you hit Harrow. You should make it there in less than ten minutes."

"What am I getting at the store?"

"Nothing. Pull around to the back side of the store, where they have their oil change and tire garage. There's no view of the street from there. Leave the car in one of the spots back there. It'll probably take a few weeks before they even notice it. But with that car's history, we can't touch it again. Joey's going to bring your bike there and will leave it leaning against the wall near the loading bays."

Jiminy's heart sank. He really thought the car was his. He said, "So, I'm driving my bike all the way back here?"

"Yup. Should take you about a half hour. Drop the car key into the first sewer grate you see. Listen, they won't be looking for someone on a bicycle two towns away from a fatal robbery, but they may be looking for someone in a black sportscar. I'm just looking out for you, my man."

That was partially true. Teeth had hatched a pretty clever plan. If followed precisely, there was a decent chance Jiminy would stay out of trouble. The problem is, though, that even with exceptionally seamless plans, it's impossible to anticipate *every* variable. And sometimes, those variables can be pretty darned random.

And so it was. Jiminy followed the plan to a tee. Well, at least initially. Surprisingly, he remembered and followed every detail leading up to and during the brutal murder of the horrible man's innocent wife. However, Jiminy intentionally ignored one of the subsequent details; a very important one that had the potential to derail the entire plan. A few other random variables also got in the way.

As the couple walked, hand-in-hand, from the restaurant, Jiminy jumped from behind the mailbox and brandished his gun. As expected, the woman screamed, while her husband pretended to be macho. It's easy to argue with a gun when you've hired that gun. Jiminy pointed the gun at the man and instructed him to deposit his wallet and wedding ring into the nylon bag. The man grumbled and threw some expletives at Jiminy, but he ultimately complied.

In truth, it was easy for the wretchedly immoral man to do, because he had previously emptied his wallet of large bills and his most coveted black credit cards. The fact that he always kept a spare condom in his wallet was something that bothered his wife, but she never brought it up. The adulterous letch also withheld the condom, knowing that he would use it later that night. As far as his wedding ring was concerned, he hated wearing it and wanted it as gone as his wife would soon be.

Jiminy then pointed the gun at the woman, who at this point was shrieking and crying uncontrollably. The woman's terrified expression bothered him and, for just a moment, he thought about his mother. Jiminy told her to put her wallet and rings in the bag. His voice was unsteady and cracking.

She immediately unzipped her purse and fished for her wallet. She was shaking and was so nervous that she dropped it onto the sidewalk. A tube of lipstick and various other items fell out and rolled on the concrete. Jiminy yelled at the woman to pick the purse up off the sidewalk and get her wallet out. She bent down, grabbed it and followed his instructions. She awkwardly straightened-up, but appeared to have some difficulty doing so.

Remembering how he needed to have the woman zip the bag closed, he gave it to the woman. He told her to put her wallet in the bag and she obeyed him. He pointed the gun at her face and shouted, "Put your fucking rings in the bag...NOW!"

So filled with terror, she didn't give a second thought to removing her favorite ring, a real showstopper with red rubies and large diamonds. She dropped it into the bag. But when it came to her wedding ring, she hesitated. It was the last vestige of what she knew deep down was a dying marriage. She struggled to get it over her swollen knuckle.

She looked at her husband as she dropped the ring in the bag. She was shocked and saddened by what she saw. Her mouth opened and her eyes widened in disbelief as he curled his right lip ever so slightly in a smirk.

Preparing himself mentally to complete the job while continuing to make it look like a robbery, Jiminy pushed on with the plan. He switched the gun to his left hand and continued to point it at her. He ordered her to zip the bag shut and hand it to him, which she did. Her uncontainable tears splashed off the bag and dribbled onto the sidewalk. Jiminy could feel the wetness of the bag when she handed it back to him.

He clipped the carabiner to his belt loop, but had to struggle with it. Using just one hand made it more difficult, but he finally clipped it on the third try.

Jiminy then raised his voice and accused the woman of holding back. He switched the gun back to his right hand, pushed the gun up against the bottom of her nose and put pressure on the bottom of her nostrils.

She winced in pain and threw her head backward. Jiminy wrapped his left hand around the back of her head and pulled it upright.

Judging from the woman's terrified expression, Jiminy figured that she probably felt powerless, just as he felt when Teeth demonstrated the same move on him. Although, he thought, this was very different. This was real for her.

Jiminy followed his script and accused her of holding something back. He threatened to pull the trigger if she didn't comply. Before she could even fathom what he was talking about, he made good on his promise and pulled the trigger.

Jiminy performed his first homicide like a contract killer. The percussion sound of his gun sliced through the poor woman's screams, silencing her forever. The bullet followed a precise path through her sinus cavity, shredded her cerebrum to bits and then exited the crown of her skull. She died instantly.

The woman's body went limp and crumbled onto the sidewalk. Never having killed anyone before, let alone with a gun to the head, Jiminy wasn't prepared for the aftermath.

He hadn't given any thought to the blood. Sure, he had caused a lot of people to bleed, but never like this. The blood, and bits of skull and brain matter were everywhere. Blood continued to spill out of her head, creating a small river that pooled-up on the sidewalk.

Jiminy was shocked by what he saw. He couldn't look at her lifeless, pathetic body any longer. He turned his head toward the bastard that paid for him to do this. At that moment, a couple exited the restaurant; Jiminy and the man suddenly had an unexpected audience. As if on cue, the man screamed at Jiminy, shouting, "You damned animal! What have you done? You've taken the most important thing from me! Shoot me now! Kill me!"

It was all happening so fast. Jiminy was in a state of shock. Instead of looking forward to collecting the rest of the money and feeling like he was in control, he felt sick in a way he had never felt before. He was filled with remorse and extreme sadness. The smell of black powder still hanging in the air accented his despair and the acrid stench burned his nose. Not only did Jiminy suddenly realize the enormity of the mistake he had just made, he also understood that his life had forever changed.

Seeing the new couple brought Jiminy back into the moment. His mind switched from remorse to self-preservation. He ran as fast as he could to his getaway car.

The couple leaving the restaurant was the first random and uncontrollable variable in the plan. They exited the restaurant just before the fake robbery and murder went down. They saw everything, albeit from a bit of a distance. However, it was bright enough and they were close enough to get a very clear view of

Jiminy. When teeth checked-out the location in advance it was in the middle of the day and he didn't notice the streetlight hanging directly over the mailbox area.

The restaurant's exterior security camera was another variable, but again, it was one that Teeth had not considered in his apparently not-so-seamless plan. That camera's recording could prove invaluable to the police.

For whatever reason, Teeth also never considered the fact that other people could and would likely be milling around at the time of the planned homicide. After all, it wasn't all that late. What he considered to be a seamless plan proved, in fact, to be a very porous one that was predestined for failure.

In addition to the couple who had just left the restaurant, yet another passerby witnessed Jiminy's getaway in the crappy black sportscar. Her curiosity was piqued when she heard the gunshot and, shortly thereafter, noticed him running from an alley to the only vehicle parked at the very back of a parking lot.

The police arrived within a few minutes. Six cruisers converged on the horrific scene, pulling the 'distraught' and 'hysterical' husband off his dead wife. The witnesses were able to provide police with perfect descriptions of Jiminy and his getaway vehicle.

The precision of Jiminy's deed, along with the husband's rehearsed performance fooled even the police. It was, as far as they were concerned, a random robbery gone bad.

The three police officers that made-up the small town's police force, along with more than a dozen deputies from the county Sherrif's office, set in motion an immediate manhunt to find the perpetrator. They fanned-out in a wide swath of the town and surrounding areas, using patrol cars, armored Emergency Service Unit SUV's and officers on foot. Armed with an arsenal of guns, tasers and other tactical weapons, the hunt was swift and serious. "Only a few roads led into—or out of—Oxchley, the small winery town where the murder had just occurred. Police quickly blocked those roads.

Fortunately for Jiminy, he had a good head start and was well beyond those road blocks before the spike belts went down. He drove slow enough to avoid attracting any additional attention, but fast enough to evade the authorities. As instructed, he took Pick Valley Road and stopped briefly at the curve next to the creek. He kept the car in the lane, got out and threw the gun toward the creek from the road to avoid making any tracks in the sand and gravel on the shoulder of the road. Although it was already pretty dark, Jiminy was confident the gun went into the creek when he heard the splash.

He proceeded to the lakeside park with the boat launch, just as Teeth told him. Once he got to the parking lot, he was glad to see that Teeth was right; it was too late in the season and too late in the day for anyone to be there. His was the only car in the lot.

With a flashlight guiding his way, Jiminy walked along the thin dirt trail to the boat launch. Once there, he clicked it off and walked carefully to the end of the dock. Out on the dock without tree cover, there was enough star light to see what he was doing and to avoid falling into the water.

Jiminy unclipped the carabiner and got ready to throw the loot bag as far as he could into the lake. He hesitated. He would get another five thousand dollars from Teeth for completing the job. But then he started thinking about the value of the dead woman's life. He had just ended her life and knew he would never be the same because of it.

Jiminy rationalized that the ten thousand dollars he earned was nowhere near the worth of her life, so he was fully justified in pocketing what was in the loot bag for himself. After all, he thought, nobody else could possibly benefit from the sunken treasure and that in itself would be terribly disrespectful to the woman. It didn't take much for Jiminy to persuade himself using that twisted logic.

He unzipped the bag, removed the wallets and rings, and shoved them into his front pockets. He looked inside the bag to make sure there was nothing else of value that may have fallen out of the wallets. The heavy rock was all that remained. Jiminy zipped the bag to close it He threw the bag with all his might and watched it soar for a few seconds before darkness shrouded its trajectory. He couldn't see where it landed, but heard it plop into the water. He then dashed down the dock and back to the car.

He stuck to what remained of Teeth's plan, doing everything as instructed up to and after keeping the loot. He made it to the big box store, where he found his ugly old bicycle waiting for him around the back of the parking lot. He jumped on it and started riding back to town as quickly as his feet could pedal. When he got to Harrow, he remembered to ditch the car key and dropped it down a sewer grate; a bit late, but otherwise, just as Teeth had instructed.

It was such a small thing, really. An itsy-bitsy, insignificant thing that should not have set in motion the line of dominoes that was about to fall. In retrospect, had Jiminy just casually dropped the key down the sewer as he drove over the grate, the whole thing would have gone unnoticed. Jiminy would likely have gotten away with it.

However, Jiminy was careful and wanted to make sure that the key actually went into the sewer. If you try to picture it, it *does* seem rather odd. The sight of a stranger on a bicycle in a small town is no big deal. However, if that stranger stops cycling, hovers over a sewer grate, reaches purposefully into his pocket, pulls out a large car key and then drops it into the sewer...well...it looks genuinely suspicious.

And Jiminy's slow-motion key drop *did* generate suspicion! Talk about the wrong time, the wrong place and the wrong people!

For someone trying to be so careful, it was surprising that Jiminy didn't notice the sign on the small building directly in front of the sewer grate. It read, "Sussex County Sherriff, Harrow Detachment Office."

Bad move, for sure. An observant deputy watched as Jiminy stopped and dropped the key. He hadn't even thought about Jiminy's resemblance to a description on a "Be On the Look Out" fax that had just come out of the machine. It was merely the peculiarity of the key drop that caught the deputy's attention.

In response, the deputy hopped in a squad car and stopped Jiminy about three blocks away from the drop. It wasn't until then that he noticed how closely Jiminy's physical appearance perfectly matched the witnesses' descriptions on the BOLO that appeared on the cruiser's computer screen. The deputy immediately took Jiminy into custody and searched him.

He didn't find a gun, but that didn't mean a lot. You'd have to be colossally stupid to hold onto the murder weapon after killing someone. He had no ID, but that was also a moot point; a simple scan of his picture or fingerprint was all it would take to identify Jiminy and his criminal past.

However, the gamble that Jiminy took when he decided to keep the wallets and rings, well, that was the first domino to fall, and it was huge.

Instead of seizing Jiminy's bicycle as potential evidence, his precious twenty-some year-old mode of transportation was simply donated to the side of the road. That rusty, paint-chipped old bike with oversized tires sat there for a few hours before a local kid decided it was his and rode away on it. *(How that decision shaped the kid's life from that point forward is the subject of another story to be told at a later time.)*

A test for gunshot residue on Jiminy's hands and arms immediately indicated positive results. Second domino. Further tests on the red splatters on his shirt and jeans indicated the presence of human blood and organic matter. Third domino. Fingerprints connecting Jiminy to his rap sheet; that was the fourth domino.

He was formally arrested and interrogated by a pair of seasoned detectives. During several hours of questioning, they learned more about Jiminy than he knew about himself. They quickly pegged him as a chronic under-achiever with low self-esteem, poor social skills and a messed-up sense of priorities. They came to the conclusion that they were dealing with someone who most often acted without thinking and who focused on immediate reward without much ability to consider the consequences of his actions.

Based on their assessment, Jiminy fit the profile of a habitual offender who likely carried-out the robbery for money and then killed the victim to watch her die for his own enjoyment and sense of dominance. If the detectives could convince the district attorney that this was the case, a short trial would likely lead to a guilty verdict and to Jiminy's agonizing wait on death row.

The detectives didn't entirely rule-out someone else's involvement in the crime, but they both thought it was unlikely that anyone would trust Jiminy with such a job, due to his limited capacity. However, just to entertain the slightest possibility that Jiminy was an underling, they dangled a carrot in front of him. They didn't expect him to jump at it, but it was there. They said if someone else paid for, forced, blackmailed or coerced him into doing the crime, they could possibly get the district attorney to agree to a plea bargain for reduced charges...as long as he testified against that person.

Jiminy cracked, but just a bit. He told the detectives that he would think about it, which surprised both of them, but they shrugged it off, figuring they were the words of a cornered rat; a desperate and pathetic little man looking for a way out.

The detectives looked disinterested and were getting ready to leave. They told him they might pay him a visit the next day or two, but not to count on it. Just as they were about to leave, Jiminy grabbed the carrot.

"Okay, I was paid to do it...to make it look like a robbery, but it was all part of a plan to get rid of that woman."

The detectives were curious as to where Jiminy was going with this new admission, but discounted it as more cornered rat ramblings. Nonetheless, they let him talk.

The first detective said, "Tell us more. I, personally, doubt that anyone else was involved, but maybe my partner is a little more...um...gullible."

Jiminy opened his lips and clenched his teeth together. He pointed at his teeth. Then he said, sheepishly, "That's who hired me. I'm no more than a fucking crumb in this. Yes, I'll admit I pulled the trigger, but I was just a tool...used by someone way more powerful than me."

The first detective said, simply, "Well, we'll look into it."

They left the room and closed the door. Jiminy spent the night locked in a holding cell at the detachment. He was weary from the events and from the interrogation. Most of all, he was terribly distraught about having killed that woman so brutally. He couldn't get her terrified expression, the sound of her screaming or the sight of her bloody, disfigured head out of his mind. It tortured his thoughts throughout the night.

The next morning, Jiminy was hauled into the local courtroom, where he was formally indicted on charges of first-degree murder and robbery. As it turned out, the black getaway sportscar had been reported stolen months before and a charge of grand theft auto was added to Jiminy's indictment. His court-appointed attorney, on his behalf, pled not guilty to all charges.

Bail was out of the question because the murder charge brought a potential life sentence or death penalty, so the judge instructed the bailiff to make arrangements to transfer Jiminy to the county jail to await trial. He was scheduled to be transported there in a few days, but would stay at the local detachment until then.

Back in his holding cell, his new lawyer, Evan, paid him a visit. He wasn't very optimistic or encouraging. Having reviewed the criminal complaint, Evan was pretty clear about the likely path of this case, which he shared with Jiminy. Basically, he said, it was an open and shut case. He explained that he would be very surprised if Jiminy was not found guilty and sentenced to death.

Evan said, "Why you would have even *considered* doing something like this in Sussex County is beyond me! You do realize that this is one of the most pro-death penalty constituencies in the nation, right? I've got to be forthright with you. I don't want you to have any illusions about what's going to happen here."

Jimmy's entire world deflated. Evan explained to him that there would have been a chance—albeit remote—for him to mount a successful criminal defense in the case. That is, if Jiminy had not pocketed the wallets and rings. However, having the most important evidence on his person virtually guaranteed a guilty verdict.

Jiminy wasn't the brightest bulb on the tree, but he more than understood how badly he snookered himself by taking the wallets and rings. Had he not been so greedy, he wouldn't have been caught with those items, which would have probably led to his release. Despite witness descriptions and a blurry security camera recording of a perpetrator that looked like Jiminy, there was no apparent connection to a guy riding a bicycle through a different town who dropped something in the sewer.

However, possessing the stolen items changed his situation dramatically. Even though the police never found the gun that he ditched in the creek, having the victims' wallets and rings made it a no-brainer. Combined with the witnesses' accounts and the security video, having those stolen items truly did make it an open and shut case.

Jiminy knew how much trouble he was in and had never been so frightened in his life. The terror that he experienced as a child when his mom's loser boyfriends punched and threw him to the ground was no match for the new dread that was settling in. Evan wasn't the only one who provided little hope. The detectives who interrogated him the previous night also made him very much aware of the likelihood of a guilty verdict leading to a death sentence.

Evan was clearly not interested in helping Jiminy's situation. He wasn't about to put much effort into a case that had such a predictably negative outcome. Beyond that, despite the need for objectivity, Evan despised what his new client had done and secretly hoped that he would be put to death. Not exactly Jiminy's most ardent cheerleader...

As Evan left the cell, the two detectives stopped by to have another chat with Jiminy. They were following-up on unfinished business from the previous day. The second detective said, "You pointed at your mouth yesterday when you suggested that someone hired you to do this as a hit. I don't know if you were coming down from some heavy pharmaceuticals or what, but what the hell was that about?"

"I wasn't coming off of any drugs. I was pointing at my teeth. And I WAS paid to do this. Teeth. That's what you need to look into. The husband isn't so innocent in this. That's all I'm prepared to say right now."

The detectives weren't really interested in what Jiminy had to say, and had already convinced themselves that he acted alone. Their visit was merely meant to be a follow-up to tie-up loose ends and move things forward. They thanked Jiminy and left.

Back in the precinct offices, the detectives laughed and joked with their colleagues about Jiminy the perp and his obsession with teeth. One officer, Justin, took a special interest in what they had to say, but he kept it to himself.

Justin was a well-connected officer who was familiar with Teeth and his enterprise. Most of his fellow officers didn't trust Justin. They would often say to each other that something about Justin's views and moral compass just seemed off.

Jiminy's last night in his holding cell turned out to be a horrendous night; the worst night of his life. He had been given his own cell due to the seriousness of the charges. He quickly realized that even a real badass cellmate would have been far more reassuring than having been left alone.

His night was mostly sleepless, but the little bit of it that he did get was filled with agonizing nightmares about a wasted life, people he had cheated and hurt, and the poor woman he had just killed. He also had chilling visions of being strapped to a slab while being executed by lethal injection.

At precisely 3:42 a.m., Jiminy awoke from one of those tumultuous nightmares. This time, he felt like he couldn't breathe; as if something or someone was choking him. He awoke in terror. In fact, he was unable to speak or breathe, because a towel had been crammed down his throat. Someone was squeezing his nose shut and he was overpowered, pinned down to his bed. His struggles were no match for the force that was draining the last trace of life from his body.

The last thing Jiminy saw was Teeth's enraged face.

It was no big deal for Teeth; he was merely disposing of a potential problem. Teeth removed the towel from Jiminy's disfigured mouth and fashioned it into a noose, tying it around his former underling's limp neck.

The prosecutor was quick to close the case; some in her office thought she was too hasty. She stamped the folder with a "Case Closed" classification and filed it away before noon the next day. She could hardly hide her delight that the case was over, the guilty party was gone for good and none of it would take-up any more of her time. As far as she was concerned, Jiminy's apparent act of suicide proved his guilt and shame; justice was done.

Teeth watched the six o'clock news from his fortified office that evening. His eyes twinkled and his smile was unusually broad and bright. He shook his head and muttered, "Pathetic, really."

He was correct.

*Reminder:

You were warned.

Perhaps a glass of wine would be a good idea right now.

TEMPRANILLO
DOUBLE VISION

Imagine being a contestant on a general knowledge type of game show. It's your turn and the host asks you to name the most widely-planted grape varietal in Spain; one that's the most important to Spain's red wine industry. Would you know the answer and win the round or take a wild and likely incorrect guess?

Tempranillo would be the correct answer, so if you ever find yourself in that situation, you can thank this book for your big win! Its pronunciation sounds like "tem-prah-nee-yo" and it's as big a wine as it sounds! After being grown, crushed and fermented, Tempranillo ends-up in over forty per cent of Spain's red wines. It's an obvious mainstay of the nation's *"vino tinto"* because of its versatility, early ripening characteristics and delicious flavor profiles.

Tempranillo can be fruity and smooth when young, but gains sophistication when aged, with flavors of tobacco, fig and even caramel. It is one of the most important international wine varieties and it deserves a prominent place in every wine aficionado's repertoire of knowledge!

I was thinking about Tempranillo, because it was the wine of focus that night at my wine club's weekly tasting. To be honest, I "tasted" a bit too much of the Tempranillo that evening. It's not a fair introduction, because I usually have far more self-control than that. However, I was a bit anxious about my overseas trip and the wine helped tame my nerves.

Eight of the evening's wines were based on Tempranillo, but the club's President stealthily slipped-in two Italian Sangiovese interlopers. As it turned out, nobody could tell the difference between the two.

By the way, I'm the wine club's secretary. I think it's more of a title than anything, because we only have formal meetings a few times a year. Those meetings don't follow anything even close to "Robert's Rules" and I've never been asked to record any of the proceedings. So yes, I'm pretty sure that my title is meaningless. All of the other meetings are, basically, our tastings.

I consider myself to be someone who appreciates fine wine. To be honest, though, I like to socialize and enjoy drinking wine even more than I do learning about wine. When it comes right down to it, I'm a member of a group of people who really like to drink wine and who found an awesome way to frequently do so while socializing.

Most of us in the club are pretty much the same. Except for James and Martha. They take it far too seriously. Sometimes they just suck the fun out of our otherwise happy drinking events.

With the evening wrapping-up, I ordered a ride-share on my phone app and waited for just a few minutes before the driver arrived. The vehicle picked me up at one of the gorgeous old mansions on Prytania Street in New Orleans' Garden District. It's where my wine club recently started hosting tastings every Wednesday evening. Up until a few weeks ago, the other seventeen wino's and I attended our weekly tastings at another stately old home, also in uptown New Orleans.

Something about those grand historic homes makes the wine taste even better! I know this is true, because the same wines never excite my tastebuds and olfactory senses at my own home or in any restaurant with quite the same depth that they do during these tastings.

After climbing into the back seat, I was struck by how awful the vehicle was. It was some sort of generic older sedan and I had to straddle a huge tear in the peeling faux leather upholstery. The gash was almost as big as my butt. The yellow-turned-orange foam peeking-out from that rip looked disgusting! I couldn't stop thinking about the plethora of secrets that it held; more specifically, bacteria, human secretions, and bits of food and drink that likely soaked-into the foam over the course of several years, if not decades.

I've never considered myself to be a germaphobe, but this was over the top! To make matters worse, the vehicle stunk. Having a good sniffer is crucial to enjoying gourmet food and fine wine. Enjoying good food and fine wine are almost as important to me as life itself! However, as much as I value my delicate sense of smell, it is a curse in situations like this.

The air in the vehicle was stagnant and dank. You know when you visit someone in their home and there's a peculiar smell that permeates the place? It was like that. As much as I know scent profiles, I couldn't pin it down. I had no idea *what* this smell was, but it certainly didn't belong in a car. One thing that I *did* know, however, was that I didn't want to be breathing it in for very much longer.

Should I put in a complaint about this rat trap of a ride share vehicle? Maybe just mention something to the driver? Nope, I decided to just let it go, but I also blocked the driver from ever picking me up again.

Speaking of the driver, he looked a lot older than his picture on the ID lanyard that hung from the rearview mirror. I wasn't trying to be judgmental, but honestly, he didn't look like he could use any more trouble in his life. My complaint would only compound his struggles. It also occurred to me that I'd been in far worse taxis in New York City.

I sat there thinking about the similarities between the Tempranillo and the interloper Sangiovese, and how it was difficult to tell the difference, when suddenly, the driver said, "We're here."

The driver had already crossed the Crescent City Bridge and made it to my house in the Brechtel area. I was so wrapped-up in my thoughts, I hadn't even noticed. I tapped the ride-share app on my phone to pay the driver and said, "Thanks." He looked surprised when he saw my twenty-dollar tip for a thirty-three-dollar fare.

I was focused on the fact that I had less than six hours to pack, get a tiny bit of sleep and get to the airport the next morning for my trip to Valencia. I had never been to Spain before and was looking forward to what I knew would be a very big change of pace.

Having consumed about the equivalent of a full bottle of wine earlier at the tasting, I wasn't in the best frame of mind or motivation to do the packing, but I had no choice. Of course, I could hardly keep my eyes open while organizing and stuffing whatever I could into a single carry-on. However, once my head hit the pillow, sleep was nowhere to be found.

Five a.m. came early; particularly when you only get two hours of sleep. It wasn't nearly enough to feel human, but I figured I could get plenty of sleep during the four-hour flight to my first layover at JFK. The second leg of my trip would take me to Amsterdam, which meant another seven hours of sleep, so as far as I was concerned, I'd be a well-rested man by the time I landed in Valencia the next morning, give-or-take some jet lag with the time change.

As soon as the plane hit cruising altitude and the seatbelt indicator disappeared, I reclined my seat and closed my eyes. Numb, lifeless, dead to the world. I was out for four hours and felt transformed into to an actual human being when I finally woke. I spent the remainder of the flight alternating between playing games and watching the GPS flight tracker on the video screen on the back of the seat in front of me.

By the end of my third and final leg of this trip, I had managed to get quite a bit of shut-eye. Once I deplaned and exited the jetway, I was struck by how modern and clean the airport was. I stepped outside to hail a taxi and was pleasantly surprised at how comfortable it was. For a coastal city in the eastern Mediterranean in June, I kind of expected it to be more similar to the uncomfortable conditions back home, but it was definitely cooler and less muggy.

The purpose of my trip was to represent my employer, an engineering and manufacturing company involved with advanced forensic technologies. It was a simple client follow-up. My schedule was pretty loose and unstructured. Bill, the Executive Sales Manager at the company, basically told me to hang-out with and schmooze some of the key players at the law enforcement organization, because they had recently made a huge purchase. It was going to be a simple after-sales relationship building trip; over the years, I'd done hundreds just like it.

Apparently, Valencia's police agency had come-up with a plan to share our embarrassingly overpriced technology with other area agencies, so I would have to meet with a few extra people than usual. But like Bill said, after those initial meetings and dinners, all I had to do was hang around and enjoy what the area had to offer.

Bill told me to let the client know that I'd be available for the rest of the week in case they needed anything or had questions. I knew that was unlikely. That was more than fine with me. I hadn't had a vacation for over a year and, even though this was officially a business trip, it sounded like most of my time would be my own. Besides, the place had everything I would normally want in a vacation; a beautiful hotel, warm weather, multiple local playas or beaches, coastal breezes and attractive single women.

Well, to be completely truthful, the "attractive single women" feature was meaningless based on my own personal history with women. I hadn't exactly taken advantage of that perk on past vacations, due to my own insecurities and shyness. Perhaps that's the same reason I'd avoided showing any interest in Melissa from my wine club, even though I'd been so damned attracted to her.

Before I got too relaxed in the hotel, I made my initial calls to the client contacts on my list. I'm aware that my mediocre fluency in Spanish likely makes it painful for Spaniards to listen to me as I go about butchering their language. Thankfully, my contacts were quite comfortable speaking English.

It was Friday, before noon, so I took the initiative to meet the two main client contacts for lunch. Afterward, they took me on a tour of their forensics lab and related facilities. Having done similar tours all over the world, I was aware of what the term "related facilities" meant and it was the one part of this job that I liked the least. The autopsy rooms weren't as shiny, clean and scientific as they look on television. What they don't tell you before your first visit to one, is that you really can't prepare yourself for the reality of what you may see...and smell.

Enough about that. I'll skip to something more pleasant. Lunch was amazing. Well, the food was amazing. Probably the freshest assortment of shellfish I've ever eaten, absolutely perfect paella and delicious, delicate white wines that I'd never even heard of.

The lunchtime companionship wasn't as amazing as the food and drink. Joining me for lunch were the Police Captain, Alfonso, and the Director of Forensics, Reyes, both from the Policia Local (the main client). It wasn't that they were impolite; they actually tried their hardest to have a meaningful conversation. It's just that it was forced and artificial.

They clearly didn't understand why I was there and why I was taking-up their time. Despite the awkwardness, I recognized that

Alfonso was hiding a huge personality. He seemed to have a very humorous side, although I think he felt that he had to be reserved and professional.

Having done this post-sales schmoozing in different parts of the world before, I understood how they felt. In North America, Germany and the U.K., clients expect the post-sales service visit and seem to almost look forward to the free lunches, dinners and other freebies. But, it's not like that everywhere and, clearly, this was one of those places where it just seemed redundant for me to show-up. From their point of view, they weren't having any problems with the tech and my presence was a bit like having to babysit your sister-in-law's kid, even though he's old enough to be left on his own.

It was my lucky day. The tour was pretty much what I expected, but the lucky part was that the autopsy slabs were vacant and clean! Bonus, I thought. Before the afternoon was done, I managed to arrange a dinner to take place the following evening, Saturday, for the same two police client reps, along with the Mayor and three City Councilors.

I also invited two more reps from other local police agencies who would be sharing our tech. Another two reps from the Guardia Civil were on my list, along with yet an additional rep from the national police force. I encouraged everyone to bring a spouse or guest if they wished.

My first day in Valencia went well and bedtime arrived at the unusually early hour of seven p.m., local time. I guess the traveling had caught up to me, despite catching that solid round of sleep during my inbound flight.

I spent most of the day Saturday trying to get the lay of the land, so to speak. The big dinner was scheduled for six in the evening. I made a pit stop to talk with the restaurant owner in advance to make sure that he was prepared for the party. I really wanted to show this group how our company takes care of clients.

Only one of the attendees arrived solo. Her name was Paula and she was a rather important bureaucrat with the "Cuerpo Nacional de Policía, CNP" which, translated to English, is the National Police Corps. This federal level civilian police force had not purchased anything from us…yet. However, I recognized that she represented a valuable prospective sales target.

When Paula arrived, I was mesmerized. My research and the pictures of her that I had creeped from Facebook and LinkedIn didn't come anywhere close to capturing Paula's natural beauty and alluring personality.

Alfonso, the local police captain, took the initiative to introduce the guests to me as they arrived. This made sense, since he knew everyone, but I was initially concerned that it looked like he was hosting the dinner instead of me.

As if he had rehearsed it, Alfonso put his arm around Paula's shoulder as he said to me, "This is Paula Serrano, Assistant to the Director of Operations of our National Police Corps."

Before I got a chance to respond, Alfonso smiled, looked at Paula with an impish wink, and said, "Paula, I know you've spoken with David by telephone, but now you get to see him in person. *I'm sorry for the disappointment!*"

I was taken aback. I thought, initially, "Whoa, did he *really* just go there?"

From earlier conversations with him, including our lunch the day before, I sensed that Alfonso had a large personality, but I wasn't prepared for his sense of humor. He must have sensed that I had a similar personality or he wouldn't have taken the risk.

"Paula, I'm very pleased to meet you," I said with a smile while shaking her hand. "But what Alfonso doesn't realize is that you and I have never even heard each other's voices since we've only communicated by email. Now, seeing *and* hearing me for the first time, you must be doubly disappointed!"

Paula jumped effortlessly into our verbal joust with both feet and said, "Well, at least I hope tonight's meal is something to look forward to!"

We all laughed and Alfonso walked over to speak with someone else.

"Let's move to the bar and we can chat. What would you like to drink?" I asked her.

I listened to her intently but have no recollection of what she said. I was hopelessly entangled in her beauty. I dove into the depth of her breathtaking azure eyes. I had no choice. Her eyes were like a drug to me; after looking just once, I was addicted and had to have more.

When she smiled, well, I'm not sure, but I think she could see my body quiver involuntarily, which seemed to make her smile even more broadly. It wasn't one of those half-baked, "I have to be polite and somewhat receptive," types of smiles. No, her smile was beautiful, honest and welcoming.

Paula's voice was just as captivating to my soul as were her eyes and her smile. Her accent somehow mingled with her breathy smooth voice and brought it to another level. I don't really know if my reaction to meeting her happened as methodically as I'm describing, being that this all happened in such a short period of time, but this is how I remember it.

Suddenly, nothing else mattered. None of the other guests, the commission from this big sale, even my position with the company; none of that mattered. It all paled in comparison to Paula. I talked with her for a good portion of the evening. Perhaps I monopolized her, but I'll make no apologies.

I remember silently thanking God that she came alone and, more importantly, that she was romantically unattached. Yes, I daftly determined that important little kernel within our first ten minutes of conversation. As the evening went on, I noticed other guests looking our way, smiling and sharing secrets. Was it that obvious? I didn't care.

The dinner was quite literally suitable for royalty. Word had gotten out that I (my company) was very generous. If there was any reservation remaining about taking advantage of my employer's generosity, it was now history!

Paula sat next to me for the dinner, which she seemed very happy about. As my guests ordered the most expensive appetizers and entrées from the menu, along with pricey wines and ancient solera brandies, I had my focus set on something else.

I sensed that my feelings of attraction and connection to Paula were mutual, although neither of us mentioned it. As the dinner came to a close, she stuck around while I said my goodbyes to the other guests. I secretly hoped she would be the last one there. Not being sure what would come next, I was just happy to see that she wasn't in any hurry to leave.

After seeing-off the last couple, I returned to the table. It was clear that Paula wanted more. Exactly what that "more" represented, I had no clue, but I wanted it as well.

"So, David, I would say that your dinner went exceedingly well," said Paula.

"I'd have to agree," I said, "although, to be honest, what's made me happiest has been my conversation with you!"

As the next words flowed from my mouth, I questioned if this was reality, because I would *never* say something like this in real life. "I know it's not the wine, but you have me quite intoxicated!"

Paula blushed. She didn't know what to say. Or perhaps she was embarrassed and wanted to make a quick exit. I blew it. "Stupid, stupid, stupid me," I thought, cursing myself.

Just as I was about to get up and make things less awkward and embarrassing for her, Paula pursed her lips and with a serious expression, said, "David. I'm not usually like this, but I feel it too."

She smiled and leaned into me. We kissed softly, gently, just for a moment, but the intensity of that moment lit a fuse in both of us. I told Paula that I needed to settle the bill with the restaurant manager and asked her where she wanted to go afterward.

"Why don't we go for a walk," Paula suggested. "I can show you this beautiful city at night and then...then we see."

I realize that men are fairly predictable. It occurs to me that I was solely focused on the "then we see" part of her sentence. It was just after eight o'clock and Paula had mentioned earlier that she was planning to take the high-speed train back to Madrid at nine. The trip was less than two hours, so she would be back in her cozy bed shortly after eleven at night. She also mentioned that the nine o'clock train was the last one until the morning.

That presented a bit of a problem, I thought. We had less than an hour before she had to be at the train station. Disappointed, due to my lack of foresight about what might still transpire, I proceeded to ask for the bill as quickly as possible.

Despite doing some quick calculations on the fly, I was surprised at how much less the bill was than I had expected. €1,672.52 is not at all a steep price to entertain twenty-two people; each of whom ordered lavish meals and drank copiously! There remained at least another few thousand Euros on my expense account for this trip, so I was in good shape for the remaining five days. And I really didn't expect to spend much if any of those five days doing any client work.

Paula slipped on her delicate white sweater that barely covered her shoulders. I asked her to begin the evening walking tour and we were on our way.

The architecture was breathtaking, but paled in comparison to Paula. I had never felt so tremendously attracted to a woman after such a short period of time. She was different. She was somehow made for me and I prayed that I was made for her. "Soulmates?" I wondered.

She stopped at a beautiful old fountain that was adorned by statues around and in the water. Paula's breathtaking green eyes met my own. Her deep gaze was so intense I felt paralyzed; I was completely under her spell. She took both of my hands in hers. We locked fingers. Such a simple thing, but the feeling of her warm hands in mine was tingly and made my heart race. She then raised my arms and playfully tried to pose me as if I were one of the statues.

We both laughed and lost ourselves in the moment. We continued to hold each other's hands. Her hands were warm and supple, yet strong and purposeful. She then caressed the centers of my palms with her thumbs. It felt sensual and I didn't want her to stop. I suddenly felt like I was in high school again.

Paula then let go of my hands and raised hers to my head, where she lightly pinched and caressed my earlobes, while bringing my lips to hers. I lost track of time as we kissed.

I noticed a giant clock on an old building and hoped it was right. According to the dial, it was 9:30; the last train for Madrid had already left. Using her own code language, I asked Paula, "Would you like to go back to my room for a drink and...*then we see?*"

"I'm looking forward to that," said Paula, her fine eyebrows raised in anticipation.

The early morning sun peeked through the thin embroidered window coverings and splashed across the lacy white bedspread. I woke up feeling both sleepy and well-rested at the same time. The sun already felt warm, especially where it rested on Paula's smooth skin. I looked around the hotel room to get my bearings and then fixed my gaze on Paula.

I remained as still and quiet as I could, trying not to wake the goddess beside me. Everything felt new and fresh. It was like I had never seen a naked woman before. The sun poked a path through the lacey window covering and its rays drew intricate swirly shadows across her breasts. I soaked-up her natural beauty and gentle curves.

Paula startled me as she woke. She smiled and said, gently, "Buenos días, mi amor." She raised her hand and rested it on my chest.

It was a moment that seemed magnificently frozen in time as we lay there silently, caressing one another and breathing in the moment. We explored one another's bodies with our hands and our mouths. I told myself that I would always remember this.

I called room service and ordered breakfast. We ate on the terrace balcony, which was far more spacious than most residential balconies in town. She never planned on staying overnight, so she didn't have a change of clothing. I generally travel very light and fit whatever I will need into a single carry-on bag, so my own options were limited. However, she was more than happy to wear my long-sleeved button-down shirt and not much else. I didn't realize how damned sexy my shirt could look!

The coffee was delicious, as was the assortment of fresh breads, cheeses and smoked meats. We ate, learned more about each other and paused from time-to-time to hold hands like teenagers.

As the city began to awaken, we saw people moving around on the streets below. They were starting their routines. It was easy to spot the folks who were on their way to Sunday Mass, just by their dress and their comportment. There was no denying it, the day was happening.

As much as I didn't want to think about this morning coming to an end, the thought crept into my mind. It was Sunday and I wondered if or when Paula would take a train back home.

She must have read my mind. "David, I will never forget our evening or this morning. But I do work tomorrow and I eventually have to get back to Madrid."

It was hard enough to accept that this special moment was about to end, but almost impossible to think about her leaving. I was grasping for something to say; something that wouldn't encourage her to just go on with the rest of her life without me, or, something that wouldn't make me seem too needy or unrealistic.

I took a chance. I thought, if this hadn't been as special for her as it had been for me, then it's best to know. After all, it would be foolish to hold onto something that's merely one-sided or sentimental.

"Paula, I can't bear for you to leave. That's how close I feel to you after our short time together. We're adults and have our own lives, but," I paused for a painfully long time, then said, "What do we do here? Just move on like it was a good time and nothing really special ever happened?"

Paula started crying. I had no idea what this meant and didn't have a clue how to read her. She said nothing for a few very difficult and very long minutes. Then she said, "David, I feel the same way. I don't want to leave, but you know I have to. What do we do? My heart and the reality of the rest of my life right now are in two very different places."

We decided to leave the negative thoughts alone for the time being. We held hands, returned to the bedroom and made love again. After showering, Paula got dressed in her clothes from the night before. I tagged-along as she did some shopping at a few local boutiques. She found a beautiful new blouse and skirt that she wore out of the shop.

After walking until our feet hurt, we stopped for lunch at an outdoor café. The rest of our day was spent laughing and sharing some of our embarrassing life stories. I told her about the time I gave my grade 11 student government election speech in front of the entire student body, not realizing that my khaki pants were stained in a most unfortunate spot. She shared with me how she bad-mouthed her new manager after being hired into a new position, not recognizing that the stranger she was talking with *was* her new manager.

I talked about my wine club back in New Orleans and she loved the idea of a club in which you just drink different wines every week. Apparently, she had never heard of a wine club before!

Eventually, the time came and we said our goodbyes. Paula hopped on the last train out at just before nine. I waved at her from the train platform and she waved back through the train window. She tried, without success, to hide her tears.

That was the last time I saw her. I had hoped that she would surprise me with a visit at least one more time, since she was only a few hours away and I was in Valencia until Thursday, but that never happened. I had considered surprising her, but I didn't get the signal that it would be okay to intrude upon her established life in Madrid. Beyond that, even though I had no plans to meet with clientele, I was required to stay in Valencia during the entirety of my time there in case there was an emergency or problem with the tech.

The rest of the week went by quickly, as I tried to tame some of the sting of missing her with alcohol; Tempranillo based wines, to be exact. I tried to convince myself that nothing had really changed. I reasoned that, before meeting Paula, I was more than happy to spend my week basking in the sun, beaching at the sea and taking in the new experiences. However, I never imagined that the most amazing experience would be both unexpected and fleeting.

I expected to hear from Paula before I left, but she ghosted me. My calls and texts to her went unanswered. I began to feel resentful, but then realized how difficult our parting was for her as well; I stopped trying and let things be.

Fast-forward to 6:25 a.m. on Thursday morning. The jet had already taxied to its final position on one of the runways and was now waiting for traffic control to grant permission to take-off.

Morning had come early, as usually happens before I get on a plane. I felt like I hardly slept, which was because I hardly slept. As with my three inbound flights that eventually dumped me in Valencia, I planned to get as much sleep as I could on the outbound return flights. This time, though, my flight from Amsterdam was going to Atlanta instead of New York and then finally back home to MSY in New Orleans.

After boarding the jet in Amsterdam, I promptly took my seat in First Class and buckled my belt. Behind me, I could hear the usual commotion of inexperienced travelers, exasperated parents with whiny kids, people who are way too happy and those who are high maintenance jerks.

It wasn't until after the "Fasten Seatbelt" indicator dinged and flashed, that I realized my seatbelt was crimping the skin near my stomach. It was becoming painful, so I unbuckled it and struggled with the mechanism to loosen the strap. Great, it was stuck. As I was trying to open and close the clasp, and pulling hard on the strap, a flight attendant promptly "attended" to me to admonish me for unbuckling. I tried to explain my problem to her, but she turned-out to be a robot. I don't like robots.

Even though the belt was still way too tight, I snapped the buckle anyway and tried to ignore it. The engines began to roar and, within seconds, the jet was hurtling down the runway and starting its ascent.

A lot of people are really nervous about air travel and have to rely on sedatives to make it through their flights. Not me. My parents traveled a lot when I was a child and they often took me and my siblings along. Like most kids, I looked forward to any time I could spend on a plane, and I guess that just kind of stuck with me. I was a happy camper as long as I could get a window seat. I still remember one of my teachers telling me when I was in Grade 2 that when you're on a plane, people below look like ants. They never did. I think I expected them to look like *actual* ants, but of course, they looked like people very far away, for about two or three seconds, until the plane was so high you couldn't see them at all.

The point is that, even though I traveled frequently and extensively for work, I am one of those strange people who actually looks forward to taking a flight. Now, don't get me wrong, the security lines, the frequent delays and cancellations, the rudeness of some other passengers; I dread these things like anyone. But I *do* like being up in the air!

The final leg of my flight from Atlanta was unremarkable and boring, and I guess I was tired, because I just wanted to be home. It's always like that; the trip *to* anywhere is filled with anticipation, while the trip home can't be over soon enough.

Monday came and my direct supervisor, the executive sales manager, poked his head around my office door to congratulate me. He said that he had received remarkably strong feedback from the clients in Spain. He also mentioned that someone named "Paula" who was high up in Spain's national police force wrote a tremendously complimentary letter about me.

As the weeks went by, I settled back into my routine. Beyond an occasional dream of Paula and deep feelings of loss that were connected to those dreams, life was about as "normal" as it ever was. At least that's what I tried to tell myself. However, I'm not obtuse and I realized that life was not at all normal in any way. That one evening and the following day with Paula was one of the best experiences of my life, if not *the* best.

I tried my best to deal with the loss and attempted on several occasions to drum-up the courage to call or message her. However, I just couldn't bear hearing her soothing voice or seeing the natural beauty of her face again, knowing that we couldn't be together.

About two months after the Valencia trip, I received a phone call from Alfonso, the Valencia police captain. He sounded serious and reserved.

"I was aware of your and Paula's, um...friendship...and I have some very bad news for you. I think it's respectful to let you know. There has been a tragic accident involving Paula and she has died."

The news shook my body and brain like a sledgehammer. Even though I knew that we would never be together again, I guess I harbored some trace of hope for the possibility. Now, I realized that what we shared was truly over.

My eyes welled-up and I tried to steady my voice. "What happened? What kind of accident?"

"This past weekend," Alfonso explained, "Paula came to Valencia for a day of surfing. She was at Playa de Levante Beach and a rogue wave overtook her. We don't know if it was her surfboard or a rock under the water, but she concussed and drowned."

I tried to say something, but I couldn't speak.

"Listen, David," Alfonso said, "after you left Spain, she confided in me. You know...about her relationship with you."

Even though I just learned that she was gone, the idea that she shared the story of our time together was, in a way, comforting. It validated what we had and made it seem as real as I felt it had been.

"Since you left, she had been spending weekends here in Valencia. I think she was just trying to relive a part of what you both had for that very short time. A short time that clearly blossomed into much more."

I thanked him and asked, "Is there anything I can do. I mean, I just feel so helpless."

Alfonso said, "Sadly, no, it's done. I would say that the only thing you *can* do, the only thing you *should* do, is to take care of yourself. The corazón, the heart, must not stay broken."

Five months went by since Paula's passing and I continued to waver between depression, disbelief and forced acceptance. I realized that time does, indeed, heal all wounds, but also knew that it doesn't mean it's easy. During those five months, I had traveled to Boston, Montreal and the U.K. It didn't matter where I went or what I did; nothing seemed to bring much joy or excitement.

I began to worry that my Valencia experience set the bar so high, that I was doomed to endure boring, miserable trips for the remainder of my career. In all truth, I came to the conclusion that it was not so much the travel or Valencia, but it was Paula that set that bar so unachievably high.

The one thing, however, that I did look forward to was my Wednesday night wine tasting on Prytania Street. Time kept its promise and the sting of losing Paula became less intense with each passing month. That's not to say that I no longer missed her or our special time together; that would *never* fade. But I was, at least, allowing myself to feel happy again and to begin living life.

I also attempted to challenge my social and romantic side more than I had in the past. In fact, I even asked Melissa out on a date, which to my surprise, she accepted quite eagerly. Maybe a bit too eagerly, I found out.

Melissa was certainly attractive enough. Her social upbringing was very similar to my own and we had similar levels of education. Unfortunately, I quickly came to realize that she was more boring than I could handle! I took her on two more dates, giving her benefit of the doubt that maybe she was just "off" on the first one, but she proved to be just as wearisome on the subsequent dates.

I have to wonder how someone with two college degrees, a fantastically interesting career and multiple talents can be so mind-numbingly boring! I thought that her quips about cats were just a mechanism to cover-up her lack of oenological knowledge. As it turns out, Melissa's scope of conversation starts and ends with felines.

All of this brings me to last week—one of the strangest weeks of my life. Don't misunderstand me. It was strange in an amazing way. It started last Wednesday. I had just finished a dinner with an old college buddy at a restaurant in the French Quarter. He happened to be in town for a convention in the Central Business District and he had a free evening, so we planned to catch-up over some Crawfish Etouffee. Afterward, I hopped on a streetcar to the garden district for my weekly wine tasting. As I was walking from my drop-off point, I saw her.

My mind was playing tricks on me. I thought I had made more progress in dealing with Paula's death, but clearly, I was no further ahead. I once heard a popular TV psychologist say that hallucinations are not a good sign. Then he said that hallucinations in the absence of drugs or drunkenness, are basically a red flag indicating that something's seriously wrong with the noggin.

But there she was. I couldn't believe what my eyes were seeing, yet I wanted to believe it so badly. It was Paula. Just about 20 feet ahead of me on the sidewalk. Okay, her back was to me, but my mind was seeing Paula from behind and not just someone who looked like Paula. Her frame and height, her hair style and color, and even her gait when walking, slightly favoring her right side; I thought I was seeing a ghost, but hoped I was not.

I was physically frozen. My feet were fused to the concrete and my legs wouldn't move. I took a few deep breaths and tried to regain some sense of reality. I convinced myself that I had slipped into irrationality, allowing my imagination to take control.

I tried to shake it off and began walking in her direction. She stopped abruptly and was struggling to get something out of her purse. She dropped her purse, the contents of which spilled across the sidewalk. I caught-up with her and approached her from the side, so as not to startle her. I asked, "May I help you with that?"

She turned toward me and I was stunned. Literally in shock. It was Paula. It *was* Paula. I couldn't tell if her expression was one of fright in response to my own apparent shock—or—if, perhaps she recognized me in the same mysterious way that I recognized her.

Stumbling for words, she said, "Oh...thank you, I, I appreciate the offer, but I'm fine, I've got this."

She spoke with Paula's intoxicating voice, but without the Spanish accent. Her alluring azure eyes, her generous smile, her body shape; I didn't understand how, but this woman standing in front of me was Paula in every discernable way, except for the accent.

I was, at once, astonished and hopeful. Yet, I was also paralyzed with fear of the distinct possibility that I was having a full-blown mental breakdown.

"Could it be?" I asked myself, "Is it possible?"

After we both grappled with the last few remaining items that had fallen out of her purse, we both straightened-up and our eyes met. I was speechless. Once again, I was drawn into her eyes; into her entire presence. I couldn't escape.

We paused and stared at each other. I felt as though I was in a trance. My heart fluttered and I felt blood coursing through my body with new vigor. I wondered if it were possible that Paula had a twin living in the States?

She smiled at me, and said, gently, "Do I know you? You look really familiar to me."

"I'm David," I said with an embarrassingly shaky voice. I tried to maintain my composure, but I feared that my fragile emotional state was obvious.

"I'm Alma," she said, "I know, it sounds like a grandma name, but it's Spanish, from my heritage. In English, it translates to the Soul."

"Absurd!" I thought. I tried to avoid thinking the obvious. But I *did* think it. And I wanted so much for it to be true. Was the universe somehow trying to tell me that Paula's soul had been reborn into this exquisite woman standing in front of me? Every fiber of my being wanted to believe it, even though I realized it was a ridiculous thought of an obviously irrational person.

We began walking together and chatting, as though we were old friends. It didn't seem odd to either of us; just comfortable.

I took a bit of a leap and explained to her that I knew someone who had a striking resemblance to her. I couldn't tell her the whole truth, which was that she was the unequivocal personification of Paula. I also didn't dare mention anything about our time together or about Paula's untimely death.

"Well, David, like I said, you also seem very familiar to me as well. It's strange, because I feel like I've known you from a different part of my life. Just walking and talking with you feels so familiar and comfortable.

"I can't explain it, but I feel the same way. It's not just that you *look* familiar." I didn't know what else to say.

"Maybe we went to school together or worked in the same office at some point in the past? How about church, a team or a club?" Alma was blurting-out some obvious possible meeting situations. She seemed as sure as I did that we had met. However, she knew nothing about how different my story was.

"I guess anything's possible, but I don't think I could ever forget someone as beautiful as you," I said.

That was so out of character for me, I couldn't believe I just said that. Alma blushed, just as Paula had blushed months ago. As we walked by the grand old mansions, I noticed that Alma had a round blue-green tattoo on the underside of her wrist. I couldn't make it out.

I asked, "What's that tattoo on your wrist?"

"It's a pearl."

"Why a pearl? What does it mean?"

"This is going to sound corny, but my middle name is Margarita. And, well, I got really tired of everyone associating my name with alcohol."

I felt dumb, but admitted my ignorance. "I didn't realize there was another meaning for it."

Alma said, "In Spain, the name Margarita refers to a pearl from the sea. My tattoo reminds me that my name is much more special than a sour drink!"

My mind wandered to connections between Paula and the pearl. It seemed like a stretch, but the more I thought about it, the more it made sense. I drew a connection to Paula's tragic demise; her surfing accident. The coincidence was too obvious for me to ignore. Alma, a woman with Spanish lineage, has a first name that means "soul" and a middle name that's something you find at the bottom of the sea.

"Anyway," Alma said, "I'm not really a fan of Margaritas; they're always either too sour or too sweet."

"So, what *is* your favorite drink?"

"I'm a wine girl. Maybe a bit too much for my own good!" Alma joked.

"I'm sure that's not true! So, what's your favorite wine?"

"That's easy, Sangiovese," she said.

"Sangiovese?" I asked. "Seriously, Italian? I really expected a Spanish varietal, considering your ancestry!"

Alma exposed her knowledge of wine. She said, "I get it. I should probably be a Tempranillo girl. The two varietals are quite similar."

"It's true! I was at a Tempranillo wine tasting last year, when someone secretly introduced a few bottles of Sangiovese into the lineup. Most of us were fooled, so yes, they are similar."

I immediately regretted saying that. I was showing-off; not a good look. I was relieved when she continued our conversation.

"But you know," Alma clarified, "Tempranillo can have a bit more of a youthful bounce, while Sangiovese is more like a mellow old friend."

Shivers fluttered down my spine. Was *she* Paula, the mellow old friend? The parallels between she and Paula were becoming too much to ignore.

"You said you were at a wine tasting," Alma said. "Well guess what? Here's a coincidence...I'm off to a wine club tasting tonight!"

Was it possible she was attending my wine tasting? She wasn't a member, after all, but maybe I missed a new member announcement. I carefully broached the possibility. "By any chance, is your tasting on Prytania Street?"

She looked surprised; perhaps a bit unnerved. She paused, as though she was having second thoughts about our 'chance' meeting. She asked, nervously, "How on earth did you know?"

At this point, I was beginning to believe that everything about our encounter was far more than mere coincidence, but I was even more certain that I couldn't talk about it. At least not yet. What I was thinking was so out there, I had to be careful. Even just casually mentioning a connection to Paula carried the risk of making me look like a stalker and scaring her away.

Trying my best to look surprised, I said, "You've *got* to be kidding me! You're not going to believe this, but I'm the club's secretary. Well, not that it really means anything other than the fact that I really like to drink wine!"

My stalker concern vanished as she laughed at my bit of humor. I said, "I've been with the club for years, but haven't seen you before. You must be a new member?"

"I just joined on the weekend, so it's my first tasting you're your club"

I made a welcome gesture, moving my open hand from my chest outward and said, "Well, let me be the first club member to welcome you to your first tasting!

We continued walking from St. Charles Street to Prytania. Alma mentioned how much she loved the old mansions in the Garden District; she said she felt quite privileged to be doing a wine tasting in one of them.

We were the first regular members to arrive. The club president was already there along with the past-president. They had just finished setting-up the cloaked bottles, glasses, water pitchers and charcuterie boards prior to members' arrival.

Alma sat next to me throughout the evening and we never stopped talking. So much so, that some of the other members sitting near us threw darts at us with their eyes to signal their disapproval of our nonstop chatter. We talked about wine, likes and dislikes, local politics and even some of our deep beliefs. I didn't learn until a few hours later that she was holding back a pretty big bombshell.

After the tasting, we took a trolly back to the French Quarter where we shared a late-night Café Au Lait and Beignets. We talked, laughed and learned as much as we could about each other.

Alma learned a lot more about me than I did about her. She revealed to me that for half of her life, she was a ward of the state, having been tossed from one grim foster situation to the next. That was about the extent of what she shared about the first 18 years of her life. After that, she landed on her feet and, against all odds, had the resilience to take her life back. She told me that she finished her degree, got a civilian administrative job in law enforcement and had lived a pretty boring life up to that point.

Then came the bombshell. Alma revealed that the little bit of her past that she shared with me was re-learned, not remembered. She explained that, about a half year ago, she had a serious surfing accident while on vacation in Florida. She didn't resurface immediately after wiping-out badly. Her friends frantically searched the water near the spot where she went down and thankfully found her. They dragged her back to shore and resuscitated her lifeless body.

"I have no memory at all of that day," Alma said. "In fact, most of my earlier memories in life; the foster parents, the bouncing around...I have to take what people tell me about my life as truth, because it's just not there for me."

I honestly didn't know what to say. I was utterly stunned by the fact that her life changed after a surfing accident. A surfing accident. Just like Paula. I couldn't believe it.

Alma continued explaining her situation. "My doctors said that the head trauma and loss of oxygen resulted in what will likely be permanent long-term memory loss. They have told me that it won't affect my ability to recall memories formed after the accident, but everything before it will remain vague."

I asked, "How does it feel? Like, what's the difference between your memories of the last six months and those that were formed before the accident?"

"That's a good question, David! It's like when you watch a movie and remember scenes from the movie. That's what the pre-accident memories are like. They are kind of patched-together from what people have told me, and from actual pictures and videos and papers. But they don't feel real. I'm really just recalling what I've learnt about parts of my life. The memories since then feel like real life."

I asked about her job and she said that the Louisiana State Patrol welcomed her back to her same civilian job when they determined that the accident didn't impact her cognitive functioning.

That was our first date. We are now well beyond dating and our relationship is as close as I could ever have imagined it could be. The intense desire and intimacy that I felt about Paula has simply migrated and grown into my relationship with Alma. For her part, Alma frequently says she feels as if she's starting a new life all over again and that she doesn't understand why, but somehow knows that she was waiting for her life to really begin.

My time, as short as it was, with Paula, is one thing that I have never shared with Alma. I won't speak of it; there's nothing positive that can come out of it. Revealing it may cause any number of problems.

There's one other coincidence I learned about Alma that will remain unspoken. A few days after our initial meeting, I did a bit of digging and found that her surfing accident occurred on the same date and at the same time as Paula's.

Alma is my soulmate; there's no question about that. I cannot describe the depth of joy that fills me whenever I'm with her. I cannot stop looking at her without being in awe of her beauty. Talking with her, loving her, sharing our bodies and our minds, these things feed my soul.

Is Alma really Paula?

Well, there are two things in life of which I am absolutely certain. One, that there's no such thing as a coincidence. And two, second chances do exist.

Stephen J. Kristof

PINOT GRIGIO
TRAINING THE NEW BOSS

Shortly after the historic blockbuster white wine Chardonnay became too popular for its own good and its style emulsified into a caricature of itself, Pinot Grigio came along and saved the day.

It brought a fresh and exciting new idea to the table for those who grew weary of what many Chardonnay producers at the time were making. Those cloyingly sweet, closed, overly woody, stodgy and disappointingly predictable Chardonnays had lost their footing. Pinot Grigio quickly became the new kid on the block, supplanting Chardonnay's prior popularity.

Pronounced, "Pee-No-Gree-Joe", this grape is successfully grown and vinted just about anywhere wine grapes are grown. The nice thing about Pinot Grigio grapes is that their low-tannin, stone fruit profile can produce white wines that are very approachable, easy-drinking, mellow and extremely versatile.

The not-so-great thing about this varietal is that it has become a bit like Chardonnay was in the late 1900s and early 2000s. That's to say that many of today's Pinot Grigio wines are homogenous, lackluster, basic quaffs that add nothing whatsoever to the sophisticated side of wine tasting, drinking and appreciation!

The main character in the next story, Thomas, was a bit like those lackluster clone style Pinot Grigio's, in that he was a crowd pleaser. Well, to be more accurate, he was a pleaser in general. He didn't particularly stand out in a crowd, didn't stand up for himself, didn't make waves, was almost always agreeable—*even when, privately, he completely disagreed*—and could have made far more of himself if only he had taken some risks along the way.

We'll catch-up to Thomas in a bit. But first, let's get to know the antagonist, who, unlike Thomas, stood out in a crowd, always made waves, was almost always disagreeable—*even when, privately, she completely agreed*—and could have become a decent person, had she merely tried. Like a cloying wine, whatever sweetness she had was sickly and overpowering. Like a stubbornly austere wine, she was closed to others' feelings. And she was as predictable as nightfall, meaning that she was like the darkness that consumed light. *Oh my!*

In a sense, she was quite the opposite of Pinot Grigio's most appealing traits; she was unapproachable, uptight and inflexible. Her name was Maddison. Maddison with two d's. Thomas and his coworkers would soon learn through baptism by fire that she was absolutely obsessed about those two d's.

Misspell her name once by dropping a d and the poor sap would hear about it for a week, miss-out on perks reserved for everyone else and have to endure several bouts of Ms. Perfect's dismissive stink-eyes. Misspell her name a second time by missing one of those crucial d's and the spiteful woman would succeed in making your work life a living hell.

Her reputation preceded her, but not in a good way. She was known to be—*not merely 'said to be'*—a thin-skinned, hypercritical, passive-aggressive, sadistic piece of shit. Overall, a hell of a good human being. A true credit to our species, don't you think?

A week before she arrived, word leaked out that Maddison was being transferred here from the Southwestern Division, where she acted as the District Manager.

Well, that's not entirely accurate. She was the "Acting" District Manager (ADM), because the previous DM, her boss, died suddenly at work from an aortic dissection, otherwise known as a torn aorta. It was a freak thing; something so unexpected for such a fit, health-conscious and energetic young man. One minute he was reviewing lines on a spreadsheet and the next, his laptop crashed to the floor and his torso slumped lifelessly over his desk.

A few co-workers who witnessed the horrific episode spread word through the company intranet that he actually died when he passed-out from being overworked and his head came in contact with a pen that was standing upright in a coffee cup. As with all epic stories, this one had the crucial elements of symbolism and surprise. The pen was reportedly emblazoned with the corporate logo; there's your symbolism. The unexpected twist? That pen plunged into the guy's left eye, traveling well into his brain, killing him instantly.

Well, he *did* die instantly, but that was from the torn aorta and not from a pen in the eye. It was a pretty clever story, though. After all, his all-too-common refrain to his workers was for them to, "keep an eye," on the accuracy of their work. Yup, clever, but unfortunately, untrue.

Too bad though, really. He was actually a pretty decent person who had a bright executive future ahead. Alas, this was his fate. Most regrettably, his premature death would shape a new career path for Maddison. Regrettable, that is, for anyone under her supervision or standing in her way.

Prior to her assuming the Acting DM position, Maddison had a rather lackluster career, serving in a variety of "Assistant to" roles that, frankly, carried little-to-no supervisory experience, training or clout. According to what Thomas had heard, the only reason she had been promoted to the position of her former boss was that too many new projects being launched simultaneously made it impossible to pull a more suitable candidate away from a more pressing role. In other words, corporate wasn't about to displace a seasoned manager into a less challenging role where things were already running pretty smoothly.

So that was that. Maddison was basically a baby, ripped from suckling at the breast of corporate milquetoast and thrust into a position of significant leadership and responsibility. When it became crystal clear that she was completely out of her depth (something that became apparent after only a few weeks), top brass sent her to the Midwest-West division to develop her management skills.

This division had a steady staff of around 130 employees, give or take a few. To be honest, nothing ever really changed a whole lot in this division. From the balance sheet to performance audits and everything in-between, it was a pretty predictable operation.

It wasn't the most profitable, but then again, it never ran in the red, consistently contributed to the corporate giant's bottom line and never caused any trouble. Damage control types and well-seasoned managers were always better used in other locations. As for the dynamic hot-shots and rising stars, they were occasionally transferred to The Midwest-West division, but only for a short time while they learned the ropes. Then, off to the races they went.

The Midwest-West and Midwest-East divisions were like brothers, but the Midwest-West was the less flashy, older brother who wore wing-tip shoes and a crisply pressed white shirt each and every day. Predictable, really.

Midwest-West was also known as the nursery. It was where the big boys usually sent fresh management to train and develop for a few years, before sending them off to somewhere more challenging. (Which meant somewhere more important.) For the most part, corporate left them alone and let them shine.

Pretty much everyone else working at Midwest-West...wasn't going anywhere. With the exception of a few stars here and there who really busted their ass and made their coworkers look weak, everyone else languished in their current position until their time was up and they got to "go home." Going home was code for retiring.

During the week after the Maddison transfer news was leaked, local staff went into deep recon and gumshoe mode, gathering anything they could about who this Maddison really was. This, of course, included her strengths and, more importantly, her weaknesses. They wanted to know precisely what her weaknesses were, so that they could do one of two things.

They had been through this before. In fact, many times before. Depending on whether or not she would be decent to them during her stint, they would choose to develop her weaknesses, training the new manager in ways that other staff in other locations would eventually appreciate. Or, they could abuse her weaknesses to make her life more difficult than it needed to be, thus encouraging her to want to move away sooner than expected. Either way, the Midwest-West staff would exploit her weaknesses.

But this time it would be different. Information surfaced that revealed corporate's real plans for Maddison. They had no intention of pushing her through the nursery. Apparently, they were giving-up on her, instead following the "Peter Principle."

The plan was to jettison her to this well-balanced, never-any-surprises division where she would be shelved for, well, the rest of her corporate life. There to stay. At least, that's what they heard.

Their collective calls and texts to associates at the Southwestern Division turned-up some pretty nasty dirt; unfortunately, none of it could be used for blackmail or persuasion.

The warnings were hard to digest. Maddison, they were advised, was socially uncomfortable, had a general lack of compassion, saw the worst in others, was outwardly self-important to make up for her lack of self-esteem and had no compunction about being a tyrant toward anyone in front of anyone else.

She was to arrive promptly on Monday morning. She had already scheduled the entire division to attend a large group meeting at 9:00 a.m. sharp. She went ahead and superseded any client meetings or pre-existing commitments on our digital calendars and blocked-off a full two hours. Following this, Maddison scheduled individual thirty-minute meetings with all Supervisors, as well as Sales Specialists, like Thomas, for the next two days. Again, she blasted to oblivion any existing commitments on any of their calendars. Thomas' meeting wasn't scheduled until Tuesday afternoon at 4:30; the last meeting of the day and the last of all of these "Get-to-Know Maddison" meetings.

The Friday before Maddison arrived proved to be a particularly difficult day for all of the Midwest-West staff. She hadn't even gotten off her plane or set foot in their facility, however, somehow Maddison managed to ruin each of their Fridays, let alone their upcoming weekends.

Over the course of that weekend, Thomas counted a total of 143 text messages from terrified and depressed coworkers who shared his angst. Although the weather was picture-perfect on both Saturday and Sunday, the weekend was ruined by the ghost of Maddison.

Fast-forward to Monday morning. Thomas had already looked at his watch four times and it was barely past 9:10. He thought, "'ll be honest, I hate her."

Hate is a strong word, but it barely described the malevolence he felt about her. Her reputation undoubtedly preceded her, as evidenced by the fact that his animosity toward Maddison developed before they even met. "Who does she think she is to come and sabotage everyone's lives, including mine?" Thomas questioned.

He pursed his lips and gritted his teeth. He had the traditional "I'm not buying any of your nonsense," body language with his arms crossed across his chest.

"She should be ashamed of herself," Thomas reasoned. "What does her mother think of her? Then again, I wonder if she even has a mother? She's probably the grizzly result of a genetic engineering experiment gone terribly wrong."

In all honesty, she didn't start well. After what seemed to be an uncomfortably forced, "Good morning" greeting, Maddison really delivered the goods.

She continued, "First off, I want to let everyone know how to spell my name correctly. It's Maddison, with two d's. I'm very particular about spelling people's names correctly, so when you email, memo or message me, please make sure that you respect me with a properly spelled salutation."

Thomas thought, "Oh God. She can't be serious! She actually went there and said that. This is horrible. *She* is horrible."

Maddison didn't seem to notice the sneering looks and rolling eyes in front of her. Maybe she wasn't at all unaware; she just didn't care. In any case, she made it abundantly clear that life at Midwest-West had simply come to an end.

Before hitting the first fifteen-minute mark, Maddison had succeeded in warning everyone that she didn't want to blindside them, but that it was likely to occur if they weren't on their toes. She also drove home the idea that she was a closed-door manager. Based on her personality, this particular tidbit sat well with everyone!

She also underscored her contempt of compassion by suggesting that anyone needing a change in work hours or schedule would need to put the request in writing at least two weeks prior to the event; a new requirement that was even extended to emergencies!

Hearing this, Thomas became enraged. He turned to Devon and whispered, "So, I guess whenever my kids get sick, I'll just have to just tell them to suck it up, because I need to give the boss two weeks' notice! This is fucking ridiculous! So, what if my wife needs emergency surgery? I guess she should have planned better."

The meeting degraded into a shit-show of obnoxiousness. Maddison's deportment was one of outright anger. There was really no reason for her to project that image, except perhaps, that her own lousy self-image wouldn't allow her to be any less uninviting.

By the same token, she was at least honest. That may have been Maddison's one redeeming quality. She actually admitted that she was an outsider and probably wouldn't fit in. That's unfortunate, but it was clear that she wouldn't bother to try. She didn't want to come here, to move here or to be here, and she would make everyone under her watch pay for it.

Thomas looked at his watch an additional 57 times before her initial get to know the horrible me meeting concluded. He would have looked at his phone or tablet instead, but Maddison made it clear in her meeting "invitation" memo that all staff were encouraged to leave their devices behind.

Within just two hours, morale amongst Midwest-West staff struck an all-time low. To say that the angst was palpable would be a grievous understatement! As it turned out, the meeting was more or less a one-way volley of threats, ultimatums, rules and over-the-top expectations.

No doubt, Maddison with two d's was a quick learner. In her mere three months at the managerial level in her previous stint at Southwestern Division, she had learned the most effective methods of steamrolling and alienating one's staff permanently.

The usual hustle and bustle—the life—of Midwest-West offices was muted for the rest of the day. It was quiet, except for the hushed complaints and commiseration in corners, bathrooms and coffee hubs here and there. People walked around like zombies with pallid complexions and stoic expressions. It was as if a bomb went off. In a sense, a bomb did go off; her name was Maddison with two d's.

At precisely 5:00 p.m., office doors opened, people rose from cubicles and the entire building emptied. The entire process took less than two minutes. It was the only time Thomas had seen anything like it in his sixteen years with the company. On a normal day, some folks would leave a bit early, but then again, they made up for it by getting in early that day or staying later the day before. Others might normally be out on client calls or working late to finish paperwork. Not on this day.

Thomas had never thought of himself as a particularly dynamic risk-taker, nor as someone who would take a stand for or against a cause. Instead, he typically blended into the background, acquiesced to whatever distasteful thing he had to do and tried to let it go. Although this was the first really bad manager he had to deal with, he tended to handle every unfair situation in his life the same way.

Try as much as he did, he also realized that merely attempting to let it go had very little real effect on his emotional state. It took this rogue manager's tirade to finally make him realize that his frustration and anger had built to a boiling point and he couldn't—and wouldn't—simply sit back and take it anymore.

For once, for the first time in his entire life, Thomas finally stood up for himself and refused to be bullied any more. It was at this precise moment that Thomas had an epiphany. He suddenly realized that his life—his time on this globe—was finite. It's not like he wasn't aware of the ticking clock in a general sense like we all are. It's just that it wasn't all that real.

Abruptly, without any warning, it occurred to Thomas that he had wasted a good part of the 46 years that God had given him, including the many opportunities that he never bothered to explore or develop.

Thomas felt as if he were facing his final moment. His life flashed before his eyes. Suddenly, a deep, gnawing, painful emotion bubbled-up from within and he was filled with regret for not doing more with his life.

For the first time, he accepted responsibility for giving-up on pretty much every significant challenge he ever faced. At once, Thomas realized that he had done little with the many talents he was given. He hadn't taken the important risks and he chose not to enjoy the fullness of life; it all became so clear.

"How could I have been so stupid?" Thomas asked himself. "How could I have never noticed my life slipping away?"

As he watched everyone else stream out of the building like programmed robots, Thomas stayed behind. He decided to confront a bully.

He didn't know exactly what he would say, how he would frame things or even where to begin, but he did know one thing; that this was an opportunity—perhaps a singular opportunity—to take back his life.

No longer would Thomas allow his fear of repercussion, concern about money or angst about the future dictate his actions on this late Monday afternoon. Instead of bottling-up his frustration the way he normally did, Thomas used it as fuel for courage to stand up for himself and for his colleagues.

Now, that all sounds warm and mushy, but life isn't always that clean and tidy. In fact, it's often messy; sometimes brutally so.

Maddison had never met Thomas and, since his personal interview wasn't scheduled until the last slot of the next day, she had no idea what to expect. Thomas scribbled-out a few notes on a steno pad. They were mostly about the unfairness of her decisions and how consistently profitable the division had been without the need for such harsh treatment of employees.

Thomas got up and stood tall. His confident posture felt unfamiliar. It was as though he had just put on a dazzling new suit. He put his paper with his notes on his desk and promptly forgot to bring it with him. He walked to the elevator like a man with a purpose and rode it up the two floors to the 10th floor where Maddison's office was.

His heart was beating through his chest and he could feel his hands shaking at his sides as he balled-up his fists with nervous energy. As he approached Maddison's office, he noticed that her door was open and the Assistant to the Division Manager, Ashleigh, had left at five along with everyone else. It was the first time Ashleigh left before six at any point in the last three years.

Thomas pushed the door fully open and walked in, feeling taller than he had ever felt before. Maddison was clearly startled and took a few steps backward toward her desk. She had been trying to hastily hang some ugly artwork on the wall and not having much luck with the task.

Maddison was taken aback. She would rather everyone in the building had left even if they *did* hate her. But not everyone left. There he was. Thomas introduced himself by stating his name and position title.

Maddison, appearing extremely rattled, said, "Um, I'm sorry. Uh, uh, who are you?" Her voice shook and cracked. "I didn't schedule any appointments after five today."

Thomas said, "That's right, I don't have an appointment." His voice was shaky, but commanding. He continued, "Again, my name is Thomas Fuller and I have been dedicated to this company, doing my best as a damned good salesperson for over fifteen years and..."

Maddison interrupted him, blurting out angrily, "Listen! You can't just come into my office...the District Manager's office...without an appointment and begin to, well, I don't know what you want, but you'll have to wait until tomorrow."

Her snub bolstered Thomas' confidence and stiffened his resolve. He said with an even louder voice, "...FIFTEEN YEARS and I've NEVER had a manager here or anywhere else come in and do as much damage to staff morale as you did in two short hours!"

Thomas didn't know what to expect and had no idea how she would react, other than guessing that she would likely be very angry and lash out at him. Regardless, he was prepared to take it and throw it back. Surprisingly, Maddison said nothing. She locked eyes with him and moved toward her chair. She sat down and appeared to have no idea how to respond.

Thomas didn't know if she was giving him enough rope to hang himself or if she had never before been confronted. His heart was racing, but it felt good. He felt alive like never before. His senses were super-sharp.

He doubled-down, saying, "You've come into a division that historically and perpetually does well. We get along. We're productive. We work as a team. Do you really think that threatening, putting-down, restricting and enraging staff is going to end well for you?"

She was stunned. Nobody had ever talked to her that way and she was at a loss for a response. She quickly calculated her position and asked Thomas, "What, exactly, did I say that you're so angry about? If you're as good an employee as you say you are, then you should be entirely fine with everything I said; I have only laid-out basic expectations of acceptable behavior in this corporation. If you don't like it, you are welcome to leave."

As she pointed to the door, Thomas said with firm conviction, "This is how you deal with confrontation to your own weakness as a manager? Instead of showing the least bit of concern about your own effectiveness, you are willing to let a profitable employee go? FINE!"

Thomas wished her luck and slammed the door as he left. The episode knocked the wind from her sails. She sat in the oversized leather executive chair for over two hours, replaying in her mind what had just occurred. It affected her profoundly, although even she had no conscious idea of how it did or what would follow.

Thomas arrived home just after six, pretty much the same time he always did. He didn't tell his wife or his kids what had happened, but they could all sense that a different man walked through the door that evening. The husband and dad they had known was gone. It was as if someone different had broken through that tough, protective shell; a man with a palpable passion for life and who, for once, knew how to smile. Although they loved him dearly, it had been for as long as they could remember, that he was merely a surrogate, a robot of sorts.

He had no idea what was next, but he was more confident about his future than he had been in many years.

Thomas felt free. He realized that hard work was ahead, but was looking forward to rolling up his sleeves. He finally had a say in what his next steps would be and was, for once, willing to take the risks that were necessary to explore his own potential.

After dinner, Thomas asked his wife to join him in the den to have a chat about the events of their day.

Thomas smiled broadly and said, "Honey, I made a decision today...an important one." His voice was unwavering and confident; it was a quality his wife had never heard in his speech.

Her eyes perked-up and Thomas could tell that his newfound passion had ignited her own. He said, "I'm ready to start actually *living* life..."

Stephen J. Kristof

ZINFANDEL
SETTLING FOR MORE

Here's a story that's just itching to be told. It simply will not wait for the pithy preamble about its own Wine Mascot; Zinfandel. More on that in a bit...

But first, you see, his voice didn't prepare me for his appearance. In fact, I can honestly say that his voice belied the way he looked. It's very common. When you hear a radio host or voice actor and try to envision their appearance, you automatically get this picture in your head that perfectly matches their voice.

At least that's what you believe; that is, until you see their picture or meet them in person. Then you realize how far off you were!

I don't know where our assumptions come from, in terms of how voices "look." You know what I'm talking about. Perhaps we attach stereotypes to voices? If so, there's likely a gender aspect to it. When hearing a deep and richly toned male voice, many people visualize a tall and muscular man with dark hair and a perpetual five o'clock shadow. A beefcake kind of guy with smokey eyes, a chiseled jawline and just enough facial character to have that irresistible bad boy look.

On the other hand, a woman's breathy, playful voice might give some people the impression that she looks tall and slender, ultra-sexy with long legs and with, well, yah, smokey eyes too. It's pretty laughable and a bit pathetic when you think about it.

Then, of course, there are the thin, hesitant, almost squeaky and somewhat nasally voices. For men, and I really don't know why this is, but I expect that kind of voice to belong to a guy who is on the short side, a bit underweight, balding, but with a way-too-thin mustache and eyes that are a tad too close to one another. I picture women with thin, nasally voices to have that quintessential librarian look, if that makes any sense.

It's kind of like Zinfandel, the wine grape varietal. Time and again, I find myself looking at the label. It doesn't matter who the producer is; if it's a Zin, I somehow think less of the wine inside than if it were a more serious contender. Somewhere deep in my consciousness I regard Zinfandel as the little guy with a brassy sense of humor, but without the weight and depth of, say, a Cabernet.

If different wines had unique "voices," I would guess that Zinfandels wouldn't sound all that sophisticated or mysterious. That's probably due to my personal bias. When I bring a Zinfandel to my lips, I often catch myself thinking that I'm somehow settling for less.

Yet, every time that silky, jammy, fruit-forward Zinfandel caresses my palate, I realize that I wasn't settling for less at all. The name, just like the voice on the radio, doesn't always match what's behind it.

More on that in a bit. But, first, you need to know about Chloe, my closest friend in the world. She broke-up with her long-term boyfriend about six months ago. They dated for just over five years and, although she was fully expecting to at least be wearing an engagement ring by the end of those five years, it never happened. Greg wanted to move in with Chloe or for her to move in with him, but she had her own ideas about getting married first before living together as a fully committed couple and eventually having a family.

It's not that I didn't like Greg. He was okay, but I never understood what Chloe saw in him. Why did she hang-on to him for as long as she did? Particularly when he made it pretty clear that he had no intention of ever getting married or wanting to have children.

I had to be careful not to say anything negative to Chloe about Greg. I learned a few years into her and Greg's relationship that disparaging him only pushed her further away from me and, to fill that gap, made her desire Greg even more. I would occasionally suggest that she was settling for less than she deserved. Her response was that he was still growing as a person and would eventually propose. She truly believed the opposite of what I thought was true; she thought that starting a new relationship with anyone else would be settling for less!

Some people are like that. They just keep hoping that their partner will miraculously change. I think they believe that if they were to move-on to a more suitable partner, it would be like giving-up on a dream, no matter how unlikely it is that their deluded fantasy would actually become reality.

Chloe was so excited before her most recent date with Greg. Unfortunately, she didn't realize that it would be, literally, their last date. Greg made reservations at the ever-popular Trattoria Brutto Grasso and told Chloe that he had something important to talk about. I personally didn't understand why that restaurant was so popular. Then again, it's nearly impossible to get a reservation there at a decent time on any night, so a lot of other people must think otherwise.

Chloe was convinced that Greg would finally pop the question during this special date. She told me she made this presumption based on his shaky voice and school boy nervousness when he asked her to meet him there. I never told her this, but I doubted he would propose marriage at a restaurant that's translated English name literally means *"Ugly Fat Restaurant."*

She drove to meet Greg at Ugly Fat, because he was working late that night and said he would have to meet here there. In actuality, he knew that he wouldn't be driving her home, so it would be better for her to have her car at the ready.

Chloe called me from her car about forty-five minutes after the "special" night began. She was crying hysterically and hyperventilating. I was able to glean from her incoherent babble, that "Dreamboat Greg," as I often called him *(although she never realized I was being sarcastic)* dumped her. In true cad fashion, he apparently waited to drop his bombshell until *after* their ugly fat entrees were brought to the table. He scarfed-down his last forkful of food and then he came clean.

He wanted out of the relationship. It came as a total shock to Chloe; she was utterly blindsided. Greg delivered the old one-two punch, saying first, "It's not you, it's me," then, "I need to figure things out."

Of course, the dumper and everyone else, except for the dumpee, knows that this is guy code for, "I found someone else and would rather be with her."

She was devastated like all of us are when this happens. When she found out about the other woman, her devastation turned to anger. Scary anger, to be frank. And then came the five weeks when she ghosted me. She was initially extremely jealous of my relationship with my fiancée, Jamie, and just couldn't handle it. I didn't blame her; I knew she would come back.

Like I said, that happened about six months ago. Chloe went through the various five or seven or how many ever stages of grief one needs to go through after a breakup. After working through it, she was in a far better place, emotionally, than she was when Dreamboat Greg was in the picture. She was happier, was being kind to herself and to others that deserved her kindness, was looking toward a better future with someone actually worthy of her, and, best of all, didn't feel like she needed someone else to be complete.

Short Stories to Enjoy with Wine, Vol 1.

Chloe had come a long way and I was never happier for her. She also signaled that she was open to a new relationship. I trusted her, but it was the one thing that concerned me. I tried to suggest that she take it slow and each time I brought it up, she just laughed in response.

This is where the voice/appearance paradox comes in. "Danny the Beach" is a local deejay for one of the more popular radio stations in the area. That's, of course, his stage name. I had no idea what his actual name was, although I wanted to believe that his first name was actually Danny.

Since Danny was a household name around here, I concluded that, regardless how many people deny listening to live radio at all, a lot of people still must.

So, how did Danny come into the picture? Chloe's mother, who is very young, very fit and very attractive at fifty-four years of age, was having lunch with one of her much older-looking high school friends. Now, don't get me wrong. I honestly love Chloe's mother, but I do not love how she looks. She needs to look more like her age. You know, like her much older-looking high school friends.

I get it. It's really a 'me' problem that I have to deal with. And I have no business having those negative thoughts about Chloe's mom, because she really is the sweetest, kindest and nicest woman I've ever met. Maybe even more so than my *own* mom. Did I just say that? Well, if I'm honest with myself, I'm a tad envious about how she looks, but hope I can look even half that good when I'm her age.

Yes, I do digress. Anyway, her mom and friend got talking about Chloe, her breakup and how she's ready to start dating again. Somehow, Chloe's mom's friend offered-up her son to go on a date with Chloe. She said that her son, Danny, worked for a local radio station.

I often listen to Danny the Beach on my way into work, as he does the morning show. He's actually pretty funny, puts me in a positive mood and plays music that I actually have on my own playlist. So, when Chloe told me about her upcoming date with him, I was really excited!

Danny has one of those ultra-smooth, clear, mid-register voices that, for a reason unbeknownst to me, tends to fill most morning radio deejay spots. His eyes are like deep pools, he's of average height, is pretty fit, dresses in a somewhat sloppy but modern style, has an attractive fade type of hairstyle and a very well-trimmed goatee.

Chloe explained how her meddling mother's matchmaking connected her to Danny the Beach. I was initially a bit jealous. Not only is this guy locally famous, he also knocks it out of the park when it comes to looks.

As I pictured Danny with Chloe, it dawned on me that I'd never actually *seen* him before; the image in my mind was merely manufactured by my own imagination. I had never bothered to look on social media or the station's website to see what he actually looks like, because it just never occurred to me to do so.

Danny was planning to pick-up Chloe at her place at 6:30 on Saturday evening. He told her that he made reservations at a really nice restaurant, followed by a show. I was hoping for her sake that he wouldn't take her to the ugly fat Trattoria Brutto Grasso!

Chloe and I promised each other that we wouldn't creep Danny's picture before her date. If truth be told and I were in Chloe's position, there's no possible way I could have been talked out of looking him up before the date!

I've been on my own share of blind dates and I've got to tell you, sometimes those surprises can be very cruel. Don't get me wrong; I'm not that superficial. Sure, looks are important, but everything else is far *more* important! The depth of a guy's character, his generosity, intelligence, positive self-image, integrity, sense of humor, ability to love and be loved...these are the things that mean the most to me.

Nevertheless, we can be cruel without ever intending to do so. I've likely caused some embarrassment and deflation by my apparent shock and disappointment with the appearance of at least a few blind dates. No matter how much I tried to hide it, I just wasn't prepared. I've learned over time to creep my blind dates in advance to prepare me for those unexpected surprises.

And, no, I've never declined a blind date after seeing a guy's picture. Sheesh! Give me a little more credit than that! Regardless, I don't have to worry about this anymore, because my guy is a keeper. I would never, ever, tell him, but hey, he's no Brad Pitt. Far from it, to be honest. But he's the most amazing man who checks-off every other box on my list and I'm so fortunate that we are together. Sorry Brad, my Jamie outshines you without even trying!

Saturday arrived and Chloe asked me to be at her place by 2:00 in the afternoon to help her get ready. I agreed, not because I thought she needed any help, but because I thought it would be fun. Chloe's the kind of girl who looks extraordinarily beautiful without so much as a dab of makeup.

For example, we went camping a few years back. One night, we sat around the campfire and drank entirely too much wine. Predictably, the next morning I deserved to look as rough as the copious amount of wine made me look. Chloe, on the other hand, was ready for the silver screen. And that was without any effort! When she puts on makeup, she looks absolutely stunning.

By 5:30 p.m. I had helped her with four different hair styles, four complete cycles of makeup application followed by makeup removal pads to start all over again, at-home manicure and pedicure treatments and nail painting. She also tried-on nine different outfits, each one as attractive as the next. For my part, I gave-up complimenting her after the second outfit. Any of them would do the trick. (Well, that is except for the appallingly dowdy green and white patterned dress that didn't belong in *anyone's* closet!)

I really wanted to stick around and meet Danny. Chloe displayed some really bad judgment by saying that it would be okay if I stayed. She hatched some lame excuses to explain why I would be there, which of course, Danny would see right through. As much as I wanted to stay, I left about 20 minutes before Danny was expected to be at her door.

I texted Chloe far too many times during her date. I don't know exactly what she told Danny, but at one point she texted me back, saying, "Danny asked me to respond to your latest probe, but only if he can start texting questions back to you!" She included an LOL and smiley face to avoid any hurt feelings. I was a bit embarrassed, but realized that I brought it on myself.

Just before midnight, my phone chimed and woke me up. It was a message from Chloe. She had just gotten back and couldn't wait to tell me about her date. I called her right away.

"Chloeeeee!" I shrieked. "Well, thumbs-up or thumbs-down, girlfriend?"

"Thumbs WAAAY up," Chloe said cheerfully.

"Did he come in to your place or just drop you off?" I asked.

"I invited him in for a drink, but he was a total gentleman. I could tell that he really wanted to come in, but he said that it was only our first date and that he wanted to be as respectful as possible."

"Kiss?" Standard protocol, I thought.

"Definitely!"

"Is he a *good* kisser?"

"Definitely!" Chloe's voice was buzzing with excitement!

"So, tell me about the date. No, no...first tell me what he looks like," I asked.

Chloe said, "I was surprised. Very pleasantly surprised!"

I said, "Go on..."

Chloe continued, "He looks nothing like he sounds. Better than he sounds; way better."

"C'mon Chloe. Describe him!"

As Chloe started to describe his features, I simultaneously did an image search on "Danny the Beach." He *was* gorgeous!

Chloe said, "He's a bit taller than me, part wavy, part spikey brown hair with blonde highlights, um, a small goatee and mustache, dreamy blue eyes, a strong jawline and, bonus, he's got a six-pack."

"A six-pack? Seriously," I asked, "how could you see if he kept his shirt on?"

"I could see the ripples under his shirt," Chloe explained.

"What's his real name?" I asked. "Obviously Danny, but what's his actual last name?"

"Danny the Beach is actually Danny Beach," said Chloe.

"What do you mean? What's his *actual* last name?"

"Beach!"

I said "Ohhh, I get it. So, what's he like?"

"I started listening to his show in the mornings this past Wednesday, you know, after he asked me on this date," said Chloe. "I never told you, but when I realized that he acts like such a goofball on the air, I toyed with cancelling our date."

"Seriously?" I said, "That's just an act. Show business, I guess. Well, you're the one who went out with him...so what's he *really* like?"

"Nothing like that, except that he has a great sense of humor," said Chloe.

"So, he's funny, but not like on his show?" I asked.

"Right. Nothing like the goofiness. He's seriously funny, interesting, knowledgeable and…now…here's something I really didn't expect…" said Chloe.

"What is it?" I interrupted.

"On the radio," Chloe explained, "he talks constantly. But in-person, he's one of the best listeners I've ever been out with. This is a new one for me. My date actually asked *me* questions!"

"Now that's a new one," I said, somewhat sarcastically.

"Not only that, he actually *listened* to what I had to say," said Chloe.

"So, when's your second date?" I asked the question rhetorically for the most part, but was surprised by her response.

"Tomorrow," she said.

You might not be able to determine a lot about people's appearance based solely on their voice, but I could tell that Chloe was smiling.

Chloe kept on smiling for the next six months. Danny proposed; it was a beautiful traditional proposal that he delivered at the end of a very special day he had planned, doing all of the things Chloe loved to do. When she called me to announce her engagement, we both started crying.

Jamie and I had just tied the knot a month earlier and, as much as I thought life couldn't get any better, I realized that life had only just begun. Chloe and Danny were married exactly one year after his proposal.

A lot of water has crossed under the bridge in the five years since Chloe and Danny's wedding day. Jamie and I had a few struggles, as did Chloe and Danny, but we all came through and the love we share with our spouses is stronger than ever.

I looked at Jamie, smiled and thought, "Dreams can come true," as we arrived at Chloe and Danny's for their anniversary party. We helped our two children, Adrianna and Tyler, out of their car seats and they immediately ran toward Chloe and Danny's kids. I can't describe the joy that fills my heart every time I see our kids playing together!

Chloe hired two certified early childhood educators to run activities and supervise the children. This allowed adult guests at the party to let loose and celebrate without worrying about or having to entertain their own children. Just before dinner, Chloe sat with me for a few minutes and privately thanked me for encouraging her to, "settle for more." It was one of those special moments in life that I know I'll tuck away and treasure forever.

Just before dinner was plated, I stood up and, raising my glass of Zinfandel, proposed a toast. Friends and family who were present were pin-drop silent, yet the mood was celebratory.

I said, "Like this glass of wine, our lives hold promise beyond labels and expectations. The covers of the books of our marriages only hint at the manifestations and expressions of love that are written in their pages. Wishing my forever friend, Chloe, and her amazing husband Danny, a very happy anniversary with a lifetime of experiences yet to live and beautiful memories yet to make!"

Stephen J. Kristof

PINOTAGE
SHIFTING CHARACTER

Have you ever tried a new wine and absolutely fell in love with it, but were then disappointed the next time you tasted it? Veteran oenologists *(noun: wine experts)* have many plausible explanations for this phenomenon; it's an experience that's more common than you may think.

Perhaps your palate was off the second time you tasted it. Or your palate may have been influenced by some other drink or food during one of those tastings. There's, yet, another plausible explanation. An important aspect of enjoying wine is that it is inseparably tied to atmosphere. It's possible that a desirable physical or social setting, pleasant music or an ambient aroma enhanced your appreciation of a wine on one occasion, but that same atmosphere was missing on your next tasting.

Maybe you tasted the wine on a Friday and by Saturday or Sunday it had degraded due to improper storage.

Pinotage is a hybrid varietal grown primarily in South Africa. It descends from Pinot Noir and Cinsault genes. Like any wine, it can change from one day to the next. It can have a velvety and luxurious charm at one tasting, but may then seem a bit cloying the next. The sophisticated and exciting layers of plum, soft tannins and umami that are often present in a Pinotage can easily take-on an overripe banana-like flavor if not produced with precision.

One difficulty with Pinotage is that its wines can vary significantly; even from the same single rootstock. And a particular batch of wine from that same rootstock can change a lot over its life. Some wines have little ageing potential and turn into lifeless, lackluster plonk. Others age gracefully and gain far greater character over time. In this respect, people sometimes imitate wine. While people aren't nearly as likely to change their character during their lives, it can and does happen.

Keep that notion in mind with respect to Brock; the main player in an unlikely scenario that ultimately thrilled the CEO at the helm of one of the most dominant organizations around. Brock is described in financial newsgroups as a dynamic, highly successful, ultra-rich, fifty-four-year-old entrepreneur.

His public persona tends to be more about his assets than *who* he is. With minimal digging, one learns that Brock has a magnificent mountain retreat in Virginia and a coastal 'get-away' estate in West Palm Beach, Florida. His primary residence is a mansion in Salt Lake City, Utah. He also owns an ultra-luxurious 120-foot yacht, which he keeps in Florida. The boat has its own staff of five, who attend to it on a full-time basis and are always on-call, regardless of whether Brock is in West Palm.

Brock made his fortune the old-fashioned way; he was born into it.

He has always had a knack for business and is more than willing to take educated risks. When he was barely twenty-five, he sold his first tech start-up venture to a major insurance carrier for $1.4 billion. In the twenty-nine years since that first ultra-successful transaction, Brock started and sold three more successful companies in different industries, each one netting multiple millions of dollars.

Now, keep in mind that while Brock is very smart, he's not particularly brilliant. His business ideas are solid and extremely profitable, but not necessarily unique. A lot of people have had very good ideas for ventures; many of them are on-par with Brock's. Many others have ideas that are, frankly, far better. However, it's difficult to compete with someone who has the kind of advantages that Brock has.

You see, when you're born into the kind of affluence that defines Brock's lineage, it's not exactly a level playing field. Brock never had to worry about meeting bankers' requirements for getting a start-up loan and his network of extremely influential contacts had little to do with his effort or affability. All of this was already baked-in before he even got started.

His degree from Princeton was only part of his education. Brock acquired exceptional business acumen through osmosis by observing his father's shrewd wheeling and dealing, along with several savvy investment schemes.

As a side note, a few of his dad's investment schemes were more 'schemey' than savvy; they involved practices that brought into question the boundaries of his father's so-called moral compass. Regardless, growing-up surrounded by such high-level financial decision making represents an enormous advantage. That type of education generates a level of confidence that easily eclipses formal schooling.

In a sense, Brock was born to succeed. His rootstock virtually guaranteed a life in which he would become increasingly affluent, living in the lap of luxury no matter how much he tried…or didn't try at all.

It's no secret that most poor people don't care much for rich people. Middle income earners often tolerate the rich because of their dependance on them. However, curiously, it sometimes happens that poor people admire and put the rich up on a pedestal. It's a psychological thing. Deep in the psyche, there's a connection made when poor or average people idolize the rich and powerful. Doing so tricks their subconscious into feeling that they are at the same level. Sure! Keep dreaming!

On the other hand, truly rich folk—that is, filthy-rich, absurdly entitled people—well, they often mollify any guilt they may feel about their own affluence by feeling sorry for the poor. Sometimes they pretend to admire poor people's courage and resilience, but deep down, they actually dislike their lifestyles and despise their lack of refinement. Rather than helping out, some ultra-rich people choose to blame their fellow human beings' desperate financial situations on their own poor choices in life. It's often short-sighted and terribly judgmental, but it's very easy to do and it makes one feel better about one's own undeserved advantages; it's easier to do than you may think.

As far as Brock is concerned, he doesn't dislike the poor, nor does he blame them for their lot in life. He actually feels sorry for them; particularly for those who work hard, but who never seem to rise above their financial distress and all the collateral damage that comes along with it. He's troubled by that disparity in life, but tries not to think about it too much.

Brock likes to help the poor financially, but only in ways that are related to "teaching a man to fish," rather than giving him a fish. For this reason, he's quite a generous benefactor of charities and programs that promote growth, independence and skills for the underprivileged and neglected. It's one truly admirable aspect of what Brock brings to humanity.

Having said that, keep in mind that Brock is, nevertheless, uncomfortable socializing with poor people or those with average means. To be fair, due to his upbringing and pedigree, he's never had any experience with poor or average people.

About the only people that Brock *has* had experience with are his fellow super-rich human beings. Now, we've looked at ways in which poor and average people view the rich and vice-versa. But this begs the question; how do affluent people regard their equally affluent peers?

Well, rich people commonly and secretly dislike their fellow rich acquaintances, but accept them as part of the package. But it goes further than that. There's the exclusivity aspect of all of this money and class hierarchy. Affluent old-money folks are members of a very exclusive "club." Interestingly, these ultra-rich people often don't care much for their ultra-rich peers. Deep down, they realize that many of them are not true and loyal friends, but are a necessary part of life at this echelon.

Plus, with whom else would they socialize? The super-rich know that anyone who is *not* part of their club either dislikes them or is trying to exploit their wealth, power or influence. It's difficult to hang out with people you feel are trying to use you or who secretly despise you because of the green-eyed monster.

Like his peers, Brock doesn't care for or trust his society friends, but feigns a fondness for them and pretends to respect their "achievements." He's wary about anyone who tries to get too close to him if their net worth is south of $500 million. He's just as guarded about those with new money, even if they do meet that $500 million threshold.

The second truly admirable aspect of what Brock brings to humanity is his relationship with his family. Brock and his wife, Jenna, have two teenaged children, Kendra and Keaton. They are fraternal twins, but their personalities are more different than they are alike. They are both seniors in high school and are presently stressing about college; which ivy league college will look best on a resume, which program will be the least boring and which campus has the most awesome social life.

For them, it's merely about making choices among the top options. Kendra and Keaton are magnificently privileged, compared to most teens their age. Unfortunately for the rest of the teenage world, it's less about decisions and more about *acceptance*. In other words, accepting a future that is far less than what they would choose if they had the kind of opportunity that Kendra and Keaton were born into.

Their mom, Jenna was not born into money. Her parents were professionals, meaning that she experienced privilege and had higher than average expectations. However, she grew-up in an upper-middle class neighborhood, worked at a video rental shop during high school and, later, as a waitress during her college years. So, although her expectations in life were high, she set equally high expectations of her personal effort, was willing to work for them and didn't see herself as entitled. Her experiences and upbringing were *so* unlike Brock's!

Jenna met Brock when they were both attending college. Brock was a Computer Engineering major at Princeton and Jenna was an undergrad pre-Law student at Ryder University. After Ryder, Jenna earned her JD degree at Seaton Hall. She eventually attained her goal of practicing social justice law.

They were both bright, but Jenna pulled ahead of Brock in the brains department; she was a gifted student with a PSAT score of 1340 and a Stanford Binet IQ score of 142. Jenna qualified for Mensa membership but had no interest in pursuing it, because she always considered it to be too pretentious.

They met at a frat party mixer night. Brock and Jenna instantly fell head-over-heels for each other. They became fairy-tale college sweethearts who eventually got married and never looked back. You may wonder who had had a greater influence upon the other? Did Brock's life-long indoctrination of affluent bias and justified privilege stealthily coerce its way into Jenna's head? Or was it the other way around? Did Jenna's belief in equality and social justice win over Brock's way of thinking?

Over time, Brock's early socialization to discrimination and class ranking dynamics grew more deeply ingrained in his mind. It must have been difficult for Jenna to resist Brock's strong influence; particularly when she herself enjoyed the enormous privilege his money provided. However, despite her abrupt transition to immense wealth once she got married, Jenna continued to see herself as an everyday person, undeserving of all of the prosperity.

Now, that's not to say that Jenna didn't really like all of the comfort and opportunity that money can buy; she loved it. But she was aware of the baggage that came along with all of it and, as a result, deliberately reminded herself to remain humble.

Back to that earlier question; who rubbed-off on whom? It's fair to say that it was pretty much a draw, although Jenna did soften some of Brock's perspectives over time. More on that later.

Jenna and the kids arrived at their West Palm Beach mansion on the fifteenth of April, the day before Brock's birthday. They were planning a modest evening reception with a handful of their 'closest' fake friends to celebrate his big day. Brock knew about it and was expecting it to be a low-key affair.

He was looking forward to his birthday party, but was much more jazzed about spending the next four weeks in Florida. Salt Lake City had been unusually cold through the winter and early spring, with dreary overcast conditions and temperatures stuck in the forties. Brock had wrapped-up his business commitments and was ready for a month-long break of boating, beaching and swimming in the balmy breeze and abundant sunshine.

No need to pack anything. Everything Brock would need was already waiting for him at his West Palm home. In fact, preparing for travel was nothing at all like the complicated and frustrating ritual that the rest of us have to endure. Most people on this globe have no idea—*seriously no idea*—how the ultra-rich travel!

Imagine showing-up to the airport on your own schedule. No need to purchase tickets, no fighting check-in and security lines, not having to worry about luggage sizes or weights, never being kicked off of an overbooked flight, never worrying about who you may have to sit next to and avoiding the baggage carrousel altogether!

It sounds like a dreamy way to travel and it really is. But when you own your own private jet, and directly employ the Captain and Cabin Attendant, the experience in no way reflects travel for the rest of us grunts. The only similarity is that both planes take off, fly in the air and eventually land.

Brock's hired limo showed-up the next morning at eight sharp to collect and transfer him to the private airfield where his private jet had already been fueled and was ready to go. The limo pulled-up to the jet on the tarmac. Brock exited the limo and quickly ambled-up the fold-out stairs. Once inside, he had a quick chat with his Captain and took a seat. Matthew, his Cabin Attendant, quietly brought him a plate of Danish and a heavy mug of freshly brewed coffee that filled the cabin air with a heady aroma. Brock didn't have to ask; that was pretty much one of his standing orders for any morning flight.

"Happy Birthday, sir," Matthew chimed cheerfully as he placed the food tray on the elegant, burled elm coffee table. The table was one of dozens of custom enhancements and amenities that Brock had ordered when he purchased the plane. The jet also had a lounging area, work desk, fully-stocked bar, working kitchen, dining table and swiveling leather upholstered captain's chairs.

Brock was seated at a comfy sofa that faced the middle aisle. He was on a phone call, so Brock simply smiled and shot a thumbs-up gesture to Matthew.

To be honest, Matthew was far more than a Cabin Attendant. For the past seventeen years, Matthew was Brock's Concierge, Flight Attendant, Personal Fixer, Walking Encyclopedia and general go-to guy. Working on a 24/7 year-round on-call basis, Matthew was on-duty on all flights, but spent even more time tending to Brock's various personal needs during off-flight hours.

He was paid very handsomely for all of this, but it came with an enormous cost; he had sacrificed having a family of his own.

Similarly, Hayes was also more than merely Brock's personal pilot. "Captain Hayes" had an illustrious career in hedge fund finance for over fifteen years before coming to the conclusion that, while he loved the money, he despised the work. He abruptly followed his true passion, flying.

In a stunning mid-career pivot, Hayes acquired the necessary hours and certifications, and worked for two major commercial airlines before Brock hired him as his own personal pilot. However, Brock applied his intellect to the job description. Hayes' financial acumen was part of the deal. Brock often leaned on Hayes for advice and occasionally asked him to take the lead on certain financial proposals when he wasn't piloting one of Brock's flights. For all of this, Hayes was also paid very handsomely, earning an annual salary in the low seven-figure neighborhood.

As Brock's luxurious plane waited on the tarmac, he read and responded to various messages on his tablet, finished the last of his coffee and pastry, and then readied himself for flight. He became aware that there was some sort of delay when he glanced at the time and realized that the plane should have already been on its ascent at least ten minutes before.

Just as Brock was about to ask about the delay, the cockpit door opened and Hayes emerged, looking frustrated. Hayes and Brock had a conversation that neither one seemed to want to have. At one point, Hayes pointed toward the back left side of the plane, where there was a mechanic's truck that was parked next to the jet's engine. Brock was so glued to his screen that he hadn't noticed the truck. On-board diagnostics detected a potential fuel-line issue in one of the two engines.

Upon quick inspection, it was determined that a large portion of the turbine had cracked. Consequently, the plane was grounded until it could be fixed or replaced; a repair that would be both costly and lengthy. There was no way that Brock was taking his own plane to West Palm Beach for at least a few days.

He asked Hayes and Matthew to scour the local area for a private jet rental option or to make arrangements to borrow one from a local operator. He was dejected to learn that nothing of that sort would be available for at least a couple of days. Brock wondered how he would make it to West Palm Beach to be with his family for his birthday.

Matthew had already been scouring alternative options on his phone. Exasperated after hitting several dead-ends, he finally told Brock that there was a final option. There remained a limited number of seats available on a regular commercial non-stop flight from Salt Lake City (SLC) to West Palm Beach (PBI). The flight was departing shortly, at 10:50 a.m., which would give Brock just enough time to be driven from the private airfield to SLC, the regular commercial airport at Salt Lake City, get through security and be boarded.

This was the best option. Otherwise, Brock would have to take an even later commercial flight or wait a few days for his jet to be repaired and cleared. The later flight had a six-hour layover at LaGuardia Airport. Even with the two-hour time zone difference in Brock's favor, he wouldn't get into PBI until at least 11:30 p.m., so he told his Cabin Attendant to book the earlier flight.

Brock's limo pulled-up to the airport in good time, but he wasn't accustomed to dealing with the chaos that's common to major airports. He despised what he felt was the inhumanity of standing in line to get through the TSA security check. When the twirling X-ray booth caught a fragment of something under the stitching of his pants, he was required to endure a manual pat-down, which he complained, loudly, was an, "...affront to my modesty."

By the time Brock made it to the gate he was far worse for the wear. He had no idea until he was seated that, when his Cabin

Attendant booked his ticket, there were no remaining First-Class seats. As the flight attendant guided Brock to the right instead of left to the First-Class section, he complained loudly, "Main Cabin? Are you serious? This is just getting worse by the minute!"

Once seated, he was infuriated with the lack of leg room, the uncomfortable body-crushing seat, the absence of elbow room and...the fact that he had to share his "row" with two other people. It was almost too much for him to take. And then it happened...

Mike and Flo, the two passengers that were trying way too hard to jam oversized carry-on bags into the overhead compartment, proceeded to compact him even further into his tiny seat as they settled in next to him. Brock was thankful that he had a window seat, so he could at least rest his head on the window and pretend to be asleep. On the other hand, he felt claustrophobic and physically trapped. He didn't like either option.

Mike held-out his hand. Sporting a genuine smile, Mike said with a booming voice, "Hi there, flight partner! My name is Mike and the Mrs. here is Flo!"

Brock's head was telling him to say just enough to be civil, but not enough to encourage any further interaction. He didn't listen to whatever his heart was trying to tell him, because he was so angry and frustrated about everything. All he could think about was how much he wanted to be on his own plane instead of on this, "cattle car," as he silently called it.

Brock eyes met Mike's very briefly and he then looked away. He decided not to reciprocate with the handshake and said in a mumbled, monotone voice, "I'm Brock. Nice to meet you." His disinterest in communicating any further was almost palpable.

Mike was of average height and build. He wore jeans and an old raggedy t-shirt that he probably shouldn't have worn out in public, no less, on a plane. Flo was dressed more respectably, but she had a "take me as I am" sort of attitude and an extremely casual way of talking that Brock didn't find particularly appealing.

At least not initially. Flo's distinctive southern drawl was syrupy sweet and, Brock felt, unnecessary. Mike and Flo were around the same age as Brock and Jenna, although they appeared to be quite a bit older.

The couple tried their best to make polite conversation with him, but Brock wouldn't have it. He confined his answers to aloof one-word responses and purposefully avoided asking any questions, as one would do reciprocally and respectfully in normal conversation. Mike and Flo didn't share Brock's pedigree, but they weren't socially inept either. They knew they were being brushed-off, so they eventually stopped trying and kept their conversation between themselves.

Even though they didn't have pedigree, Mike and Flo exhibited far more class than did Brock. Rather than judging and dismissing him as a rude and arrogant individual, they took the high road and left room for more forgiving explanations. Flo typed the following phrase into her tablet and angled it toward Mike, but just enough that it was out of Brock's view. The message read, "I feel sorry for him. Who knows what he's dealing with? Illness, death in the family...unresolved issue? He certainly seems unhappy."

In a sense, they were right. Brock *was* unhappy. Sure, he had privilege, power and endless choices, but his affluence didn't bring the joy, love or contentment that he longed for. He was happy in his marriage and loved Jenna, but there were so many distractions and false idols in his life that he didn't fully *experience* that love.

For the remainder of the flight, Brock said very little, fiddled with his tablet now and then, and glanced out the window. He overheard the hushed conversation taking place next to him. He learned that his row companions had just attended a relative's funeral in Salt Lake City. They were flying to Atlanta, where they would be shuttled to an off-site long-term parking lot, pay the parking fee and drive their minivan back home to the suburbs, Kennesaw, to be specific.

As Brock considered their situation, it suddenly dawned on him that Matthew had apparently made a mistake about the flight that he was now very much into. This wasn't a non-stop flight at all! It was making a stop in Atlanta.

Brock pressed the little orange overhead button to call for a flight attendant. The attendant arrived promptly and he asked her how long he would be waiting in Atlanta before boarding the last leg of his trip to West Palm Beach.

"Just about an hour between flights, sir," the flight attendant said. "But it's just long enough to grab a quick snack or to refresh yourself after disembarking this plane and hopping back on the next one. You'll be home before you know it!"

She wasted her cheerful response on Brock. He was too focused on the inconvenience and hassle of a layover. He moped about his misfortune for the remainder of the flight, rarely acknowledging Mike or Flo.

About 45 minutes before landing, the co-pilot came on the overhead speaker system with an ominous message. An unusually late nor'easter was causing havoc all along the east coast, with punishing snow, sleet and rain effectively shutting-down all forms of transportation from Maine to North Carolina. Airports throughout the region were closed and thousands of flights had been cancelled.

As the co-pilot explained, this also meant that thousands of planes that were expected to make connections elsewhere were grounded and going nowhere...including the next jet that was expected to carry Brock from Atlanta to West Palm Beach. Passengers unable to make this connection would be refunded the entire cost of the flight, including a generous credit toward a future flight. That, of course, was of no consolation to Brock.

At once, Brock grabbed his phone and registered for the in-flight wireless service. He first texted Jenna to let her know what was happening and then Matthew, who he had hoped would navigate other options to get home quickly from Atlanta. After urgently exchanging texts with Matthew for about 30 minutes, Brock looked exhausted and dejected.

Mike tried, once again, to reach out to Brock.

"Looks like your plans have been masterfully screwed-up by Mother Nature. I'm really sorry."

"Yah, that's one way of putting it." This was the first time since the plane took off that Brock maintained eye contact with him for more than a few seconds.

"I don't mean to be nosey, but I'm concerned," Mike said, "it looks like whoever you're texting isn't able to find you another flight home?"

"No. Nothing at all. Flights are cancelled obviously all along the eastern seaboard, but it seems all over the country as well," Brock replied. "At this point, I have no idea how I'm going to make it to Florida, let alone West Palm Beach."

"Are there any other options? How about renting a car and driving the rest of the way?" Mike asked.

"Already checked. Not many options at this point. I suspect that by the time we get off this plane there won't be many cars—if any—left at the rental agencies." Brock's tone grew increasingly despondent.

"Well, you'd still be looking at a nine-hour drive, so that's not an option unless you want to get home in the middle of the night," said Mike. "I don't' know about you, Brock, but I'm not a fan of highway driving after dark. Just not safe in my opinion."

"Hmm. I hadn't even considered that." Brock pursed his lips as he thought about something and then said, "And there are no air rental services or private planes available either."

"Damn!" thought Brock. He had inadvertently shown his hand. He hadn't intended for the couple to know about his affluence; he realized from past experience that it doesn't usually end well.

Mike had heard what Brock said about renting a private jet, but he assumed that Brock was merely joking about it. Mike added, "Ha! That would be a nice option to have! Maybe I should just call my pilot and have him bring my jet around to take you home! Wouldn't that be a blast!"

Brock returned a smile and breathed deeply as he realized Mike assumed he was just kidding. He returned his gaze to his phone and texted Matthew, asking him to reserve a nice room for the night at a decent hotel in Atlanta. He also asked him to book a private jet service for 10:00 a.m. the next morning.

He wasn't happy about missing his birthday celebration and texted Jenna with the bad news. She wasn't too concerned. She returned the text, saying she was happy he wasn't caught in the storm or worse. She said they'd simply reschedule his birthday. She ended with an animated hearts kissing emoji.

While he was exchanging texts with Jenna, Brock didn't notice that Mike and Flo were talking about him.

"I can't imagine you're going to get a flight until sometime tomorrow," Mike said. "Do you have a place to stay? I mean Flo and I were just talking about your situation and, well, we don't really know you, but what kind of people would we be if we didn't offer a meal and somewhere to sleep to someone in need?"

His response was, expectedly, ingenuine. "Thank you, your offer means a lot to me, but..."

Flo interrupted him, saying, "Look, why don't you take advantage of our offer. We're good people, it's a genuine offer, we live in a nice house in Kennesaw and our two kids are away at school, so it's quiet and we have a comfortable guest room just waiting for you.

"And Flo is an awesome cook," Mike added. "C'mon Brock, let us be your hosts for the evening. It would actually make us very happy."

As the words escaped his mouth, Brock couldn't believe what he was saying. "Are you sure? I mean, I don't want to put you out. My assistant is currently working on finding me a hotel room in Atlanta, so..."

"Nonsense. Take our offer Brock! You might even enjoy yourself!" said Mike.

"Okay. I'll take you up on it. Thank you. This means more to me than you realize. Um, I hope you know I can be a real pain in the ass!"

His attempt at humor was uncharacteristic, but ever more than that was his willingness to spend the night. This wasn't Brock. Not by a longshot! Brock didn't understand why he had agreed to it, but he had done just that.

He began thinking about reciprocity and realized that despite his kindness in supporting numerous deserving causes and endeavors, he would never, ever, offer a stranger a seat at his table or a room in one of his homes. He found it incredibly sincere that this couple would extend the same offer to him, especially given that they had no idea of his wealth.

For the short remainder of the flight, Brock continued to question whether he had made the right decision, but he stuck with it. He had no idea how his simple decision would be so pivotal in terms of how his life was about to change.

Overall, it was a rude awakening! Brock gained an appreciation for what air travel is really like for almost everyone else in the world. However, as shocking as the airport and flight experience was, it paled in comparison to having been whacked around a dirty and rusty old shuttle van that transferred he and his unlikely hosts from the airport to the offsite parking lot. He wondered aloud if the vehicle was road legal; a comment that set the three of them into muted, but genuine, laughter!

As he climbed into Mike and Flo's minivan, Brock reflected on the fact that, despite being such a common vehicle, he had never been in one before. It was at that moment that Brock had an epiphany. Despite a plethora of exotic and exclusive experiences throughout his life, he had clearly missed out on some of the most common things that most people know very well.

Driving home, Mike took a chance and stayed on I-75, driving straight through the city rather than taking the loop around it. His bet paid-off, as traffic was remarkably clear all the way from the airport to Kennesaw. Brock was oblivious to the time during that hour-long drive. He was actually engaged in real conversation with real down-to-earth people! Not only was he the one asking questions, he was actually listening to Mike and Flo's answers like he cared about what they were saying. And, surprisingly, he actually *did* care.

Before they got home, Mike turned-into the local big box department store to pick-up a few grocery items for the evening's dinner. Brock took advantage of the opportunity to do a bit of shopping and went off on his own.

It was yet another first for Brock! He had never so much as turned into the parking lot of such a store, let alone entered one. Nothing could have prepared Brock for the experience. Rubbing shoulders with extremely common people of all stripes and sizes was almost too much for him. However, he actually felt a sense of accomplishment as he foraged for essential toiletry items, underwear, a pair of track pants and an athletic t-shirt.

Mike and Flo didn't quite understand how Brock managed to travel without any luggage, but they didn't press him about it.

Twenty minutes later, they were back on the road. Their home was five minutes from the big box store.

Brock's concern about staying in a dump was erased as the minivan pulled into Mike and Flo's driveway. Their house was far nicer than anything Brock had imagined. It was a stately two-story, detached, modern red brick home in a beautiful upscale neighborhood where everyone kept their properties neat and well maintained. Brock wondered how the couple could afford what he considered to be a mid-level executive type of home.

Once inside, Mike showed Brock to the guest room. It was comfortable and well-appointed. It even had an ensuite bath, for which Brock was tremendously appreciative. Brock took a shower and changed into the casual clothing he had purchased earlier. He then went downstairs and joined Mike in the den, where he had been watching a basketball game.

Brock and Mike moved outside to the backyard deck, where they enjoyed a few glasses of red wine. It was a Pinotage; a South African wine that a member of Mike's sales team gave him as a Christmas gift. Neither man had ever tasted the varietal before, but both were pleasantly surprised by its full body and plummy flavor.

The sun began to set as evening crept up on them. The Atlanta area often experiences chilly evenings in early spring, but that particular night—Brock's birthday night—was surprisingly warm and cozy. As the two men finished the bottle, they shared some laughs and discussed current events. They were both on their best behavior, being careful not to cross the invisible line of politics.

They eventually moved inside and joined Flo in the kitchen, where she was working on dinner. Mike, a Sales Manager for a large medical instrument manufacturer, shared insights and experiences gathered along the way during his long career. At one point, Flo joined them and talked about her twenty-three years working as a "Technical Customer Care Specialist" for a corporate call center. She explained that she lost her job over a year ago when hers and all of the other jobs at the call center were eliminated. She sounded so bitter and defeated when she explained that the work had been transferred to India.

Brock blushed momentarily when Flo shared the story. He didn't dare mention it, but he happened to own a majority shareholder position in the same company that cut her job. In fact, he felt downright ashamed because it was his idea and his influence that led to that decision. He thought, "Here's this woman being selflessly kind and generous to a complete stranger who...basically...fired her and everyone else she worked with."

He had trouble digesting the reality of his own responsibility for her loss and changed the subject abruptly. Not that he actually cared, but to divert conversation, he asked the couple why they decided to move to Kennesaw.

As Flo talked about their move, Mike opened a second bottle of wine. He poured a glass for Flo, and then refreshed his and Brock's glasses. He suddenly grew quiet and appeared puzzled.

Brock noticed his change of mood and said, "You look like you're trying to solve a difficult math problem! What's up?"

"I'm just thinking back to when we first met on the airplane. You seemed so stiff and didn't want to talk at all. Turns-out you're a good guy after all!"

"Umm, yeah, I should really apologize for being so rude. I'm sorry about that."

It's okay. We don't like to probe. It's none of our business anyway!"

Brock felt embarrassed and struggled to explain his behavior. "Um, yah. Let's...let's just say that I'm still learning about some things in life that, well...that I should have learned a long time ago."

"Enough said. I'm just glad that I met a new friend and that we get to spend a bit of time enjoying each other's company."

Brock smiled broadly and raised his glass of wine, clinking it against Mike's and Flo's glasses. His toast was simple and sincere. He said cheerfully, "To new friends!"

Over the next few hours, Brock enjoyed a scrumptious home-cooked dinner and learned more than he had expected to about his new friends. He found out that Mike and Flo's two kids didn't end-up where they wanted to go for college, but they nevertheless invested tremendous effort and work ethic along the way. As for finances, they explained that although they saved for their kids' education, it wasn't nearly enough. They expressed how guilty they felt about the inevitable outcome; the unsavory gift of expanding student debt.

Brock was disappointed to hear about their kids' situation and silently reflected on his own twins' privilege. He was surprised that they were so open with their own miserable financial situation. He didn't understand why they weren't embarrassed admitting to still owing over two hundred thousand dollars on their mortgage.

Their debt and lack of savings was a situation that Brock found nearly impossible to fathom. Mike explained that he wished to retire soon, but there was no pension plan to collect, and he and Flo's joint 401K investments were equally dismal.

Brock was taken aback not only by the truth of their meagre circumstances, but even more so by their jovial attitude toward them. They laughed and joked about the fact that they, "...didn't have a pot to piss in," that their minivan was in need of transmission work and that their second vehicle, a sedan, was a virtual torture chamber during warm weather, because its air conditioning hadn't worked for over three years.

When Mike and Flo shared their perspective on spiritual devotion with Brock, he asked what they got out of attending religious services. They were puzzled with his question and were even more confused by his disdain about their habit of donating money to their church, to the homeless and to others in need.

How on earth, Brock wondered, could Mike and Flo justify giving away money to those sorts of causes without stewardship or proof of effort? It seemed even more incredible to Brock that they would donate anything at all, considering how little they had.

There was one other thing that he found difficult to come to terms with. Despite their mounting debt and dismal financial forecast, this couple lived their lives with a sense of freedom that he could never come close to experiencing. Whatever love they shared was no doubt challenged by financial stress, but their love for each other seemed deep and authentic. Brock was also perplexed by how much joy his hosts appeared to derive from the simplest things; it was remarkable to him and he found himself beginning to wish for the same capacity.

After dinner the trio ended-up in the great room, where they sat by the fireplace and sipped on a fine old Spanish solera brandy. Perhaps it was more than mere chance, but it happened to be Brock's favorite after-dinner spirit. He was thoroughly surprised by his hosts' exquisite taste, but bewildered by their hierarchy of values. Despite being as financially stressed as they were, they apparently saw it as a priority to enjoy a tiny bit of something that they felt was very special. To offer something as special as this to him when they clearly had so little for themselves also seemed peculiar to Brock.

It was a concept with which he was completely unfamiliar. He had always perceived money as an instrument to amass for more power and to spend on one's insatiable desire for whatever one wants. Instead, Mike and Flo used money as an instrument to pay for what is necessary in life, to help others who need it more than they and to reserve just a bit of it to enjoy something extraordinary.

Brock tried hard to process all of these conflicting thoughts, but his lifelong devotion to affluence made it virtually impossible to do so. However, he started to question some of the core assumptions that had prevented him from truly growing as a human being.

As the brandy grew closer to the bottom of each of their snifters, Flo tried to dig a bit deeper into Brock's work and family life. Up to that point, he had been fairly vague about his personal and work life. Brock felt bad about holding back and being evasive; they had been so unguarded with him that he really wanted to be honest. At the same time, he didn't want to ruin things by revealing too much about his extreme wealth.

Flo's distinct Georgia-style southern drawl that initially irritated Brock had been growing on him. He wasn't aware of it, but suddenly caught himself wanting to hear more of her charming accent. Each of her words lingered and danced around the room like autumn leaves frolicking gently in a light breeze.

"So, Brock," Flo said, "you mentioned earlier that you're married to your lovely bride, Jenna, that you also have two kids in college and that you have a small vacation getaway in West Palm Beach."

"Correct! You're paying attention!" Brock smiled, paused and lifted the snifter to his lips, savoring its last few drops.

Brock thought about his family and how much he missed seeing them on his birthday. He was far more emotional than usual. It was debatable whether that was caused by the alcohol or the questions swirling around in his head. However, the next thing Brock said was so uncharacteristic.

"I'm very blessed to have such a wonderful family. Jenna is my better half—and I mean that sincerely; she doesn't merely complete me, she improves me! And then there's our kids who just eat-up whatever life has to offer them. Kendra and Keaton constantly bring me hope, wonder and laughter."

As mushy as Brock's response was, Flo, the ultimate romanticist, began to tear-up a bit.

Realizing how head-in-the-clouds he had sounded, Brock said, "Okay, let's get real. The kids *do* bring me hope, wonder and laughter...but they *also* bring me weekly heart attacks and give me misgivings about bringing them into this world!"

Brock paused while they all shared a laugh, then said, "Seriously, I'm going to miss them terribly! Next year, they'll both be off to college, most likely living in different parts of the country. Yup, with kids, it's always a calamity, always an earth-shattering problem; it never ends. But, you know, I'm really going to miss them!"

A tear pushed its way out the corner of Brock's eye and he wiped it with the back of his hand. He was embarrassed to be showing his emotions so liberally.

Flo shook her head in agreement and said, "Oh, I get it! Christian and Lily aren't nearly as far from home as your two kids will likely be, but we miss them so much it hurts."

Brock said, "I guess Jenna and I are in for a change."

Flo moved the conversation away from its melancholy trajectory and said, "True, but to be honest, we're still on the phone every day. You know, they seem to need a lot of, um..."

"GUIDANCE!" Mike interrupted.

"Exactly, Mike!" Flo said. "I mean, you want them to be independent, to learn their own way, to make mistakes, but..."

Mike interrupted again, "Must they make so many of them?"

The trio raised their empty glasses and toasted their common frustrations as parents.

Afterward, Mike pushed on with questions about Brock's career. "Okay, and your job...you said that you're an entrepreneur? Tell us a bit more about that. What kind of business do you own?"

Brock was uncomfortable holding back, but he knew he had to be cautious. "So, the thing is, I'm not running any business right now. I'm an entrepreneur, not a manager. I love starting new businesses, but I don't have the patience or attention span to keep them going over the long term."

Flo and Mike looked puzzled.

"Over my career, I've started several different businesses. Some flew and others crashed very badly. But I've been very fortunate to have sold four of them."

"Wow! Sold *four* businesses? That's awesome! What *kind* of businesses are we talking about…like, in what industry?"

"Well, several. Honestly, I'm easily bored and, after a while, want to move onto something different. Insurance, energy, personal computers and corporate data security. Stuff like that. That last one, the data security company, it was actually my very first business to sell and it's still my biggest win of all."

Flo looked fascinated. "That sounds so interesting! So, you're a tech wizard?"

"I wouldn't put it that way, Flo. At least I don't see myself as a tech guy. I mean, I am a Computer Engineer in terms of my college degree, but I think that title is too limiting."

"You like to keep your options open," Mike said. "I get it. You're a very smart and courageous man, Brock. I've got to tell you; I really admire that you took chances in life. You took the road less traveled and look where it got you. You are a self-made man!"

"You're being too kind. The road less travelled, well, maybe. But self-made man, I don't think so. Honestly, I've had advantages that others haven't and I simply exploited them." This was the most candid Brock had been.

"So, what's next for you, Brock?"

"A.I."

The two letters hit a brick wall. They had no idea what Brock was talking about. He was kind; he back-peddled a bit so that they didn't feel embarrassed.

"Most people haven't heard of A.I. or don't really understand what it is. A.I. is. Artificial Intelligence. Basically, it refers to using computers and programs to make decisions in ways that are similar to how humans think. In other words, the program changes and expands as it gathers information, which it uses to influence future decisions."

"That's intriguing," Mike said, but cautioned, "...it also sounds a bit scary. I don't know if I'm comfortable with computers making decisions that, maybe, people should be making."

Shaking his head in agreement, Brock said, "That's a very wise observation. A.I. has the potential to be used in ways that remove the human element from decisions that we should absolutely be making. It's *very* scary. There's also the question of whether an A.I. system can have consciousness? This is all part of why I'm exploring it as a business opportunity."

"Interesting," Mike said. He and Flo both appeared concerned.

"You see, that's my entry point. Developing a platform that *prevents* A.I. from becoming a problem."

They lingered in the great room for another hour, during which time they broached many different topics. Mike uncorked a third bottle of wine and conversation continued to flow as liberally as did the drink. Although Brock was a bit more open with his personal information than he had planned to be, his hosts still had no idea that he was as absurdly rich as he was. He was also careful not to reveal that it was his birthday. It wasn't that he wanted to hide his birthdate or his age. it was simply because he didn't want Mike and Flo to go to even more trouble on his behalf.

Eventually, the time had come to call it a night and get some sleep. As Brock made his way to the guest room, he studied the many framed family photos that were proudly arranged on tabletops and upon the walls of the stairway that led to the second-floor bedrooms. He felt himself becoming emotional and suddenly realized how wrong he had been in the past to have pre-judged people based primarily on their respective wealth, occupation or social class.

Brock reflected on the artificial lines he had drawn throughout his life that effectively excluded people without regard to their kindness or integrity. He thought about the similarities shared between his own family relationships and those of his hosts. He also began to feel ashamed for harshly judging those with far less than him. He now realized that many of those people were likely more genuine and generous than he had ever been.

The fact that his "common folk" hosts made the authentic gesture of welcoming him into their home, providing him with a delicious meal and giving him a place to sleep bothered him; *he* was the stranger after all, not them. It was hard for him to reconcile their generosity with the fact that he would never have been so welcoming and kind-hearted. It then occurred to Brock that Mike and Flo offered all of this in spite of the fact that he had treated them poorly and acted like an aloof jerk for most of their flight.

Brock pondered the irony of it all; Mike and Flo appeared to enjoy a freer life than he, despite their mounting debt and lack of possessions. He began to regard his many extravagances and possessions as trappings of affluence that weighed on him like burdensome baggage.

With all of these new and unsettling thoughts spinning around in his head, sleep didn't come as easily as Brock had hoped. He reached for his phone and began surfing various social media and newsgroups, hoping to distract himself and get some shut-eye.

An hour later, still awake and agitated, he called Matthew to enquire about the status of his plane. He was happy to hear that the engine damage wasn't as serious as first thought, and that the jet had already been repaired and cleared for flight.

He asked Matthew to have Hayes fly the plane to the closest regional airfield overnight. Of course, this meant that Matthew would also be onboard for the trip. Brock wanted to be wheels-up no later than ten the next morning, so that he could still enjoy most of the day in West Palm Beach. Matthew took about twenty minutes to make some calls and complete the arrangements.

Even though it was past two in the morning, Matthew didn't hesitate to call Brock with the details, knowing full well that he would still be awake. Hearing the details and knowing that plans were set helped put Brock's mind at ease. A large suburban SUV was scheduled to be at Mike and Flo's home at nine-thirty the next morning. After a short drive to the convenient Cobb County-McCollum Regional Airport, Brock could expect to board his refueled Gulfstream.

Brock was happy that he'd be back with his own family shortly, but that didn't mean he was unhappy about spending the night at Mike and Flo's home. A change was clearly under foot. The old Brock would have been mortified to have to bunk at a stranger's place.

This was different, he thought. He was already feeling somewhat wistful about having to leave his new friends. And to be sure about that point, he actually felt that these folks *were* friends.

He called Jenna just before going to sleep. It was so late that when she answered the phone, she sounded startled and disoriented. She asked what was wrong, as if she expected to hear bad news or an emergency of some sort.

Brock apologized and tried to calm Jenna. He then brought her up to speed on his itinerary. They ended-up talking for nearly an hour. Much of their conversation was about Mike and Flo;

Jenna said that she would love to meet them. However, she also kept asking Brock if she was speaking with "her husband," because although he *sounded* like him, *what he was saying* sounded nothing like him. Their telephone conversation involved a level of intimacy that they had not shared or felt in years.

Bacon, eggs, freshly brewed coffee; there aren't many other aromas that so convincingly pry-open the eyes at six-thirty. Morning came quickly. Brock slept like a log since drifting off at nearly three o-clock. However, despite only getting three and a half hours of sleep, he hadn't felt so well-rested in months.

He was bowled-over by Mike and Flo's exceptional hospitality. During breakfast, he dropped the bombshell. He had no choice. Although they were new friends, Brock considered them to be some of the most genuine friends he had. He felt that it was wrong to be anything but fully upfront with Mike and Flo. Regardless of their reaction to his admission, not sharing it with them felt dishonest.

"Guys, I've got something to tell you that you're probably going to find, well, um, shocking. I really hope this doesn't change your impression of me."

Mike and Flo looked at each other, their eyes widening, as though they were about to hear something awful—perhaps even criminal—about their new friend's past.

"Everything I told you last night about my family, my personal life and my career is true. But it's only half of the story. I apologize, but I withheld some pretty important details. I consider you to be my new friends and could not leave without being totally honest."

Mike said, "Whatever it is, Brock, I'm sure it doesn't matter. We've all done things in the past that we'd like to erase. It doesn't change who you are now."

"No, it's nothing like that," Brock explained. "When I mentioned to you that I've had advantages in life that most others don't, what I really meant is that I was born into a family that has a lot of wealth and privilege going back generations."

Mike and Flo seemed unfazed.

Brock tried his best to paint a picture of his lifestyle without sounding arrogant. That was almost impossible.

"Let me put it into perspective. My 'little' getaway in West Palm Beach—the one I'm leaving for today—it's an enormous estate with its own staff. My cozy little home in Salt Lake City is what most people would call a mansion and my mountain retreat in Virginia is embarrassingly large; it's like I own a big chunk of the forest. I have a 120-foot yacht waiting for me in Florida, and my private captain will fly me on my own private jet today. All of the other toys that you would imagine going along with all of that stuff, well, that's what we're talking about."

Brock didn't get the reaction he expected. In fact, his big bombshell landed more like a tiny sugar cube splashing gingerly into a cup of coffee.

"Brock," Flo responded, "full disclosure, we've not been totally honest with you either."

"How so?"

"A few of the things that you said during dinner last night just raised some flags and we...well, um, we got curious and our curiosity got the best of us. So, once you went off to the guest room, we checked you out on the internet. You're a lot easier to search than you might realize!"

"Look," Mike added, "you have a lot of material things and wealth, but everybody's got their own situation. We talked about it before going to bed and we both agreed that we're thankful we met and dined with and got to know you *before* we learned the rest of your story!"

Brock asked, "Why is that?"

"All of that other stuff—the money and the mansions and the boats—they don't define you. However, to be completely honest, knowing about it may have influenced our opinion of you; it's just human nature. Instead, we got to know YOU, the person, not your stuff," said Flo.

"...and we hope that you still regard us as your new friends, as much as we do you...you know, outside of all the trappings," said Mike.

"Truthfully," Brock replied, "it should be *me* asking that same question. Do you still see me as a friend?"

Brock didn't want to hear their answer, so he didn't wait for one. He interrupted his own question, saying, "Look, I was miserable yesterday when I learned that I had to take regular commercial air and even more miserable when I found out I was stuck in the Atlanta area overnight."

He shifted his gaze downward slightly, as if looking through their necks, and said, "All of my social friends and business associates are cut from the same very entitled and socially judgmental cloth. You guys are different and I mean that as a huge compliment. In a very short time, you've taught me a lot more than you may ever realize, and I would be honored if you regard me as your friend."

The trio continued to talk over a second cup of coffee. Mike asked a lot of questions that started with, "What's it like to..." Flo had her own questions, that focused more on Jenna and the kids, in terms of how Brock maintained such a good family life despite all of the distractions and commitments.

Once breakfast was finished, Brock took the initiative to begin rinsing dishes and cutlery before placing them in the dishwasher. As he was helping-out, he had a proposal for Mike and Flo.

"Guys, I was talking with Jenna about this last night before I fell asleep and she would really like to meet you. A driver will be here at 10:30 this morning to pick me up and take me to a small airport near here, where my jet will be waiting to take me to West Palm Beach."

Mike and Flo glanced toward one another.

"So, what we're thinking is, we would love for you to join me on the trip and be our guests for the next week. What do you think? Will you come?"

They were blindsided. They had no idea what to say or how they even felt about the offer. Mike said, "Can you give us a moment?"

"Sure! Take your time. I just have to shower, tidy your lovely guestroom and put my things together. It's seven-thirty, so that gives you almost three hours to get yourselves ready, dress, pack *very* lightly and do, *literally,* nothing else!"

Flo smiled and said, "You definitely have our attention!"

"Look, you just got back from a family funeral, so I'm sure you could both use a bit of downtime to recharge. You mentioned on the plane yesterday that the funeral coincided with your two-week planned vacation—a fully-paid vacation that was non-refundable. Not only did you lose the cost of the vacation, but you had to bear the cost of full-fare round-trip tickets to Salt Lake City.

Basically, your vacation fund is shot. Mike, you have over a week left in vacation time, but can't afford to do anything with that time. Ouch! That's damned unfair! Seems to me, my offer is perfect timing. So, guys, are you with me?"

Mike said, "You do make a compelling argument."

"I promise it will be an awesome time! You'll get to meet Jenna and our two kids. It was also my birthday yesterday, so…"

Flo interrupted, "It was your birthday! I wish we would have known! Well, happy belated birthday Brock!"

"Thank you, but I'll have an even better birthday if you join me and my family. Jenna really wants to meet my new friends who, as she said last night, have opened my eyes. And I want to thank you for giving me a gift that's far more valuable than money or things."

Flo asked, "But with just a few hours left, there's no way I could pack! I wouldn't know where to begin!"

Despite her declaration, she could barely hide her excitement. The slightest bit of reassurance and she was ready to go.

Brock said, "Pack a little, pack nothing at all. It doesn't really matter. Did you notice how I didn't even have an overnight bag yesterday?"

Mike said, "Yes, but you were simply going from one home to another, where you have everything you need. We, on the other hand, don't have anything waiting for us."

"True, Mike, but it's not an issue. Believe me, whatever you need to wear, use, eat, drink, play with...can be very easily had. There are a lot of things in this life that I can't do, but when it comes to stuff that can be bought...that's the easiest of all!"

Mike was concerned about crossing some imaginary line and potentially overstepping Brock's kind offer. He said, "Brock, I'll lay it on the line here. This new friendship of ours, well, uh, it's not based on your wealth and I don't want us to be taking advantage of that wealth. You understand, it's not the reason we want to be friends and not the reason we would be your guests. Right?"

"Listen...Mike, Flo, good friends help each other as they're able. It's not a stretch for me to be your host and show you a good time. I like you guys and I know Jenna will too!"

Brock paused and studied their expressions. He wasn't sure if they understood how insignificant his offer was in relation to his own abundance. He tried to put it into perspective.

"Much of what I can do really has nothing to do with my effort. I'm not special; just born into a pretty good situation. But what I can do is to share. So, no, you're not taking advantage of anything but an effortless and honest eagerness to share a little bit!"

Brock's tone became a bit more serious as he said, "Listen, I'm proud of the fact that I share a lot of money with good causes and charities that build people up; however, I'm *not* proud of the fact that it is the very least that I can do. It really doesn't take any effort or special sacrifice to throw money here or there at this or that. And to be brutally frank, most of the people in my and Jenna's social circle have more than enough money for themselves and for thousands of others. Even if they *did* actually need money, I don't trust them and would never regard them as *true* friends.

"You, on the other hand," Brock said, "are genuinely good and trustworthy people who I'm honored to call my new friends. Let me share a tiny bit of my wealth with you. Please let me host you as you hosted me."

"YES! We'll go," chanted Mike and Flo simultaneously. The sparkle in their eyes and their sing-song voices reminded Brock of when his kids were very young and had just found out they were going to Disney.

Before Brock went to the guest bedroom, he could barely hide own excitement. "I'm thrilled! What a wonderful birthday gift! And, hey, I guarantee you've never had such easy air travel in your lives. About packing, pack very lightly. It's going to be pool, beach, boat, open-tab shopping, eating and anything else you want to do, but I want you to be as comfortable as possible."

Mike's smile faded slightly. "You know, we don't have designer clothes. It's more like, um, big box fashion and I use the term 'fashion' very loosely! How do I say this? Basically, Brock, we don't want to embarrass you or Jenna."

"Particularly," Flo added, "in front of your own social circle."

"If dressing like regular people would embarrass me or Jenna, we wouldn't be very good hosts, would we? Anyway, I've got a secret to share. Unlike the rich 'look at me' celebrities and influencers, people with our kind of money dress *comfortably* as much as possible. Designer this or that may look good on television, but it's often uncomfortable as hell! Jenna and I have a bunch of fancy-schmancy clothes, but we only wear that stuff when we have to. Truth be told, I'd rather not have to wear it at all!"

Brock's assurance helped erase any remaining apprehension Mike and Flo had about their upcoming trip.

"One other thing," Brock said, "what about your kids? Do you want them to join us for part or all of the week? Jenna and I would love to have them and you never know, maybe our kids will become friends as well."

"Thank you, Brock. You're being more than generous. I'll mention it to them, but I doubt they'll come, because they are both into their mid-terms."

They went to their respective rooms to get ready. Of course, time went by much faster than expected. A hulking black suburban arrived early and waited in the driveway. Mike heard it pull in and looked out the bedroom window. He joked with Flo, saying that it looked like the kind of armored vehicle they saw recently in a movie that secretly shuttled the President.

Brock climbed into the limo a bit early in order to do a conference call with Captain Hayes and Matthew, going over some pre-flight expectations and getting them up to speed with the new passengers.

Just before arming the home alarm, Mike gave Flo a huge hug and said, "This is so exciting! We've never done anything like this before! And I wouldn't want to do this with anyone but you."

Based on their child-like expressions, Brock's routine travel reality was like a dream for Mike and Flo. Merely being driven to the small jet's fold-out stairs was clearly a thrill. They joked about feeling like big-wigs for a change, and said it was just a notch up from their regular economy coach experience.

Once aboard, the couple looked around the interior. Their mouths were agape, evidently amazed by the décor and features. Having never even seen a photo of a private jet, they had no particular expectations, but what they saw clearly exceeded any that they could have imagined.

Mike peeked into the lavatory and smiled broadly, saying he couldn't believe it was on an airplane and explaining that it was more spacious than his main floor bathroom. Flo said she was smitten with the little kitchen and bar area.

Once Brock's plane hit cruising altitude, Matthew brought out a beautifully polished charcuterie board loaded with an assortment of fine cheeses, smoked meats, bread and dried figs. He placed it on the dining table and took drink orders.

It was a short flight from Atlanta to West Palm Beach. So short, in fact, that Mike and Flo shared the sentiment that it was the first time they could remember wanting a flight to last longer.

The week in West Palm Beach went by quickly. As expected, Jenna quickly embraced Mike and Flo's new friendship and delighted in their visit. The foursome shared candid conversation and abundant laughter. The unpretentious tone all but erased the ostentatious appearance of the estate and of the yacht.

As the week drew to a close, the two couples had to say goodbye. Life's commitments go on. Brock and Jenna joined their guests in the drive to the airfield, where Brock's private jet was waiting to fly Mike and Flo back home to suburban Atlanta. Hugs, tears and laughter ended their visit.

Although Mike and Flo's children were unable to join them for this trip, Brock and Jenna had already set a date for their two families of four to meet a few months down the road for an all-expense-paid week at a Caribbean resort, followed by a few days at Brock and Jenna's mountain retreat. They were all looking forward to it.

Almost home; the hired limo turned the corner onto Mike and Flo's street in Kennesaw. Two brand new high-end vehicles were in their driveway. Before Brock flew them to Florida, Mike had parked their own vehicles—the rotting minivan and the torturously hot unairconditioned sedan—in the garage.

Mike and Flo wondered aloud if their kids took a break from college and had some well-to-do friends over. As the limo pulled-up to their home, they could see the giant bows and gift tags. The cars were 'no strings attached' gifts from Brock and Jenna!

They were awestruck, but the reality of the gesture hadn't fully sunk-in. Shortly after bringing their luggage inside, Flo shuffled-through a pile of mail; a couple of overdue bills caught her attention. She hastily logged onto their joint banking platform and froze. She called Mike to confirm if what she was seeing was actually on the screen.

Their combined mortgage and line of credit no longer showed a negative sum of $ -214,870.14, but rather, a simple and beautiful "zero." There was also a single deposit to their joint savings account, transferred from a bank with which they had never dealt. Five million dollars had been deposited.

Mike slowly lowered himself onto the chair next to where Flo was sitting, his eyes never leaving the screen. For several minutes, the couple appeared genuinely stunned and remained silent.

Brock and Jenna couldn't wait to hear from their new friends. It wasn't that they wanted to bask in the warm and fuzzy glow of Mike and Flo's gratitude. They just wanted to share in their excitement! It truly warmed Brock and Jenna's hearts to know that they were able to make such a crucial impact on their friends' lives; something they knew would remove so much stress and anxiety. Best of all, they were happy to do it without a prid pro quo sort of mentality.

Before they had a chance to digest the enormity of how much this would unburden the financial pressure they had been feeling and enhance their lifestyle, Mike and Flo's doorbell rang. A delivery driver was at the front door with a wooden box; it was a case of wine. A personal note written on parchment paper was nestled between bottles of the familiar Pinotage.

Scrawled in thick blue ink was the following sentiment. *"This is just a small fraction of my appreciation for what you've done for me; opening my eyes…such hospitality to a complete stranger! I'm still stunned by your generosity of spirit! I am a new person because of both of you. What you gave me was probably the most valuable gift anyone's ever given me. Love Brock (and Jenna)"*

As true friends, the two families would share fellowship over the long term, celebrating various occasions and milestones, and even taking trips together. During that time, Brock increased his philanthropic deeds; in fact, generosity became one of his most rewarding passions. He surrendered much of the stewardship that he had previously attached to his works of charity, and gave more freely and unconditionally to whomever it would bring the broadest smiles and deliver the greatest impact.

It's often said that money is merely a tool. It's said more often, though, that money is the root of all evil. Both have elements of truth. The decisions we make about how we use money say far more about us than about money itself.

When we adore money, its irresistible charm massages our egos with entitlement, while it distorts and diminishes our opinion of those who have little or none of it.

But, when we detach ourselves from the deceptive status that money promises, we defeat money's ability to control us and steal our happiness. Refusing to worship money allows us to see others according to their true human value. Rather than allowing money to destroy relationships, using it as a tool can help build relationships.

RIESLING
THE SWEET SPOT

If white wine made from the German grape varietal Riesling is not part of your repertoire of wine drinking experience, it definitely should be. More on that in a bit.

Then again, if you tried Riesling decades ago, but have avoided it since, you need to know that today's fine Rieslings may be nothing like what you remember! You may recall the wine as syrupy sweet and rudimentary plonk; frankly, not appealing characteristics at all.

Earlier bad experiences with Riesling may explain why a lot of people think there are far better white wine options on the shelves. However, that outdated reputation is neither accurate nor warranted! That's not to say your palate was mistaken. The problem is that for many, their introduction to Riesling wasn't actually Riesling at all! Cheap, sweet, basic, watery Liebfraumilch and other Riesling imposters served as a false introduction to the varietal from the 1970s through the 1990s. So, depending on your age, this may resonate with your own experience.

True Riesling isn't necessarily sweet; delicious Rieslings are crafted up and down the residual sugar scale, from sweet to dry. Depending on the winemaker, the weather and, especially, the soil, the varietal can result in wines that are youthful or gracefully aged. They're fruit-driven wines with flavors that range from citrus-like to succulent stone fruit. And they need not be basic! Good Riesling is most often delicate with complex layers of flavors and aromas.

More wine drinkers everywhere in the world are beginning to discover (or rediscover) true Riesling; a fine wine that has ancient roots in Germany, but which, today, is successfully grown and vinified in many regions around the globe.

Okay, enough on the wine lesson! Here's a short and sweet story that's sure to melt away the stress and leave you smiling. It starts out with a planned daytrip to the beach. Wine, of course, is on the menu!

Lisa and Stuart had just graduated to the "empty nester" stage of their life together and were trying their best to navigate the scary and unfamiliar waters. Their oldest child, Robert, had already moved far away five years earlier. He became a journeyman toolmaker and had to follow work that had all but moved out of town.

Robert and his wife were expecting their second child. Lisa and Stuart were happy to be grandparents, but the distance made it difficult to nurture what they had wished would be a closer bond.

Now that Lisa and Stuart's youngest child, Alyssa, had left the family home to finally live in her own "starter" house, the atmosphere was lonely and depressed. During their first dinner as forlorn parents, Lisa and Stuart began to replay in their minds the whirlwind events of the last five years; milestones that seemed to speed by with ruthless cruelty.

When Alyssa graduated from high school, Lisa and Stuart planned a huge graduation party to honor her over-the-top academic achievement. She was a model student, earned exemplary marks, and was into everything like a dirty shirt. She was voted Valedictorian and led the student government in her final year.

Robert, still living at home at that point, was so proud of his little sister.

That fall, Alyssa would be attending a major top ten college that was just a thirty-minute drive from the family home. She was accepted into a highly competitive program in International Relations which, in itself, was a major accomplishment.

Alyssa's education fund would easily have covered her rent and food costs had she decided to stay on or near campus, but instead, she wanted to stay at home and commute to school. Lisa and Stuart breathed a collective sigh of relief when Alyssa announced her decision to stay put, as they were nowhere near prepared for her to leave.

Alyssa worked full-time that summer, just as she did the previous two summers. She was a Tour Guide for a local historical venue. It was a huge and storied grand old mansion that was, basically, a living museum. The grand ballroom, solarium and parlor rooms were available to rent for weddings, business conferences and lavish parties. Alyssa loved working in the place and, as she guided tourists from one room to the next, she often imagined herself living there as a member of the storied old family that built the mansion.

In order to attend her own party, Alyssa had to book off a Saturday in August, which was not an easy thing. However, her supervisor approved it because Alyssa was the hardest working and most dependable summer employee she had, and as her boss, she couldn't chance losing Alyssa. Lisa and Stuart wanted to make sure that they had the party before Alyssa started college.

Just a week before Alyssa's big graduation party, Robert called a family meeting and dropped the bomb. He shed a few tears as he announced that he took a new job in a new state over a thousand miles away. His tears were heartfelt, but were the smallest of all of the tears shed that evening. Robert's blues were tempered by the excitement of stepping into the great wide open.

However, his departure created a very deep chasm. It took all of Lisa and Stuart's fortitude to put on a brave face when Robert moved away, concealing their own grief at his relocation while also supporting him as good parents must. Unfortunately, Alyssa's heart was broken when he left the house and moved away. Growing up, she and Robert were each other's best friends, and she never fully recovered from his long-distance move.

Alyssa's graduation party went ahead, despite the downcast mood and Robert's absence. Eighty-four guests included family, along with close friends, neighbors and Alyssa's own closest friends; some of whom she had known since nursery school. It was fully catered, with an open bar, live music and ample food. Lisa even rented a massive outdoor bouncy castle for the little ones and hired an adult-aged babysitter to watch those kids like a hawk.

Needless to say, a party like that takes quite a bit of planning. As the couple did that planning, the prospect of their only child eventually leaving their home was increasingly on both Lisa and Stuart's minds. With Alyssa deciding to commute to school, the eventuality was delayed, but the nostalgia and melancholic feelings brought on by their realization cast a pall over their plans.

Before the party even happened, the couple had another realization. Deep down, these devoted parents had been somewhat aware of the detachment they felt from one another, but the stress of the big event made them actually face the reality and talk about it. Although they both cared for each other deeply, there was no arguing that they had grown apart and their passion had long left the station. They got so caught-up with the day-to-day bustle and family demands, that they were spent, with little energy or desire left to work on their own relationship.

Planning for the party led from one tiny disagreement to the next, each one bigger and more hurtful than the last, eventually blowing-up in a doozie. It was actually a good thing. The fight brought the deteriorated state of their marriage to the forefront and allowed Lisa and Stuart to come to terms with what needed to be done.

For the first time in two decades, Lisa and Stuart had an honest and open talk about their relationship, and agreed to make mending it a priority. They talked about what would be left over once Alyssa actually did move out and agreed to make sure that they wouldn't be blindsided like so many other parents are when their kids fly the coop. They both recognized that if they waited to focus on their relationship until Alyssa was done college, there would be nothing left in the home except for memories and material stuff.

The party went on without a hitch and it was the success they had hoped for. Despite Robert's absence, the mood was celebratory, guests were genuinely happy to be there and, most importantly, Alyssa felt that her hard work had been recognized.

The party came and went and life's busy pace replaced its memory. Predictably, as summer wound-up, Alyssa's anxiety ramped-up. Her life was about to change significantly. Moving from a familiar place where she was confident and in charge to the murky unknown of being a lowly freshman at a big college was understandably unsettling!

It's not like Lisa and Stuart ignored the inevitable in terms of living as a pair in their home rather than as parents with live-at-home kids; in fact, they discussed it often as Alyssa and Robert were growing up. However, they had trouble understanding how some of their friends couldn't wait for their kids to move out, while they struggled with accepting the same inescapable event with their own children.

Nevertheless, it *was* inescapable! Just a few years after finishing her degree and beginning her career, Alyssa did move out and was settling into her own first home. She was finally starting to get a feel for what it's like to live on one's own and was fully immersed in making her own decisions about what her place looked and felt like. Calvin, Alyssa's fiancée, was a fine young man who earned Lisa and Stuart's enthusiastic approval. The wedding was planned for the following year.

Lisa and Stuart had only just dipped their toes into the unfamiliar and somewhat frightening new waters of living together again without children in the house. Robert's exit was, at that point, a five-year-old memory, but the wounds of Alyssa's departure were fresh and raw. Lisa and Stuart were about to discover a new way of living, regardless of whether they were prepared for it or wanted to do so.

The challenges of living as a solitary married couple were real and concerning. Even though the couple committed to renewing their relationship five years prior, there was one question that continued to cause them to have sleepless nights.

"Have we done enough to keep our own relationship alive and well, so that it continues to thrive *after putting so much time and attention into raising our children?*

It's a good question to ask. Regrettably, some couples with children never think about it before it's too late. Worse yet, some ignore their relationship with one another. They allocate every last drop of love and attention to their offspring, until the well has dried-up and there's nothing left to spare for themselves.

It happens all too frequently. Once the kids are gone, "Mr. and Mrs. Who Are You?" suddenly realize that they no longer know each other and don't care to go through the process of getting to know each other again. They've lost interest in their partner's interests. Pastimes and activities that one partner finds appealing are often the polar opposite of what the other finds interesting or pleasurable!

Over the years, our partner's idiosyncrasies that once seemed 'cute' become pet peeves. Full disclosure; that happens with or without kids. But having children at home provides a buffer for the couple's growing intolerance with each other's annoying behaviors. When the kids eventually do move out, those pet peeves suddenly become major points of contention; the starting point for hurtful arguments and worse.

The strange thing about all of this is that so many couples are oblivious to the growing chasm of daylight that separates them. They often don't see it until it's too late. The result, quite predictably and unfortunately, is marital breakup. Fortunately for Lisa and Stuart, they recognized and jumped on the problem early enough. They *did* take the proactive steps necessary to reinforce their relationship and bring themselves closer.

While it was unplanned, Alyssa's exodus from the family home coincided with Stuart's retirement. He had been an investment manager with a major bank. Lisa wasn't far behind and she, too, retired a few months later from her job as a dental hygienist. With Alyssa on her own, the couple's newfound freedom was a bit of a letdown. Their mood was not unlike how one feels after returning from an awesome vacation; it was great while it lasted, but then it's over…now what?

While they were still working stiffs, the couple dreamt of taking exotic trips, trotting around the globe without a care in the world. Having been formally retired for only about four months, those plans had not yet come to fruition. Lisa and Stuart decided, instead, to take a bit of time to acclimatize to their new and less hectic life as retired people before hopping around the world.

The transition from work to retirement carried with it some predictable emotional adjustment. Fortunately, Lisa and Stuart didn't identify themselves as much with their respective careers as they did with being the best parents and spouses that they could be.

They kept their promise to nurture their ailing marriage during the five years after Alyssa started college. That, in itself, helped a great deal in helping to make the transition to retired empty nesters a far easier one to navigate. They were both ready to retire and had enough interests—some shared, some solitary—to avoid being bored. They were just a bit lonely and found it difficult to avoid trying to derive comfort and solace from the past. Predictably, the more they found themselves mired in talk about their happy past as a family with kids living at home, the more depressed they would become.

They tried their best to keep busy. Lisa had her weekly wine-and-chat book club meetings, while Stuart enjoyed golf with former colleagues who retired before him. They enjoyed tending to their flowerbeds and landscaping together at home. They also took day trips, visited local wineries, had leisurely lunches and dinners out during what used to be the 'work week' and took a few overnight trips not too far from home.

However, they just didn't seem happy. The problem was that all of that "busy-ness" was just that; they were merely distracting themselves and passing the time while continuing to be emotionally fixated on the past.

Before autumn arrived with its cooler breezes and the familiar smell of fallen leaves, Lisa and Stuart decided to drive to the beach and enjoy what might be one of the last summery days for another six or seven months. The nearest decent beach was a couple of hours away by car.

They were looking forward to the daytrip and, the night before, packed everything they could possibly need. They spent far more than the two-hour drive time gathering and packing everything they could possibly need or want for their afternoon at the beach. When Stuart joked that they had packed everything except for the kitchen sink, Lisa shrieked with laughter, showing him a couple of giant popcorn tubs that she had filled with water and stowed in a corner of their SUV's trunk. Apparently, she *did* pack a version of the kitchen sink!

Being that they had a lot of travel experience, the couple knew that the unexpected can and does happen, and that insight led them to be as prepared as possible. They packed enough tissues to outlast a flu, enough paper towels with which to clean a house, enough water and soft drinks to satisfy a large and thirsty group, enough sandwiches, snacks and candies to feed an army, enough bandages, alcohol wipes, bug bite balm, antihistamines and stomach pills to fill a medicine cabinet, and enough sunscreen to cover themselves and everyone else at the beach! Oh, yes, there was also a bottle of wine, but more on that in a bit.

Yes, they were prepared. However, they were only prepared for the things they could anticipate. Of course, Murphy's Law had other plans...

They got an early enough start to the day. Well, not exactly. They woke up early, but one thing led to another and before they knew it, their planned eight o-clock departure became noon. So much for their plans to get to the beach by ten in the morning! The weather was absolutely ideal for a long day at the beach; it was sunny, hot and humid. Only now, they would have four hours less of that ideal beach day.

Lisa and Stuart had driven about half-way to their destination. They tried hard to convince each other that getting to the beach by two was fine and that it would still give them four hours until they needed to pack-up and start driving home.

It might have been okay, but they would never find out. The vehicle's alert system chimed. Stuart suddenly found himself fighting with the steering wheel, as the SUV tried to pull sharply to the right. The timing was terrible, as he was trying to pass a tractor-trailer at that precise moment. Icons on the dashboard video panel flashed a bright red and warned that the air pressure in one of the tires was dropping rapidly.

The pressure read twenty-five psi, then eighteen, then twelve. It took only a few seconds until the tire was completely flat. Stuart somehow managed to regain control of the vehicle, slow down and avoid hitting the large truck. He safely pulled over to the right shoulder. When traffic had cleared, he went out to personally verify what the tire warning had already told him.

Stuart got back in the vehicle and drove it with its floppy pancake tire a few more feet away from the right lane. It was as far as he could go. As bad luck would have it, the shoulder had narrowed just before the blowout, so there was very little room left. Cars and trucks were whizzing by so closely that Lisa and Stuart's personal chariot swayed each time anything passed by them.

As it turned-out, despite all of their preparation and packing, the one thing that they were *not* prepared for was a flat tire. Stuart laughed nervously, saying that he hadn't changed a tire in 30 years. He didn't even know if there was a jack under the spare 'donut' tire that was hidden under the trunk's felt-covered flip-up floor. After some investigation, he did find a small scissor jack under that tiny toy-like tire, but he had doubts about how exactly to use it and wondered if it was actually sturdy enough to hold 4,000 pounds of steel, rubber, plastic, oil and gasoline.

After some tense discussion about the situation, Stuart thankfully came to a sane decision. He conceded that the flat tire, which was on the side of the car closest to traffic, was far too close to that traffic for *anyone* to attempt changing it, let alone someone who had no idea what they were doing. He called the roadside assistance service that was part of the vehicle warranty.

Two hours later, a tow truck finally arrived. Their stomachs were now sore because they had eaten half of their rations while waiting. They were also exhausted. And stressed. And hot. And frustrated. And miserable. This was *not at all* what they had planned.

To make matters worse, the tow truck driver said that, although he could tow their vehicle to an auto repair garage in a small town not too far from their location, they were not allowed to join him in the truck for that short drive. Sure, it was a short drive, but it was a very long walk; a walk down the shoulder of a busy interstate to an exit five miles down the road. That didn't sound like much of an option.

The driver's shirt was embroidered with a cursive "Mitch" on its pocket. Mitch, if that was really his name, clearly didn't like the verbal interaction part of his job. He was fine communicating with vehicles and winches and jacks, but not so much with human beings. His one-word answers to the couple's barrage of questions were, basically, grunts. He did manage to blurt out something at one point that sounded a bit like, "Uber."

A million questions flew through Stuart's mind. Is it even possible to hire a taxi or a ride-share to come pick-up a fare at a mile marker on an interstate? How long would *that* take? What happens *until* they arrive? Was the area even safe or did some urban war zone loom over the crest of that particular section of the highway? And what about the intense heat? Stuart shuddered as he thought that they might even die from heat stroke, sitting in the hot sun on the side of the road and breathing-in all of that gas and diesel exhaust.

Frustrated to no end, Stuart finally asked Mitch if he was nuts, expecting them to walk on the highway or wait for a hired ride. This didn't exactly endear him to Mitch who was gruff and neanderthal-like to begin with. He implored Mitch to allow them to ride in the cab of the truck with him, but the driver said he couldn't do it because of insurance reasons.

Okay, that's actually the translated, cleaned-up version of Mitch's confusing response. His word-for-word murmur sounded more like, "Mmph. Umln. Ahhmm, No damn way. Aehhnnpt...ahhh... you can't be in tow with me. Ain't not possibly. Fuckin' insurant company sent no." Of course, this accurate description of the strange sounds and tangled-up words that came from Mitch's mouth, doesn't include the generous amount of saliva that landed on Stuart's cheek and shirt.

Mitch turned his back to the couple and finished pulling their vehicle onto his flatbed using some sort of motorized cable. Stuart had never stood so close to a tow truck and was surprised at how effortlessly the winch pulled the vehicle up on the tow platform.

Lisa managed to generate some well-timed tears, a talent she learned in an elective drama class during her college years. She laid it on thick and whatever she said along with those tears did the trick! Well—full disclosure—maybe the tears helped, but there was something else that was likely more persuasive.

Stuart handed the guy a fifty-dollar bill and said, "Mitch, here. Take this. Please, if you won't help us out of a sense of decency, do it for some extra cash. No questions asked."

The driver grabbed the fifty greedily like a raptor strikes its prey and, in the process, left a smear of dark grease on the bill.

The guy then mumbled, "My name's not Mitch," as he crumpled the money and shoved it into his front right pant pocket.

Stuart, looking confused, said, "But, your badge says..."

"Shirt's from the guy I replaced."

Stuart would have found the guy's response seriously hilarious had he been in a better frame of mind. The driver never did volunteer his actual name and Stuart dared not ask. Instead, he assigned a secret nickname to the driver, which he thought was funny and fitting, yet dared not repeat it to anyone else, including even Lisa.

In a gallant gesture, Stuart volunteered to go in first. He knew that Lisa would want no part of sitting next to the driver. He opened the heavy door and lifted himself toward the chewed-up, filthy seat. It was a bit more of a struggle than he expected.

Then it happened. The stench hit him like a ton of bricks. The air was dank and smelled like stale cigars. "No, wait," Stuart thought, "it's not just cigars. There's something else in the mix...it's...it's...oh God! It's years of overripe perspiration."

To make matters worse, far worse, neither the air conditioning nor the vent fan worked and, yet, the windows were rolled-up; this did a superb job of sealing-in the putrid air. Stuart began to wonder if, perhaps, he and Lisa should just walk along the side of the interstate."

Too late for that. By then, the couple was all in, but they still weren't prepared for how awful it would become. The interior looked as disgusting as it smelled. It was a veritable hazmat situation! Crumbs of unknown food in varying sizes, half-eaten French fries and something that looked like morsels of cheddar cheese covered the floor. There was enough decaying food to provide a couple of meals for a wild animal, but it was far too disgusting for even a rat to want to eat.

As Stuart hovered over the ripped upholstery, he noticed a mystery stain splattered randomly across the seat. Lisa had just lifted her small frame up to the cab and, after choking on the rancid air, saw the stain too. However, she observed that it had a thick texture.

Neither Stuart nor Lisa wanted to know or even imagine what had created those textured stains, but they reluctantly lowered their butts onto the seat. At once, they both regretted wearing shorts. It was hard for either one of them to ignore the horror of what kind of bacteria or secretion was attacking the back of their thighs and knees.

Although Stuart tried to maintain a one-foot gap between he and the driver, that didn't happen. The driver squished-up against him like a fifty-pound bag of potatoes leaning against a soft loaf of freshly-baked bread.

The sound of the massive truck engine, chugging and snorting, mingled with the squeaks and clangs coming from their own vehicle that was reluctantly bouncing and shifting on the flatbed. This bizarre concerto of sounds was the only thing heard during the entirety of their trip to the nearby town's only auto repair garage. Not a word was spoken.

Lisa opened the truck's door before the driver had even come to a full stop in the garage's parking lot. She was so anxious to get out, she ambled out of the truck and onto the pavement like she'd done it a thousand times before, even though she had never before been in a vehicle that was so high off the ground. Stuart was not far behind.

They virtually ran toward the only guy in the auto repair shop. He was using a flashlight to look at something under an old pick-up truck that was on a lift above him. He was the sole mechanic and owner of the shop.

It seemed that luck's tide had finally shifted from bad to good. The mechanic cheerfully said that he could have their flat fixed in about fifteen minutes. His only concern was that he would have to charge the couple an extra five bucks on top of the usual fifteen-dollar flat tire repair cost due to the rush nature of the job. For a moment, Lisa actually entertained the plausibility that, somehow, the bizarre tow truck experience vaulted she and Stuart back in time to the 1950s.

After realizing that she and Stuart were not stuck in some sort of time travel wormhole, Lisa whispered in Stuart's ear, "He can't be serious? He didn't sound like he was joking, but the price this guy just quoted is idiotically cheap."

She half-expected the mechanic to laugh at them before announcing some exorbitant fee, since they were, basically, out of options and in the middle of nowhere. After all, a captive customer is an easy mark. "Maybe this is his M.O.," she wondered. "Put the customer at ease and then drop the bomb of some unnecessary but scary sounding scam repair that'll end-up costing us thousands of bucks."

Nope, as it turned-out, the guy was serious about the price and honest beyond to a fault. He turned out to be friendly and sociable;

a polite and talkative man who the couple felt they could trust. He was *so* unlike the tow truck driver. Lisa was so distraught from their exchange with the tow-truck driver, that she couldn't help mention something about him.

"I'm *SO* glad we got dropped-off here! You have no idea how scared we were having this blowout in the middle of nowhere. Now, I don't know if you know the tow truck driver, but thank God you're not him. I'm sorry, but he was not a very nice person."

The mechanic had a comfortable and relaxed way of speaking. It wasn't lazy talk; he was very easy to understand and enunciated his words very clearly, but he was so calming to listen to. Lisa thought he sounded something like a farmer leading a yoga group, if one could imagine such a thing!

"Well, first, Ma'am, you're not in the middle of *nowhere*...you're HERE in Rockin' Rockford! I know it's not much, but a person can be pretty happy in this microscopic dot on the atlas!"

He paused for a bit and added, "And, yah, I know Willard."

Lisa and Stuart both scrunched their faces when they learned the tow truck driver's real name.

The both said, in unison, "Willard?"

The owner said, "Yah, Willard. Like the rat. He *is* a rat. Let me guess, he waited for you to offer him extra money to take you with him, right?"

The couple nodded in response. Curling his lip and feeling a bit embarrassed, Stuart said, "Cost me fifty bucks!"

The owner just shook his head and said, "You're lucky that's *all* he got from you. I never trusted that guy and never will."

Stuart asked, "Something wrong with the wiring in his head?"

"Nope. Something wrong with his soul."

The owner invited the couple to have a seat in the front office while he fixed the flat. He encouraged them to help themselves to a cup of hot coffee from the pot on the filing cabinet. They respectfully declined, explaining that they were already too hot as it was.

As they waited, they looked around the office and were surprised by how old fashioned everything looked. It was a dead zone for technology; the office somehow evaded a world that had managed to spring up everywhere else around it. However, Lisa and Stuart recognized that there was something comforting and peaceful about it.

In truth, the shop owner was entirely up to date on his training in advanced motive power computerized repair programming, systems and procedures. Although his front office was completely retro, he could work on any current vehicle like a factory-trained pro...because he was one.

Lisa admired the old "Gulf Oil" wall clock that was still ticking and keeping perfect time, even though it had been almost forty years since the brand ceased to exist. She noticed that all of the old signs and memorabilia were authentic and original, compared to much of today's fake memorabilia that's manufactured to *look* old. She always noticed stuff like that.

She and Stuart took a moment to decompress from their stressful day. They were too tired to talk. The longer they soaked-in the peaceful silence in that office, the louder all of the ambient noises became. The old clock's tick-tick-tick ricocheted off the plaster walls. Its sound was punctuated by a hissing noise that belched intermittently from the coffee maker. The mechanic's air ratchet produced a loud grinding noise that escaped the garage and crept into the office. They could hear its whirring echo as he removed each of the wheel's lug nuts. The combination of all of these sounds suddenly became deafening!

Sound can sometimes be odd like that. It's like when you move quickly from a noisy environment to one that's almost entirely silent. Initially, the vacuum of sound contrasts drastically from the cacophony you just came from, but within a short time, the barely audible little noises become perceptible, then obtrusive and, eventually, thunderous; they simply can't be ignored.

Stuart was about to say something about all of the sounds, when Lisa blurted-out, "Stuart, it's nearly four o'clock and we're still an hour away from the beach. We need to make a decision."

Stuart looked surprised and said, "Oh, honey, I just assumed we had already made that decision. It's way too late to keep going. We'll get there just in time to set-up the chairs and umbrella, sit on the beach for a half hour and then we'll have to start packing-up to go back home."

"Yup, you're right. The universe is trying to tell us something. Let's just cut our losses and turn around. We'll be home by five and we can throw some shrimps on the grill."

Stuart looked defeated. He was disheartened about missing-out on a beach day and wasting what was likely the last summer-like opportunity of the year. Shrimp, he thought, wasn't likely going to be much of a substitute.

Lisa sensed his disappointment. "Okay, honey, it's not the beach, but we'll crack open that Riesling that's in the cooler in the trunk. We'll have a few glasses on the patio and forget about this day!"

Stuart agreed. "Sure, but I'll honestly need a bit more wine than 'a few glasses' considering the day we've had!"

"Perfect."

Just then, the shop door opened and the owner let the couple know that their car was ready. Stuart handed him a fifty-dollar bill—his second fifty of the day—and said thank you. The owner started to walk over to the cash register to get change, but Stuart wouldn't hear of it.

Their SUV was still on the shop floor. As they walked around the tools and lifts, they joked at how their special day at the beach never happened.

The owner was observant. He was a good listener because he was interested in people. He asked, "Where were you planning to go before your tire made other plans for you?"

"Port Sterling Beach," answered Lisa.

"Well, that's a shame, especially to have missed out on a day like this. Probably the last hot beach day for a long time. You watch, next week it'll be cold and windy. It's like this every year. Just changes so quickly and before you know it...fall and winter are here and the beach is abandoned."

Then he said something that caught the couple's attention.

"Listen, folks, I don't think your beach day has to be a total bust. You're already at the beach. Why don't you enjoy our local sand for a couple of hours? You've got some time to play with now, since it's obviously too late to drive all the way to Sterling and back."

Lisa was intrigued. "I didn't even know there was a beach here!"

"Oh yah, it's not big. In fact, it's pretty small, but that's what I like about it. It's not really on any maps—well, at least not on the phone maps and GPS ignores it too...and you know...that's actually perfect for me and most of the folks who live here!"

Stuart asked, "How far is your beach?"

"Five minutes from the shop floor. Hey, you're already here. Even if it's not your cup of tea, no loss, right?"

"You're right! Thanks so much for suggesting it!"

"Absolutely. You guys seem like nice folk. Just turn left from here, go straight for two miles, take a right turn onto Main Street and then a quick left on Beach Road. You're there."

"Thank you."

"You're welcome. But I'm going to ask you one favor. Please don't mention it to anyone back home. I think fate brought you here today. But we here in Rockford like to keep our little secret...well...a secret."

The couple agreed, thanked the mechanic and drove off. The stress and frustration brought on by the day's events quickly evaporated; it was replaced with the same excitement and anticipation with which they had started their day. They made it to the beach quickly and were surprised to have their choice of parking spot. Their vehicle was one of only three in the entire lot.

A thick line of trees and underbrush separated the parking area from the beach, concealing whatever kind of shoreline the couple would soon discover. Lisa suggested that they leave the beach chairs, umbrella and other gear in the vehicle until they first checked it out. She ran down the curved crossover boardwalk that led to the beach. She laughed and playfully danced like a schoolgirl, challenging Stuart to a race. Of course, she waited to announce her challenge until she was out of sight and had an unfair lead.

Lisa screamed, "OH MY GOD!"

Alarmed, Stuart sprinted to try and catch-up. His facial expression revealed his genuine concern with what Lisa had seen...or...with what or who was confronting her. After all, neither of them had ever even heard of this beach. With his heart racing and becoming short of breath, Stuart's imagination ran wild. Gruesome scenarios began to play out in his mind. As he rounded the corner, he finally saw what Lisa was shrieking about.

The scene was like something out of a fantasy movie! Although the beach was on the small side—only about two hundred yards wide—it was spectacular! The entire beach was crescent shaped, curved from one end to the other; it was a true bay. Exotic trees and flowering shrubs dotted the landscape, and the sand was among the finest soft white beach sands anywhere. This was a surprise, since all of the other beaches in the area had coarse brown sand scattered with jagged rocks and tiny sharp shells that made it uncomfortable to walk on. The local sand would often puncture the bare feet of those who dared walk on it.

Only three other people were there; a young couple that appeared to be very much in love and a single woman who was consumed by the book she was reading. They were off in their own respective worlds, seemingly oblivious to Lisa and Stuart, who quickly flung-off their sandals, ran to the water's edge and dipped their toes in the water. The water was warm, clean and clear; its gentle waves rolled in rhythmically and foamed at the edge.

The sun had just begun its slow descent toward its eventual setting; twilight wouldn't arrive for another four hours, so they had ample time to enjoy the late afternoon sun. Lisa and Stuart retrieved their beach chairs, umbrella, cooler and beach bag. They set-up their gear and got busy doing nothing but admiring and soaking-up every aspect of the magical experience.

It was the epitome of serenity. The beauty, the tranquility; it stood in stark contrast to the frenetic, overcrowded, beach-on-steroids place that they had originally planned to visit. Lisa and Stuart had found their perfect place and decided that it was unlikely they would ever return to the beach they had originally planned to visit.

Their perspective changed. The couple sat and talked about their eventful day and about how their feelings had evolved as the day progressed. They agreed that they both needed to work on their faith, because in the end, it all worked out even better than they could have planned. They felt, ultimately, cared for and loved.

Perspective is an interesting thing. Lisa and Stuart's few hours in paradise slowed-down to the point where it was as if God's very finger pressed the pause button. They didn't feel rushed at all. Quite the opposite was true; they had as much time as they could possibly enjoy. In fact, their two hours felt to them like a full day.

The setting's striking beauty and serenity opened a door for the couple to feel comfortable confiding in each other with a degree of openness and honesty they had rarely shared in their life as a married couple. They both felt more as one than they did as individuals. They also felt the magic that this special little beach was hiding. It wasn't an illusion; in fact, it was one of the most authentic of all the experiences they had ever shared!

Their only disappointment was that their time was limited to two hours. However, during that time, they talked, laughed and enjoyed their newfound intimacy for what felt like far longer than the clock revealed.

Lisa and Stuart shared their mutual apprehension about living as empty-nesters and opened-up about their feelings of loneliness. They agreed to appreciate the miles they had traveled, but to avoid becoming stuck in the dangerous quicksand of the past. More importantly, they made a commitment to focus on the present, keeping plans in motion to make happy new memories for years to come.

As they talked, their collective perspective became one of looking forward to, rather than worrying about, the rest of their life together. For the very first time, Lisa and Stuart were looking forward to their next chapter in life. They smoothly slipped into recharge mode without realizing it.

It wasn't until the couple hit the road for their return home that they began to understand how the day's events conspired to bring them to what would become their secret, special beach. The late start, the tire blowout, the gruff tow truck operator and the kind mechanic each had their own part to play in a majestic performance that came together exactly as destiny had planned. The hurdles of the day were necessary, for had they not jumped those hurdles, Lisa and Stuart would have had just another day at the beach; a nice day, perhaps, but not the truly magical experience that destiny had in store.

As for the date of their daytrip, it became for them a special anniversary; one they continued to celebrate for many years. The couple's love and dedication to one another only grew stronger with each visit, as their favorite beach unveiled new, lovely secrets that it had held in confidence for them since they first met.

SHIRAZ
IDENTICAL TWINS

Australia is known for Shiraz. This varietal's grapes produce full-bodied, liberally fruity red wines that are popular with wine drinkers around the world. In the glass, Shiraz has a deep, purplish-red tinge; it's often so dark it appears nearly opaque. When it comes to Syrah, France is known for its full-bodied, almost opaque and liberally fruity wines that are popular with wine drinkers around the world. In the glass, Syrah has a deep purplish-red tinge; it's often so dark it appears nearly opaque.

No, you didn't misread the preceding paragraph and, yes, it's repetitive. You see, Shiraz and Syrah grapes are identical. The two names refer to the same grape with the same lineage. Depending on where or by whom it's vinified, this wine grape is referred to as either Shiraz or Syrah. But, despite the different names, they're identical twins. The grape was born in France, where it was dubbed Syrah. When its vine stock arrived in Australia and flourished on their soil, Australians opted to name it Shiraz.

The Shiraz or Syrah grape isn't limited to Australia and France. The United States, Spain, South Africa and many other wine producing nations grow and make wine from this varietal, and do so very successfully!

Regional expressions of the grape vary in terms of taste and structure, with some areas producing wines that are more smoky, more plummy or more peppery than others. However, the similarities outweigh the differences and most red wine drinkers who are familiar with the grape agree that it makes a wonderfully robust, fruity and bold libation.

It's interesting how identical twins can be so much alike, regardless of the environment or individual experiences they had growing-up. You've likely read true stories about identical twins who were separated at birth, only to be reunited much later in life. In almost every such case, the twins' shared similarities are uncanny. They often have unnervingly parallel career trajectories, personalities, interests, skills, religious beliefs and even favorite vacation spots!

This brings us to the story of Elizabeth Balynta, Senior Historian for the East Wentworth Historical Society in Massachusetts. She had worked for the Society for the last ten years and was looking forward to eventually retiring from that job. The position was a daunting one, in terms of the time and focus it demanded. But Ellie, as she was warmly known by family and friends, had an extraordinary capacity to accomplish far more than others, given the same amount of time.

In addition to her challenging and busy responsibilities at the Society, this forty-eight-year-old dynamo also served as a highly popular sessional instructor at Dartmouth. She loved teaching and the prestige that came with being a professor there, but limited herself to one course per semester. She knew her limits. What she found most satisfying about teaching was the opportunity to share her insights and experiences with students who were only too eager to absorb them.

Ellie was somewhat of a household name in historical circles. She had published dozens of groundbreaking papers in influential journals, based on her extensive fieldwork and research. Her primary focus was on bridging the gap between historical events and similar ones occurring in modern times.

Ellie was extremely perceptive when it came to recognizing those relationships, which made her predictions about future events and outcomes uncommonly accurate. She was devoted to the truth that history revealed. Her mantra was George Santayana's famous quote, *"Those who forget their history are doomed to repeat it."*

For Ellie, history was more important than the present or the future. It's not that she wasn't interested in the future; it's just that she understood how an awareness of our past can help predict and, more importantly, *shape* our future. While current pop psychology advises people to leave the past in the past and, instead, focus on the future, Ellie advocated for the opposite. She believed that the present was a product of the past and that the future will, quite predictably, be determined by the past. With knowledge of the past, the future can potentially be made better. Well, at least she hoped that others would follow that kind of ideology.

Ironically, as a teenager, Ellie despised the mandatory history classes she was forced to endure in high school. Her teacher should have retired several years earlier. He was devoid of any enthusiasm or the kind of spark that can ignite kids' imaginations and bring a subject to life. He had made his important professional role increasingly cushy, rarely, if ever updating his material or teaching methods. The utter boredom that he created for himself permeated his entire presentation, which soured virtually every one of his students on what should have been a fascinating subject.

It wasn't until her second year in undergraduate studies that Ellie discovered how much she really loved History. As a freshman, she was initially accepted into a Fine Art degree program. From an early age, she had a keen appreciation for all forms of fine art; painting, sculpture, even pop-art. She loved reading about art, creating art, and visiting art galleries and stores.

What Ellie didn't expect, however, was that her university art program would involve so much reading about art masters and the history of art. As much as she was smitten by creating art works, she was absolutely entranced when it came to delving into history.

Up to that point, Ellie had been so sure about her future—becoming an artist or a museum curator—but, for the first time, she felt lost and unsure. Not surprisingly, her first-year academic performance was nowhere near her potential; something that deeply embarrassed this rather brilliant student.

As her first year came to a close, she made an appointment with the Dean of Student Services to explore other options. Thankfully, the Dean was as astute as he was compassionate, and, as such, he took the time to find out what *really* made Ellie tick. Although his well-crafted questions seemed like nothing more than casual conversation to Ellie, it didn't take long for him to discern that she would surely thrive in a future focused on the past. And so, Ellie's path was forged.

The Dean's own history influenced his future, shaping him into the wonderful person he had become. Decades earlier, a particularly perceptive high school guidance counselor prevented him from dropping-out and starting full-time work at a supermarket. That counselor recognized the future Dean's special gifts and helped push him in a far more fruitful direction.

Starting with her second year, Ellie's college experience proved far more successful, challenging and satisfying. She really loved being a student and was fascinated with her studies. Not only did she excel in her new major, history, she also continued to feed her craving for artistic creativity.

Her favorite artistic medium was watercolor, which she continued to practice throughout her adult life. She painted breathtaking landscapes and florals that could each have easily fetched hundreds of dollars had she sold them. Instead, she gave away most of her paintings to friends and coworkers, and donated others to various charity auctions. She framed and hung some of her favorite works in her own home.

Alongside her own paintings, Ellie also hung a variety of works from other artists; some of whom were up-and-coming and others that were well established. She became quite the art collector and could have easily switched career tracks in that direction.

Had she done so, she likely would have been just as successful as she was as an historian, but her true passion was firmly planted in the past. History was her gig. She loved it and was widely respected as one of the top twenty living historians on the planet. Her position as Senior Historian with the Society grew more important and notable than it would, had anyone else held the job.

Ellie had full autonomy over the special projects and research papers she chose to pursue. She made things happen just because she wanted a challenge. Senior faculty at Dartmouth didn't require her to do them, since she was just a sessional professor. Neither did the Historical Society she worked for. No, Ellie initiated this extra work because of her own personal drive and commitment to her discipline.

She had just published a research paper that drew a lot attention and critical acclaim for its poignant and troublesome comparisons of certain Civil War era perspectives and modern-day political developments. She found herself spending increasing amounts of time fielding requests for media interviews regarding that paper. She somehow found time to squeeze in some of those interviews.

However, Ellie wasn't one to bask in the limelight. Instead, she was already well into her next big project before the ink had barely dried on the Civil War paper. It was the first study of its kind to track the descendants of different early American workers who served as full-time staff at some of nearby Newport's grand old mansions.

She started research for this new study by exploring family trees of randomly-chosen mansion staffers from the mid-to-late 1800s and early 1900s. Ellie's hypothesis was that descendants of these early mansion staffers—children, grandchildren, great-grandchildren and great-great-grandchildren—right up to the present day, were statistically more likely to work in formal roles of direct personal subservience to the affluent and influential.

The work proved tougher than she had expected. While modern day genealogical databases helped her to more easily trace family trees branching from those ancient maids, butlers, gardeners and such, something else stood in her way. Ellie found that researching the people at the end of those branches—the most recent descendants of those early mansion workers—was increasingly obstructed by privacy measures. Those measures were put in place to protect the privacy of average people who, in the digital age, had become increasingly at risk of becoming victims of identity theft and personalized scams.

Ellie found workarounds that relied primarily on social media networks. Perhaps it wasn't the most scrupulous way to go about her work, but it made her research possible. Ellie managed a whopping seventy-two different bogus social media accounts under different pseudonyms, each of whom had "his or her" own network of friends.

Of course, the real Ellie didn't actually know and had never personally met *any* of those social media friends. She was surprised by how blindly real people accepted friend requests from complete strangers; fabricated ones at that! She thought they were reckless for opening themselves up to complete strangers, but was nevertheless thankful that they did.

In order to keep track of each fake account, what they did and who they 'knew', Ellie maintained a mountainous database of copious notes and reminders for each of her seventy-two counterfeit characters. She rationalized her dishonesty with the idea that it was an innocent means to a much more important end. She also knew that her publicly published work would never reveal the names or identities of anyone she studied.

Her control group consisted of over two-hundred and fifty randomly chosen Americans who lived and worked between 1850 and 1925. People in this control group had to have been employed in random occupations, unlike the test group who were all, basically, paid servants who had worked on the island of Newport, Rhode Island during that same time period.

As Ellie dug deeper, she began to notice a trend. She really didn't know what to expect when she began the study. She had a hunch based on patterns she had noticed in the past, but wondered if there was a statistically provable correlation. While she couldn't yet prove that such a statistical relationship actually existed, she sensed that she was moving toward that conclusion.

A few months into the study, Ellie was thrilled to see that a trend was beginning to confirm her hypothesis. An unusually high number of descendants of the test group worked as present-day full-time paid personal service workers. More extraordinarily, those same workers were often dedicated by employment to a single wealthy and influential individual or to a defined group of them. Many of the original Newport workers' descendants turned out to be dedicated concierges, personal chefs, full-time housekeepers, au pairs, personal secretaries and estate gardeners. Some others worked in jobs serving affluent members of private clubs, such as yacht clubs, golf and country clubs, and executive clubs.

As much as Ellie enjoyed doing this research, it caused her to feel melancholic at times. Mentally climbing the family trees and exploring peoples' lives among the branches was sometimes exhausting. It got her thinking about her parents, which released a cascade of bittersweet memories.

Ellie was an only child. Her parents were truly beautiful people who were full of life and love, and who shared it so generously. Growing-up, Ellie often thought about how much happier her family life was compared to what she observed in her friends' families. While her friends would complain about having to be with their parents for special occasions and vacations, Ellie excitedly looked forward to those family times.

Tragically, her parents passed away shortly after she earned her first post-graduate degree. They died instantly in a horrific car crash caused by a drunk driver. He was a repeat offender who hadn't suffered as much as a scratch from the wreck and who, lamentably, got off without legal punishment or consequence. Ellie was devastated by the loss. She found solace in delving into people and relationships in history.

She didn't understand why the family tree research for her new study was causing her such emotional upset. Throughout her professional career, it had been comforting to explore the lives of people who were no longer living. Perhaps, she thought, it was because she was becoming increasingly aware of her age. That led her to dwell on the fact that she had no family other than distant relatives; kin that she never met or only rarely saw.

She dated only occasionally and had never married. Historical research usually supplanted the loneliness that would otherwise permeate Ellie's days and nights. This time around, though, it was having the opposite effect. Fortunately, she had a close-knit group of friends and was starting to spend more time with them.

Ellie found herself wondering, once again, what it would have been like to have had a twin sister. The idea of being a twin was odd, because there was no reference point for it. None of her friends, colleagues or distant family members were twins. Heck, she had never even had a conversation with a pair of identical twins. Yet, for some unknown reason, she had *always* yearned for a twin sister.

The idea was so persistent that Ellie often felt that she actually *had* a twin sister. She didn't understand it, but sensed it throughout her life. When she was just three years old, Ellie would frequently ask her mother where her twin sister was. She even had a name for her sibling; Emily. Her mother brushed it off as the creative mind of a child who had invented an imaginary friend. However, her mom was also astonished at the depth of detail Ellie would provide about her seemingly missing sibling.

As she got older, Ellie's insights and thoughts matured, but her nagging yearning for a missing twin sibling persisted. At forty-eight, she tried to tell herself that it was a silly spillover from her childhood years. Yet, part of her consciousness never let go.

It had been a hectic work week; Saturday morning was a welcome respite. Her week was a blur. Mid-term marks were due for her class at Dartmouth, she had to complete and submit the all-important annual budget for the Historical Society and she had committed to several media interviews related to her last published study. Somehow, she checked-off all of those boxes and made it through the week, but, understandably, was feeling spent.

After such a demanding week, most people would sleep-in and then drag around sipping coffee 'til morning turned to noon. Not Ellie. She woke promptly at seven on Saturday morning and couldn't wait to start her day. The air was cool and fresh, which lured Ellie into going for a short run.

Following her run, she made coffee and prepared a sensible breakfast of granola topped with yoghurt and fresh berries. Ellie showered and dressed casually. She threw on a comfy pair of jeans and a short-sleeved plaid cotton shirt that hung relaxedly on her petite frame. She had an appointment with a local antique dealer who had something of relevance to her research on the Newport mansion workers and their descendants.

The dealer had recently procured a trove of old Newport pictures from an area resident who had been holding onto a dusty old box of them for quite a long time. It was handed-down over successive generations of her family and ended-up in her lap years ago.

Stephen J. Kristof

The woman never gave much thought to the box, nor to the meaning of the old pictures it held. When her mother gave her the box for "safe keeping", she opened it and took a peek inside. It was filled with black and white prints on old fashioned photo paper and pictures on metal plates that looked a bit like negative engravings, neither of which interested her in the least!

Her mother told her that the photos, "...might be worth something someday," but couldn't explain who or why anyone would want to buy them. As a result, the box sat in the woman's fruit cellar gathering dust for decades.

The woman was aware of some vague history surrounding the photos. From what she could remember, her great-grandfather saved the pictures and a collection of artifacts from a temporary museum in Newport that had burned down in the 1920s. Certain ancestors in her family tree apparently pilfered the memorabilia years ago and sold-off what they could. Although they kept the photos, none of her long-departed relatives cared much about them since they had little monetary value.

When she first received the pictures, the woman connected with several antique dealers, none of whom had any interest in acquiring them at any price, let alone for free. She didn't know what to do with them, but couldn't bring herself to throw them away, so she babysat and eventually forgot about them.

Recently, however, the woman rediscovered the old box of pictures during a basement clean-up and finally decided to part with it. She called the most prominent antique dealer in the region, who offered her ten dollars for the lot. The woman happily snapped it up. She could have cared less about the pictures, yet pitching them would have made her feel guilty; the antique dealer offered her a perfect solution and the ten bucks paid for her gas.

For his part, the dealer recognized the significance of the rich history contained in the box, so he decided to start calling local historical societies and museums. Ellie was the first one he spoke with. After giving her a basic idea of what was in the box, he told her that he didn't want any money for the photos, but wanted to make sure they wouldn't just sit in a box again for another hundred years.

Ellie was excited about the donation, not just in terms of her official role with the Historical Society, but also, as it might relate to her current research study. She hoped that at least a few of the photos would feature people living and working at the Newport mansions. If so, she believed that it would prove helpful in her research.

Ellie turned her car hurriedly into the antique shop's parking lot and came to an all-too-abrupt stop next to the front door. She was more than anxious to get her hands on those photos! Thanking the dealer profusely for his generosity and for making the effort to find a good home for the pictures, Ellie dumped the box in her trunk, sped-off and returned home.

She quick-brewed a cup of coffee and turned-on her mug warmer. She was getting ready to dig-in. Regardless how busy she was—and she was *always* busy—she often reminded herself to stop and smell the roses. It was something that she read in a book when she was a teenager and it stuck. Whether it was the act of physically smelling something pleasant in her immediate surroundings or simply taking a break and appreciating the moment, Ellie understood how important it was to ground herself in something that would be known in the modern vernacular as "mindfulness."

Ellie took a deep breath and savored the rich aroma of freshly brewed coffee as it mingled with the unmistakable scent of musty old paper. It was a funky combination, but something with which Ellie was well experienced; in fact, it was one of her favorite smells.

Sitting at the kitchen table, Ellie flipped through the first few the pictures in the box. She was in awe at what was revealed by that little peek. She then continued to sift through some of the other photos, being careful not to disturb their order. From what she could tell, *everything* in the box pointed to life in Newport during a time span from the Gilded Age to the Progressive Era.

Of course, there were the expected photos of extravagant parties featuring mansion owners; many of whom made their fortunes in coal, plantations and industry. But the photos offered far more than just that. Former presidents, politicians, and affluent movers and shakers of the day had also been immortalized in photographic gelatin and silver, while partying and being entertained lavishly at some of the opulent mansions.

For Ellie, though, the most powerful images depicted different full-time mansion workers. They were the very people upon whom Ellie was basing her work! She studied picture after picture, featuring dozens of different butlers, servants, maids, chefs, gardeners and other assorted service workers. These low-rung workers appeared in more of the images than the powerful people they served. It was an absolute jackpot!

Sometimes things just work out. Your payday comes due. The stars align. In Ellie's case, typewritten labels had been glued to the backs of most of the pictures. They had annotations identifying specific dates, functions and the names of the people who appeared on them. This would significantly support her sleuthing work and cut her research time dramatically.

Ellie was mesmerized by the pictures in the box. She was so focused on what she was doing that she didn't realize she lifted her empty coffee mug to her lips at least a dozen times. The wistfulness that she felt earlier while doing family tree research was gone; it was replaced by a sense of wonder and excitement. The old Ellie was back!

The kitchen clock's hands kept circling, but Ellie was unaware of just how much time had gone by. She hadn't moved from the kitchen table for hours. She found it impossible to escape the lure of those fascinating old images. By five o'clock, Ellie's stomach growled, reminding her that she hadn't eaten a morsel since her morning granola. She ordered some pizza for delivery, since she had no intention of stopping what she was doing to make dinner.

And then it happened. A woman in one of the photos initially caught her attention. The more Ellie looked at her, the more intrigued she became. She was Ellie's identical body double. From her facial features to her light hair, to the little dimple on her left cheek that appeared when she tried hard not to smile; it was as if she were looking in a mirror.

The woman had a petite frame, just like Ellie and stood with the same unique gait; her left foot flat on the ground, with her right knee bent to support her elevated right heel. It was astounding.

She didn't know what to think. Was it a mere coincidence? Could it be something more than just a fluke? Absolutely not. If all of her years as an historian taught her anything at all, it was that the world is exactly as it seems, and that events and occurrences are predictable and logical. There had to be a rational explanation for this ancient woman's and Ellie's twin-like appearance.

Ellie flipped the photo over. The inscription on the back read, "Elizabeth Pawley, local Art Dealer and Historian. 1879." The caption further indicated that the woman lived and worked in Boston. It explained that she was a frequent visitor to the various Newport mansions; she was a purveyor of many of the finest paintings and sculptures that went into those massive homes.

Yes, Ellie read it, but she was strangely oblivious to the bizarre connections that the inscription revealed. She turned the picture over once more to get another look at the woman. She had no idea why, but her mind started to wander back to that lifelong, unfulfilled sensation of missing a twin sister. She hadn't been thinking about her childhood imaginary twin, but her name, Emily, kept bouncing around in her skull.

Without warning, the "Emily" soundtrack stopped playing in her mind. It was overtaken by the obvious connection revealed in the inscription on the picture. She wondered how she had missed it? It hit her like a ton of bricks. Ellie so closely identified with her pet name that she overlooked something shockingly important. The woman in the picture who looked so much like her was also named Elizabeth. Ellie then finally processed the other shocking similarities. She was *also* an historian. And just like Ellie, she was also addicted to fine art.

She was floored, but tried to maintain a grip on reality. She thought there had to be some logical explanation. Was it possible, she wondered, that the woman in the picture was in some way related to her?

Then she thought, "That doesn't even make sense! Sharing a common first name has nothing whatsoever to do with sharing family lineage. What was I thinking! I know my family tree inside and out, and there's not a Pawley among them!"

No, it wasn't at all likely, she realized. Ellie's parents were first generation Americans. Her paternal and maternal grandparents had all immigrated to the US in the 1940s, and each of them were the first children in their respective families to leave the 'old country'.

The idea that something bigger—something supernatural—was at play, began to gain traction. It bubbled-up from the back of her mind as a set of tangled feelings and then coalesced into conscious thought. No, she wouldn't let herself go there. Ellie dismissed the thought as pure hokum. She refused to loosen her grip on her firmly planted concept of reality; a reality that relied on logic and rational thought.

She chalked it up to a tremendous coincidence. Yet, a tiny part of her wanted to believe. Their shared first name aside, she couldn't reconcile the similarities that she and Elizabeth shared in their dimples, their petite body shape and bone structure, their shared unique gait, and their identical facial appearance.

Could it be a simple trick of genetics? "Surely," Ellie thought, "two different unrelated individuals living on the earth at different times in history could somehow share very similar DNA. Why not? Of course, it's just a rare coincidence and nothing more...Right?"

Well, at least that was the explanation that Ellie used to try and quell a few uneasy ideas that she couldn't stop from pestering her. How likely was it that two unrelated people divided by a hundred years could look so alike and share nearly identical career experiences and interests? What about the notion that they lived in the same general area, separated only by a bridge of time? She had no rational explanation for these *truths* and that's what disturbed her most.

The doorbell interrupted her thoughts. She paid the pizza delivery boy with cash and couldn't wait to dig in. She ate like a starved animal, wolfing-down seven large pieces of pizza without chewing any of them very much. It was quite uncharacteristic for her, but she wasn't paying attention to what or how she ate. She was more focused on fighting-off the strange coincidences that were tormenting her.

Ellie poured herself a glass of Shiraz from a bottle she had opened a few days earlier. It tasted a bit off and wasn't nearly as good as she remembered when she first had it. Nonetheless, it was still drinkable and after just a few sips, helped calm her nerves a bit. As she tried to settle her mind, Ellie went back to the picture and started examining it more closely, looking for something that would unravel the string of coincidences and restore her rational world.

Was there something she missed? What clue was hiding in plain sight, waiting to dispel the mystical nonsense? And there it was. A wristwatch. Elizabeth was wearing a wristwatch; a functional piece of jewelry that wasn't invented or manufactured in production until the 1920s.

Ellie felt her tight shoulders loosen. She took a deep breath and smiled. She found the clue she had been looking for. The picture was a hoax. Someone probably Photoshopped the woman into a scan of an actual period picture from the old mansion, printed it on black and white photo paper and then stuffed it into the box as a joke.

But her authority as a renowned historian told her otherwise. She was also too smart to believe it, regardless of how much she *wanted* to explain the unexplainable. Ellie's smile turned to an expression of disappointment when she used a loupe to take a closer look at Elizabeth's 'watch.'

It wasn't a watch after all. It looked a lot like a watch, but when viewed closer, was revealed to be a Victorian mourning bracelet with a black oval face decorated with inlaid gold. The date on the picture's inscription matched a time when these bracelets were quite popular.

Ellie poured another glass of wine and continued to study the woman in the picture. She wasn't prepared for what she was about to discover. It was something rather frightening. She suddenly felt breathless and light-headed. She dropped her glass on the kitchen table. The glass broke into shards and the wine it held created a small river that narrowly missed the coveted box of pictures, meandering to the edge of the table and dripping onto the floor.

There it was. Elizabeth had a distinctive scar just above her right wrist; a scar that was identical to one on the front of Ellie's own wrist. Ellie had fallen off her bicycle when she was nine and landed on a large piece of a broken soda bottle that someone had thrown onto the street. The wound was deep, so her mother rushed her to the hospital to get stitches. The resulting scar looked like half of a butterfly; the same exact pattern in the same exact location of Elizabeth's scar.

Visibly shaken, Ellie was finally ready to accept what she was averse to even considering just minutes before. Not everything within the realm of our human experience is empirically provable. She surrendered to the possibility that something supernatural was at play, although she had no idea what that could be.

Life has obligations and must go on. Ellie continued to conduct research for the study and fulfilled the demands of her normal paid work for the next two weeks, but she couldn't shake the angst surrounding what she was finally convinced was something supernatural. It was on her mind, day after day, from the moment she woke to the next morning. Ellie finally believed that she and Elizabeth shared a genuine twin relationship, but was baffled to explain how or why.

Almost a full month after Ellie first saw the picture of Elizabeth, she made another startling discovery. This time, it didn't just present itself to her; she used all of her resources to dig for it. During that month, Ellie spent as many hours as she could, scouring old records and documents in the storage basements of several of Rhode Island and Boston's historical institutions. She had the privilege of access to these facilities that most people would never gain, based on her vast network of connections and her impeccable reputation.

She was on a mission to find out everything that she could about this mysterious Elizabeth. It consumed her. She was able to glean a lot about the specific renowned artworks she sold, to whom she sold them and at what prices. Ellie was surprised at how detailed that information was. However, there wasn't a great deal that she could find about Elizabeth's personal or family life.

While sifting through a variety of related documents in dusty old banker boxes, Ellie stumbled upon a personal letter to the wife of a Newport mansion owner, postmarked May 14, 1892. Ellie was already aware that the woman was a summer resident at the mansion; even when her husband was off doing business, which was most of the time. She was known among various socialite circles to throw the most magnificent parties.

Despite her great affluence and ostentatious taste, she also maintained close friendships with many people who were neither wealthy nor influential; the idea of which was, frankly, preposterous at the time. Nonetheless, she was known to be a woman of great integrity and generous spirit.

However, the most exciting thing about the letter Ellie had found was revealed in the return address on the envelope. So, who had written this letter to the rich mansion owner? It was none other than Ellie's body-double, Elizabeth Pawley. It turned-out that they were very close friends. What a find!

Ellie couldn't wait to read the letter. As she carefully opened the fragile envelope, she smelled a whiff of parchment mold. Being an historian, she had fallen in love with old paper smells many years ago and found it to be comforting. With all her experience reading ancient letters and sifting through archives, she could instantly tell merely by smell, whether writing paper was made before or after 1850. Prior to 1850, printing and writing paper was made from animal and cotton fibers. Ellie loved the different smells produced by old papers; for her it was a job perk!

As if in slow motion, she pulled the letter from the envelope ever so carefully to avoid damaging it. Her portable lamp illuminated tiny specks of antique dust. The particles sparkled and flitted about like tiny fairies as they swirled around Ellie's hands.

The letter's personal tone suggested the mansion owner was more than just one of Elizabeth's art clients. Ellie gathered that they must have become very close friends. The letter revealed some very sad news.

"My dearest friend,

It's been too long since we've had the opportunity to enjoy each other's company. I miss being with you so dearly. Regrettably, I have some very disheartening news to share with you. A heartbreaking tragedy has come my way.

Last week, my twin sister, Emily, succumbed to consumption. I feel as though part of my soul has been ripped from my body. Emily and I were the very best of friends and I can't bring myself to thinking about life without her.

Tuberculosis has taken so many good people, but I never dreamt it would take my beautiful sister Emily. Never would I have imagined she would be gone at such a young age. She and I were so much alike. It does not seem real, yet I know it is. Sleep is only sporadic and comes with much difficulty, but when it does, it is tortured and tense. My sorrow knows no depths.

I hope you understand that I cannot bring myself to see anyone at present. Perhaps you would find room in your social calendar to receive my friendship at some point in the late summer?

Please pray for Emily's soul and for comfort in my grief.

Your sincere friend,

Elizabeth"

Ellie's entire world was swirling dizzily. She had never felt so unanchored. She became short of breath and felt as though she was losing control. Sweat beaded on her forehead and her vision blurred. Ellie experienced panic attacks in her youth and when she was overwhelmed by her graduate courses, but she hadn't experienced one since.

Fortunately, she recognized what was going on and regained control as quickly as she could to prevent a full-blown breakdown. Her cognitive behavioural therapy from her college days kicked-in and she immediately regulated her breathing. She opened her purse and dumped it on the table, grounding herself by looking at her keys and other familiar items. Within minutes, Ellie felt in control.

She paused and looked at the letter; the very source of her anxiety. She spoke to herself, saying silently, *"Okay, just regroup here, Ellie. You're a professional. Let's figure out what this means. Whether or not it seems rational doesn't matter, because you've just found what you've been searching for... a clue."*

Ellie tried to decipher what the letter meant, examining it from the perspective of a detached historian, as though she were not part of the equation. That's easy enough for anyone to *say* they're going to do, but to actually detach oneself from something so huge and personal is impossible!

She took on the elephant in the room, focusing on Elizabeth's twin sister's name, Emily. Of course, Emily was the name that Ellie had given her imaginary sister when she was just a little girl. It was the same name she continued to give to a missing sibling; one that she never really had. She reminded herself that no matter how much Emily seemed real, she wasn't. That was logical. Yet, her continuously nagging feeling of missing a twin sister, well, that was neither logical, nor explainable.

The fact that Ellie's identical body and name double from the late 1800s had to bury a twin sister who was also named Emily...it was just too much to digest.

Ellie drew a mental map of the different coincidences that started her on this path, beginning with her own insatiable desire to meet her twin sister who was never born...or was she?

She thought about how, even as a child, she felt like she had a twin. How did her three-year-old self somehow know that her twin's name was Emily? She then drew a thicker line, linking Elizabeth's hauntingly similar half-butterfly scar to Ellie's own half-butterfly scar on the same part of her wrist.

She was out of explanations. Ellie knew that *something* connected her with Elizabeth Pawley and Elizabeth's twin sister Emily. However, she had no idea what...or who it was. Ellie racked her brain for three weeks, trying to come up with an explanation for what it all meant and how it related to her unremitting sense that something central was missing in her life; that there was another missing part.

Everyone around her could tell that Ellie was dealing with something. She seemed preoccupied and distant. Something heavy was obviously bothering her, but no one who knew her dared broach the subject.

Another Saturday morning came around and, as usual, Ellie was up early. It was her favorite time of the day on her favorite day of the week. Each Friday evening, she would set her coffeemaker to automatically begin brewing a fresh pot at 6:00 a.m. She loved waking to the heady aroma, as it wafted from the kitchen to her bedroom.

This morning, though, she was on auto-pilot. She didn't even notice the aroma and got straight to work at the kitchen table. There were still hundreds of historical Newport mansion pictures and about a dozen documents remaining in the box that she hadn't yet seen.

Despite having the will to wake early, she looked haggard and drawn. The weight of the mysterious twin enigma had clearly taken its toll.

Ellie was programmed in college to do her research methodically. Choosing pictures in the order in which they were arranged in the box began to bore Ellie. Uncharacteristically, she plunged her hand into the middle of the box and plucked out a picture.

Somehow, she wasn't very surprised to see Elizabeth Pawley in that picture. She fully accepted that the connection between her, Elizabeth, and Elizabeth's twin sister, Emily, was supernatural, whatever it might be. So, it made total sense that a 'randomly' selected picture wouldn't be so random after all.

The image depicted Elizabeth having tea with another woman in a massive, extravagantly decorated parlor. Based on the inscription on the back of the photo, the other woman in the photo was the affluent woman who owned the summertime mansion. She was the *same* woman that Elizabeth wrote the letter to; the letter in which she shared news of her sister's passing.

Ellie had prepared herself to use the day to plow through the box, making as much progress as possible in her ongoing research project. Now, instead, she had to deal with the very puzzle that had been tormenting her for the past three weeks. Half of her wanted to cry and escape. The other half was too focused on discovering answers to run away.

The inscription on the back of this new photo didn't appear to provide any further clues. It simply identified Elizabeth and the mansion owner, along with the year, 1893; just a year after Emily's death.

Ellie took a long sip of coffee and then flipped the picture once more so she was facing the image. She raised the picture and held it in a shaft of filtered light coming from the kitchen window. Ellie studied *everything* in that picture. From the beautiful crystal candlesticks on the fireplace mantle and the bobeches around them to prevent melted wax from making a mess, to the parlor palm trees and opulent draperies.

There was a book on the table between where Elizabeth and the rich woman were seated. She hadn't noticed it before, but now it caught her eye. Elizabeth's hand rested partially on the book, suggesting that perhaps it was her book and that she had been discussing it with the woman. Ellie reached for her loupe and examined it closely.

The name of the book's author was obscured, but its title was readable.

The Special Bond Between Twins; Metaphysical Transmogrification Over Time

"Trans...morg...rif...What the?" Ellie thought to herself.

She had never heard the term before and rushed to search the internet for an online explanation. She quickly learned that it referred to some sort of metamorphosis or change, in terms of something or someone's physical form or appearance. Okay, she thought, but what does it have to do with twins or the metaphysical aspect of this so-called process happening over time? And why was the book there in the first place?

Ellie pieced-together a very basic possible explanation. What if Elizabeth was so unconsolably distraught about the loss of her twin sister that she searched for a way to see her again? An unearthly way? Perhaps the book contained some bizarre, yet scarcely plausible path to that end.

What would anyone do in such a circumstance? Of course, find the book! And that's exactly what Ellie tried to do. She began looking online, but found absolutely nothing referring to or even remotely similar to the book's title. Being an historian, she had access to searchable databases of manuscripts and rare documents that the average person would not, but even those failed to provide any reference to such a book from the 1800s or since then.

Ellie spent the balance of her Saturday calling specialty bookstores—particularly those that focused on antique and hard to find books—but none of the owners had ever heard of such a book. So, she did what any good sleuth would do; she used her imagination!

Ellie pushed beyond the usual limits of her thought process. She wondered if it was possible that the book provided methodologies—however strange or unlikely—that would claim to 'rematerialize' a dead relative's soul.

"Did I just go there?" Ellie smiled, thinking about how silly this was all beginning to seem.

She realized that her theory was *way* beyond the pale, but explored it anyway. Perhaps Elizabeth had brought the book to her rich friend to get her opinion on whether she thought it was possible to bring her sister back to life at a different time in the future. Further, could Elizabeth travel in time to reappear in her then resurrected sister's future time?

Well, even if she was correct about what Elizabeth was discussing with the rich woman and trying to make happen, Ellie realized that it had little to do with her own puzzle of how *SHE* connected to Elizabeth and to Elizabeth's sister. Further research provided no new answers. Elizabeth's trail went cold.

Six months went by and Ellie eventually completed and published her research study. The paper was widely endorsed and applauded by her professional community.

As time went on, her feelings of missing a twin sister grew even more intense, however, she never uttered a word about it to anyone. Nor did she reveal anything about Elizabeth Pawley, Elizabeth's deceased twin sister Emily or the strange book in the picture. Ellie realized that there was no upside in speaking about them publicly. She also knew that publicly tangling herself in the enigma would irreversibly tarnish her professional reputation and credibility.

As the years passed, Ellie eventually moved through the twilight years of her life's journey. She still often thought of Elizabeth and Emily and, from time to time, even tried unsuccessfully to have conversations with them. However, Ellie never considered the possibility that she and Elizabeth were, in fact, the same person living at different times.

Eventually, our earthly existence does come to its natural completion and our soul moves forward. After exhaling her last breath, Ellie finally learned the truth.

In her magnificent new spiritual state, she understood how the last puzzle piece fit into the final remaining hole. It merely needed to be rotated. Elizabeth somehow succeeded in her attempt at transmogrification. In the late 1800s, she played with time and tipped mystical equilibrium.

Plucked from her previous life as a Gilded Age historian and art dealer, she was metaphysically plunked by rebirth into a new life over a hundred years later. The re-born baby Elizabeth radiated energy that inspired her new parents to choose her name. She was and always would be Elizabeth, or "Ellie" for short. Becoming an eminent historian and artist was already in the cards. However, even though it was over a century later, Ellie still yearned for her twin sister.

Missing her twin over the course of two lifetimes finally came to its conclusion; Ellie was finally at peace. As Ellie crossed the threshold between mortality and immortality, Emily joyfully ran toward her, embraced her warmly and welcomed her home.

We humans may try to mess with elements which we do not understand, but, ultimately, the divine plan will prevail.

Stephen J. Kristof

AMARONE
LOVING DEEPLY

Love at first ~~sight~~...*taste*! Did you know there's a type of Italian wine that's so lovely, its name sounds a bit like the Italian word for love? When Italians talk about love, they say "Amore." It's fitting that "Amarone," contains all of the letters needed to spell Amore, because most people who first try it fall head over heels in love with this exquisite red wine!

Amarone is a rich, velvety-smooth, full-bodied red wine from the Italian wine producing district of the same name. When you read the word Amarone on a wine label, it means that the contents were grown and vinified in that district, but even more importantly, that a very specific and unique method was used in its production. That particular vinification method is at the heart of what makes these wines so distinctive and sought-after!

The entire process is complicated! As a DOCG (*Denominazione d'Origine Controllata e Garantita*) certified wine, it's not Amarone unless several rules are satisfied. To give you just a glimpse of how it works, here are a few examples. The principal grape used in the blend must be the Corvina varietal. All grapes that go into an Amarone wine have to be grown within a well-defined boundary in the Valpolicella region. And the vines that bear those grapes must be trained to look like pergola trellises.

Okay, fine, but what makes Amarone wines so texturally rich, highly colored and intensely flavored? Before crushing to release the juice, the grapes are spread-out and dried on racks for a few months to an almost raisin-like appearance. As they dehydrate, the grapes become far more concentrated. And *that* is precisely why Amarone wines are so dark, rich, full-bodied and dense. At least sixty per cent of the grapes' moisture is evaporated before they are pressed into juice!

One result of this unique winemaking method is the rather high alcohol content found in Amarones. You see, although more than half of the water is gone, the grapes' sugar remains intact; and don't forget, alcohol is a byproduct of fermented sugar. This means that you may *feel* Amarone's effects more quickly than you would by drinking the same amount of any other red wine!

Like Amarone's unique and bold character, the main subject in our next short story is Giuseppe; an elderly Amarone winemaker who grew up and lived in the Verona region of Italy. The head of what had over the years become a major corporate player in the Italian winemaking landscape, Giuseppe was also the patriarch of a large family. His wife, Gabriella, their six children and several grandchildren were the world to him.

Having grown, harvested, crushed, dried, fermented and sold excellent Amarone wines for the better part of his eighty years, Giuseppe earned his stripes; he was revered as an authority in the corporate world of wine. As well, despite not having earned a formal education, he was highly respected for his financial acumen. His company, quite simply, would not have become the power player that it became by merely producing good wine; Giuseppe's innate understanding of investing, marketing and forming business relationships was remarkably insightful.

The sprawling winery and estate had grown over the years. When Giuseppe was only twenty-two years old, he purchased a small patch of land using a meager inheritance from his father.

Almost sixty years later, his winery sat on the same spot, but its acreage had grown steadily over those years. As demand for his wines increased, Giuseppe wisely purchased adjoining and nearby properties; all of which had the ideal soil and micro-climate for growing Corvina grapes. He was particularly shrewd in his approach to those landowners. He researched the land, schmoozed the owners and snapped-up their properties at just the right moment before competing interests would otherwise have driven-up the prices.

In terms of the distribution of his wine company's wealth and power among his six children, Giuseppe masterminded a brilliant arrangement. He wanted to reward his three children who chose to carry the family wine business into the future. However, he also wanted to share the family wealth with his other three children, supporting their choice to pursue different career paths.

Giuseppe gifted the three who decided to go in other directions with extremely generous career-starting lump sums of cash. It was theirs to do with as they wished. They could each invest, spend or use it to start a business, but since they decided not to stick with the family business, they would have no future share of the winery company.

Those three children never regarded the arrangement as punitive. They were more than happy to be given their share earlier in life. If invested properly, with the advantage of decades of compounding, each of the children's eventual share of wealth could easily be equal to what they would otherwise have received had they chosen to stay with the winery.

Giuseppe and Gabriella were very specific about every nuance of estate distribution. It's a difficult pill to swallow, planning for one's own demise, but Giuseppe and Gabriella understood just how important it would eventually be. They had both witnessed ugly rifts and disharmony among siblings when such financial arrangements were too vague. They knew that when that time eventually arrives, it's far too late to reverse such chaos.

The three children who chose to dedicate their career lives to the wine business, two daughters and one son, were supported through college, where they each studied winemaking, finance and marketing. After graduation, each sibling worked hard and fully earned their respective appointments to crucial executive roles within the company.

When Giuseppe turned seventy, each of the winemaking siblings received an equal one per cent share of the company; it wasn't much to start with, but this arrangement continued with each passing year. At eighty, Giuseppe still held a majority position with his seventy per cent share, but the three children's full and equal ownership was also baked-into his will. As an incorporated family business, Giuseppe held the position of C.E.O. and Chairperson, with his children each eventually assuming a 33.333 per cent share of the company either before or upon his demise.

These types of arrangements showed Giuseppe's shrewd side. However, he was, more than anything, the archetypal family man. Nothing made him happier than the gift of time spent surrounded by the love of his family.

Let's be honest. If you've been gifted with a close family and cherish time spent with relatives, you understand that it isn't always easy! Not surprisingly, Guiseppe and Gabriella also experienced the difficulty, frustration and heartache that are often necessary parts of parenting. Nevertheless, their devout faith carried much of that weight through the years. As Giuseppe approached his eightieth birthday, he felt pride in being the best father he could have been.

His contentedness with life was also buoyed by his devotion to Gabriella. He had always treated her with respect, and tried hard to fill the gaps of patience and to smooth the rough waters that inevitably occur over the course of a long marriage. He would never have considered Gabriella as his soulmate; partly because such things were not spoken of in traditional Italian culture and partly because such a notion would have sounded like pure nonsense to him! However, they *were* soulmates, if such a thing exists, as much as two could ever be.

In terms of his career, Giuseppe was proud of what he built from mere grapes, but he maintained a strong sense of humility. He despised arrogance, even though it would have been very easy for him to have yielded to its allure. His unwavering faith and the role modeling of his own parents were the building blocks for his humility.

As much as he rejected his own entitlement and praise, he disavowed it in others who leaned heavily on their own success or title. To Giuseppe, it really didn't matter who you were! High-ranking politicians, business tycoons, celebrities, geniuses—he met them all—in Giuseppe's eyes, they didn't automatically earn his praise merely because of their power or pedigree.

While she quietly enjoyed seeing him do it, Gabriella would often assume a stoic expression, as Giuseppe knocked the haughty from their precarious perches by looking at their value to other human beings. In the same way, she was openly delighted whenever he would place others on that perch for their integrity and the positive impact they had on others.

For the milestone of his eightieth birthday, a huge outdoor party was held on Giuseppe and Gabriella's estate. Everyone who mattered to Giuseppe was there. Gabriella, their six children, nine grandchildren, Giuseppe's three remaining siblings, and dozens of his friends and neighbors all gathered to celebrate the fact that he was part of their lives. The first guests arrived in the early afternoon and the party carried-on well into the evening.

Everyone who was invited showed-up, except for Antonella. Antonella respectfully declined. She was Giuseppe's childhood sweetheart who never stopped loving him, but who never did get married. Old families in the region were closely entangled with one another and knew each other's business; accordingly, everyone understood why she couldn't bring herself to attend.

The party was big, but the tone wasn't at all fancy; perhaps that was one of the reasons guests were so relaxed and generous in spirit. The casual nature of the party matched the rustic, yet, beautiful landscape. Guests soaked-in breathtaking views of neatly tended trellised vines, old farm buildings and lush green hills in the distance.

Although Giuseppe and Gabriella hosted the party, their children helped a great deal with the preparations. As one would expect, they went over the top to keep all of their guests well fed and equally well lubricated. As for the lubrication, Giuseppe tapped two of his private selection barrels of wine for his guests to enjoy. Each barrel held the standard 300 bottles of red gold, so there was a lot to go around!

Of the two wines, the real prize was a thirty-year-old Amarone that was just hitting its peak. It was a dreamy brick-red colored wine that oozed intense flavors of black cherries, truffles and almonds. It had tamed, soft tannins that contributed to the wine's silky mouth feel. Guests were gifted with this spectacular Amarone twice; it filled every glass they drank during the party and, then at the end the party, each guest was gifted with a specially-labelled bottle from the same cellaring.

The second wine selection was a five-year-old Valpolicella. Although it wasn't anywhere near the blockbuster the Amarone proved to be, it was still a very respectable red wine in its class and was more suitable for guests who wanted a more quaffable, light and easy-drinking wine.

A third wine option, a white wine, was also served, but only when a guest requested it. Not surprisingly, few did. It was not unlike the old Italian riddle that goes, *"Quando un vero italiano beve vino bianco? Quando il vino rosso finisce!"* Roughly translated, it means, "When does a true Italian drink white wine? When the red wine runs out!"

The final libation was also from Giuseppe's private cellar. The fifty-year-old grappa had the punch of jet fuel, yet with an unctuous smoothness and delicate aromas of peach, flowers and white raisins. Although none of the guests abused the grappa, several younger men clearly enjoyed toasting with it. Giuseppe was amused seeing them standing in circles, singing together and shouting with laughter as they did shots of his grappa.

The food was both abundant and delicious. However, unlike a typical Italian social gathering, Giuseppe's party didn't have a scheduled sit-down dinner. Instead, and in keeping with the casual tone he wanted his party to convey, food was continuous throughout the afternoon and evening. Uniformed waitstaff—the only formal element of the party—roamed the grounds with so many different delectable offerings there were too many options from which to choose. Guests were well-fed with an endless stream of Steamed Shellfish, Raw Finfish Ceviche, Cheese Canapés, Beef Carpaccio, tiny nests of Capellini pasta drizzled with dozens of different inventive sauces, Antipasti boards, Carbonara Arancini balls and slices of Thin Crust Pizza.

It was enough to feed a literal army and nobody should have wanted more, but Gabriella still insisted on having a pastry table set out later in the evening. Many guests were entirely and irreversibly stuffed by the time the desserts came out. Instead of trying to force more food down their impossibly overworked gullets, they opted, instead, to stuff to-go boxes with scrumptious slices of Tiramisu and Rum Cake, along with brioche glazed Sfogliatella's and Cannoli's.

After dinner, Giuseppe and other men his age along with some of the more intrepid women in attendance had their own dance with the grappa. Giuseppe led the charge, pouring the precious brandy-like essence into large snifters. The grappa warmed each of their throats and lifted their moods. Laughter ensued as they reminisced around the wood-burning brick oven.

Three different groups of strolling musicians provided live music and added to the celebratory ambience. The size of the estate allowed two of the groups to play far enough apart from each other that they didn't compete for sound. The third group filled-in for the others on rotation as each took its break. This element of live music was the final ingredient that resulted in an absolutely magical evening!

After the last guests left, Giuseppe and Gabriella's children stayed behind to help with the clean-up. The catering employees and waitstaff did their own part to move things along. Giuseppe wanted one of the three strolling ensembles to stay behind for a while. The other musicians were happy to get their pay and make their way home. Italians refrain from placing cash currency into peoples' hands, as it is seen as rude. Instead, as is customary, Giuseppe had placed the cash into envelopes bearing each musician's first name, which he handed to them at the end of the night. He generously decided to double their arranged fee, which made the musicians smile excitedly when they peeked inside their envelopes.

Giuseppe asked the last few musicians to continue playing their beautiful music as he and Gabriella mused about the party. The four musicians—a singer, a guitarist, a violinist and an accordionist—played traditional Italian folk music under a nearby gazebo. They were close-enough to enjoy, but far enough away to blend-in with the nighttime ambience of tree frogs and crickets.

As they sat in half-reclined lawn chairs, the couple held hands and talked. The evening sky was wondrous, ablaze with stars! Far from the glare of city lights, the countryside location allowed the full grandeur of the night sky to radiate its glory. The heavens painted a stunning picture of countless twinkling lights. Even the densely packed Milky Way as visible.

He threw a few hardwood logs on the fire and a plume of sparks escaped the chimney, swirling and floating up, eventually dancing among the stars in the night sky. When he was thirty, Giuseppe built the wood brick oven, which he simply referred to as, "the fireplace." It had stood the test of time.

Have you ever had a moment that was so singular, so extraordinary, that it eclipsed the beauty and joy of all other memories? A moment in which the elements conspire to create an atmosphere so charged with enchantment that it feels as though you are in a movie? This was such a moment! Giuseppe, at eighty, and Gabriella, at seventy-seven, had never in their long-married life together shared a moment with such sheer magic. They had also never before felt so intensely in love as in that instant!

Time stood still as the couple sat and talked for hours into the night. The catering company had long ago packed-up and left. Their children had also returned to their own homes. The last of the musicians had finally packed-up their instruments and left an hour before with their own special envelopes in hand.

Giuseppe and Gabriella were finally alone at the end of a very long and happy celebration. Embers glowed and flickered among the logs in the fireplace; puffs of smoke wafted from the chimney, lightly scenting the cool night air with the inviting sweet scent of burning applewood and dried, old grape vine trunks. Gabriella grabbed a large woolen blanket from a drawer in the outdoor kitchen.

They moved their chairs a little closer to the fire and pulled the blanket around their two bodies, up to their necks. Neither one realized that their conversation had drifted into sleep, but a deep and restful sleep ultimately took over. Giuseppe and Gabriella shared the same dream that night. They held hands and flew among the stars, watching as their beautiful life unfolded below.

Stephen J. Kristof

SANGIOVESE
BELIEVING IN SOMEONE

Of all the wine grape varietals in Italy, which one is the most quintessentially Italian? The answer would be Sangiovese; there are more Sangiovese vines planted in Italy than any other variety. Pronounced *"san-joe-vay-zee,"* it's the backbone of the infamous Chianti, but is also used to make many other wines, both in blends and as a single varietal.

Sangiovese is grown primarily in Italy, but it has also found some favor in vineyards located in California and Australia, along with other smaller plantings elsewhere in the world. Although it adapts well to different types of soil, it is a thick-skinned grape that needs long warm summers to ripen.

So, what's the difference between Chianti and Sangiovese? They would be the same, except that in order for a winery to sell a bottle with the word "Chianti" on its label, it must consist of a minimum of eighty per cent Sangiovese grapes that were grown and vinified in specific regions of Tuscany.

The taste and nose of Sangiovese wines varies greatly, depending on the soil, microclimate, differences in seasonal weather from year-to-year and winemaking techniques. Some Sangiovese wines can be rich, dark, brooding wines with complex structures and tannins that require over thirty years to fully mature.

On the opposite end of the spectrum, many other Sangiovese offerings are light-bodied, brightly colored, approachable and soft on the palate. They have cherry and strawberry taste profiles, and are intended to be consumed within a few years of bottling.

Despite this broad range, any style of Sangiovese wine tends to pair well with an equally broad range of classic Italian foods, including Spaghetti Bolognese (pasta made with tomato meat sauce), Lasagna, Roasted Chicken, Braised Veal, Roasted or Grilled Lamb, Pizza, Sausages and Bistecca (i.e., T-Bone or Ribeye Steaks).

Regardless of your food pairing or the label on the bottle, two or more glasses of Sangiovese wines are happiest when clinked together in toasting and being enjoyed by family and good friends!

That clinking sound is the starting point for the last story in this collection. Have you ever noticed that 'clink' sounds aren't always the same? The deep tone of two full wine glasses tapped against one another sounds nothing like the brighter sound that's created when those glasses are almost empty. It's an entirely different sound when wedding guests enthusiastically tap their silverware against glasses or cups in an attempt to goad the newly minted bride and groom into kissing each other.

The clinking sound that Tony heard most often was the distinct sound cutlery makes when it hits other flatware as it's thrown into a dishwasher. As a busboy and back-of-house dishwasher for the last four years at a fancy Italian restaurant in downtown Toronto, he had heard enough clinking utensils to last a lifetime. However, he despised the work itself far more than the sounds associated with doing that work.

If you've never worked as a busser, you can only imagine how boring and gross the job must be! Maybe you've never thought about it, but handling complete strangers' used tableware and the partially consumed food, saliva, and occasionally unexplained substances clinging to all of it is, in a word, nasty. However, it was even worse for Tony. Being a germaphobe, the job was a very bad fit.

Regardless, we all need money to live and this is what Tony accepted as his role in the career side of his life. He was a single, twenty-three-year-old man who saw himself as a boy and generally seemed that way to others. Five years earlier, Tony narrowly graduated from high school and did so only because of the extraordinary interest and effort of his guidance counselor, Mr. Robbin. That teacher did what all of the best teachers do; he saw potential in Tony and worked passionately to get him to realize and capitalize on it.

However, not every effort in life produces the desired result, no matter how ardent that effort may be. It was unfathomable to Tony that he had any potential at all. Nevertheless, Tony was handed a golden opportunity; one that he, himself, didn't really earn or deserve.

Thanks to his friendship with the local community college's registrar, Mr. Robbin managed to land Tony a spot in a Culinary Arts diploma program. The opportunity was reserved for graduating high school students who were said to be at risk, but who had the potential to be successful in a culinary career.

To be fair, Tony took a whack at that college program, but unfortunately, Mr. Robbin was no longer there to push him forward. Tony thrashed about in the unfamiliar waters of post-secondary education, where one is able to do as much—or as little—as one wishes. Tony chose the "as little" route.

He floundered in that program for almost a full year, before deciding to call it quits and move on with life. Well, that's not entirely accurate. He was actually *told* to leave the college by that same registrar who said it was time he moved on.

Losing his student aid and having no way of paying for rent and food, Tony got a job in the culinary industry, but just not the type of job that was near his potential. He literally went from floundering at academics to cleaning flounder and all other types of food off people's plates.

There's nothing at all wrong with Tony's job. Bussing tables and washing dishes is one of the more common occupations out there; people have been doing that type of work as long as human beings have paid others to feed them.

However, it wasn't right for Tony. He loathed the work. For him, it wasn't only gross and even dangerous from a germaphobe's perspective, but was also a constant reminder of his failure in college. Deep in his psyche, Tony knew that he could do something more satisfying with his life, but his negative self-talk was too overwhelming for his conscious self to believe it.

The first day of October felt like autumn in Toronto. The crisp wind blew sharply from the north. Tony's phone buzzed at eleven o'clock. He would have overslept and would had been late for his noon shift, had it not been for that alarm. Sleeping-in was understandable, considering that Tony had been playing games on his small TV until four in the morning. It was not entirely understandable why he did so most nights, but that's a different story.

Tony eventually rolled-over and sat up on the edge of his bed. He had left the window sash open all night. The chilly air hit his bare chest, which made him want to crawl back under the warm blanket. He resisted the urge and got up. He pushed-up the accordion-style paper blind all the way and looked out at a rather dismal part of the big city.

Surrounding him in every direction were towering clones of dreary, institutional-looking apartment buildings. In such an environment, there's no room for nature or beauty; that is, unless one considers tagging and random graffiti to be fine art, and piles of refuse, discarded furniture and twisted metal to be sculpture.

Suddenly, a bit of nature managed to intrude on the bleak urban scene and catch Tony's eye. A single leaf fluttered past him, dancing in the breeze as it whirled up, swirled down and bounced up again, as if a master puppeteer were dangling it from above. The leaf was not only a harbinger of fall, but unbeknownst to Tony, foretold of an even bigger change in his life.

He managed to get to work a bit early for his shift, punching-in at eleven fifty-six a.m. He almost always punched-in at the precise minute that his shift began, with the exception of when he showed-up a few minutes late, which was more often than not. Lunch service at the restaurant had just begun and diners were streaming in. The late shift guys had mopped the floors and set the tables the night before as usual, so Tony's first order of work was to begin bringing water to the guests.

Tony couldn't put his finger on it, but something felt strange about that day. From the dancing leaf to the mood in the restaurant, things didn't seem normal. At one point during the two-hour gap between lunch and dinner service, Tony learned why things seemed different.

The owner, Rob, called everyone together for a pop-up meeting in the main dining room. He had closed the doors of the restaurant when the last of the lunch guests left; this was unusual in itself. Tony wondered what was up?

Rob and Chef Eric stood in front of the bar. Everyone else, the sous-chefs, line cooks, the sommelier, the bartender, all of the servers and Tony's fellow bussers were seated at the dining tables. Taking a cue from Rob and Eric's grim expressions, the staff were collectively nervous.

"Thank you for coming together here. First, I want to let you all know how much Chef Eric and I appreciate all you do each and every day. I want to thank each of you for what you contribute to the excellent food and service that our patrons have enjoyed for the past twelve years."

Rob's delivery was monotone and serious. Tony sensed that nothing good would follow. He was right.

Rob paused for a few moments and sighed. His hand glided through his hair several times like he was brushing it. He continued, saying, "I don't know any other way of saying this, other than to let you know that our beloved restaurant is closing."

An immediate and collective gasp followed. The emotional shockwave was palpable. A few employees immediately started crying, while others asked, "What," and "Why?" Still, others, were in disbelief or hadn't completely digested the statement.

Chef Eric, who had a financial stake in the establishment, stepped forward and cleared his throat. His voice was usually confident, booming and authoritative. This time around, his voice was trembling and weak. Shaking his head from side to side, Eric said, "I...I...I'm sorry. I know this comes as a huge shock to all of you and, believe me, it was the last thing we wanted to do. But we can no longer ignore the financial losses that continue to accumulate month after month."

Filomena, known to everyone as simply "Fil," was an outspoken server who had worked for the restaurant longer than anyone other than Rob and Eric. She stood up and shouted, "How on earth are you losing money? This makes no sense! We're busy busting our asses every lunch and dinner, and we see the receipts. You're frickin' *raking* it in!"

Rob tried to explain. "I get it. You see the guests, you see the money and the charges. Yes, it *is* busy. But what you don't see is the other side of the business. The expenses are out of control! Eric and I have tried to do everything possible to cut costs without cutting quality."

Eric interrupted Rob, saying, "And we can't keep raising prices. You've got to have noticed that each time we do, we lose business."

Rob continued, "The rent is becoming impossible to pay and it's going up again in November; we couldn't even afford the rent two years ago. This latest increase is the nail in the coffin. Rising food costs, your own wages, skyrocketing utilities—electricity, heating, air conditioning, cooking gas—it's a no-win situation."

Tony was usually the last one to say anything in a group. His mind would often wander and he didn't pay attention, so he would routinely ask others to repeat or explain what was said. Uncharacteristically, he stood-up and asked the question that was on everyone else's mind.

He said, his voice unsteady, "When is it closing? How long do we have?"

Rob and Eric looked at each other. It appeared as though neither one of them wanted to answer the question. Rob crossed his arms on his chest and looked down at the floor. He said sheepishly, "The doors are closed. We're not having dinner service tonight. We are closed effective immediately."

As one would expect, some elements of the group became angry and combative. They began shouting at the pair, asking why they weren't given more time to prepare financially, saying that it wasn't fair. A few of the more vocal staff began hurling obscenities at them.

"Guys, please. We have a plan for you. We're not leaving you hanging!" Eric found his strong voice. He squashed the chaotic din, hammering away at the same sentence until everyone was quiet. "We have a plan for you...LISTEN, we have a plan for you. EVERYONE! AGAIN, WE HAVE A PLAN FOR YOU!"

The clamor subsided. Eric lowered his voice and said, "You don't know this, but Rob and I have not taken a paycheck since May. Look, we're not asking for sympathy, but I want you to know that even though we have not been paid and have gone into a lot of personal debt, we avoided laying-off any of you. We didn't even cut your wages or your hours."

Rob stepped-in, saying, "We just can't continue to do it. There's nothing left and we're maxed-out on credit. That's why we're closing today."

Once more, the group started to become agitated. As one would expect, they didn't care about their bosses' financial trouble or sacrifice; they couldn't see beyond their own imminent loss.

Rob tried his best to calm their most immediate concern. "Listen, you will all get paid your regular wages for the entire month of October, but you don't need to come to work. Use the cushion to find another job, while you continue paying for rent and food...on us...for four weeks."

Eric added, "Please get to work. File for unemployment if you have to, but...be kinder to yourself and get another job as quickly as you can. We don't care if you start working somewhere else tomorrow, Rob and I will continue paying you till the end of the month."

While Eric was talking, Rob went behind the bar and grabbed two very expensive bottles of top-shelf cognac. He arranged enough snifters for everyone there and poured a generous shot into each one.

Rob took over and said, "So, I hope you can find it in your heart to forgive us and to understand that we've done everything in our power to keep this place—and your jobs—going. This is the very best we can do for you. I just wish there was *more* that we could do."

Tony and his coworkers were quiet. Shellshocked, but finally accepting of what was happening. Tears flowed as the finality of it sunk in.

Rob said, "We have a meeting here with our bankers and lawyer in about twenty minutes, so we're going to have to shut things down, but we're asking if you would kindly join Eric and I in a goodbye toast before you leave."

For the first time in years, instead of feeling frustrated about his work, Tony was genuinely worried. He was too overwhelmed to think about what would come next for him. He took one of the cognacs from the bar counter.

Holding his own snifter, Rob began his toast. "Very soon, this restaurant will be a mere memory. But this restaurant's financial misfortune could never take away the beautiful relationships that came of it, the many laughs we've had together or the way we've all been there for one another to help get through rough times. Wherever the wind takes us, let it be to better places and even happier times. We will never forget you. Cheers!"

Their toast was heartfelt and emotional. It was classy, if you could call it that, but one thing for sure was that as all of the employees left the restaurant, not one of them begrudged Rob or Eric. It was clear to all that they really did do everything possible to prevent the closure.

Realizing he wouldn't be getting a free meal that night, Tony stopped at a supermarket on his way home and grabbed a hot meal to go. He had a million questions about his own future, but didn't want to think about any of them. It wasn't until that moment that Tony realized his work had distracted him from considering doing something else with his life; something that he wouldn't hate. Maybe...just maybe...something that he would actually look forward to and enjoy doing.

After a few days of feeling sorry for himself, Tony resolved to live a healthier life, beginning with getting to sleep at a decent time. He got help from a friend to put-together a decent resume and soon after hit the bricks. As much as he wanted to break-free of the busboy and dishwasher routine, he realized that it was all he knew.

Fortunately, Tony found new work just a few days after he began his job search. Thanks to an excellent reference from Rob, he was able to get into a popular restaurant that paid even more than he earned previously. Tony's new boss, John, had worked in the catering and hospitality sector his entire life and personally knew everyone on the culinary "who's who" list in Toronto.

Not only was John well-connected, he also loved taking on a new project. Just a few days after Tony began working as John's newest busser, John recognized something special in him. He decided that Tony would be his next project. Tony didn't realize it at the time, but he really did need a guidance counselor in his corner once again.

Ninety days had passed and Tony was still working as a busser for John's restaurant, still disliking the dishwashing part of it and continuing to feel rather depressed about his lot in life. However, there were some positive changes in his life; his increased pay and an added responsibility.

He was no longer merely taking food *away* from tables; he was also running food *to* customers. It was that additional task that opened a door to what could be a better future. Although John recognized Tony's affability immediately, he also recognized that Tony wouldn't see it in himself until it was tested. As John predicted, Tony began to sense that there might just be more to his personality and skill set than he had previously thought.

Once Tony began to believe in himself, John took a gamble and promoted him to join his team of waitstaff. Trying to erase any chance of failure, John overindulged Tony with training before he was fully engaged in the new job. Again, as predicted, Tony rose to the challenge and in no time showed that John's gamble was paying off.

Tony quickly began earning higher tips than most of his peers and actually looked forward to going to work; something that he had never previously experienced.

The one thing, however, that John could not and did not predict was about to occur. After putting so much time, effort and trust into his protégé, John was disappointed beyond words when it happened. Having never believed in himself in any significant way, the unfamiliar shot of confidence went straight to Tony's head. He was unprepared for any measure of success and reacted to it badly.

It didn't take long for Tony to alienate himself from most of his coworkers. He came across as an arrogant jerk, boastfully elevating himself at every opportunity and rudely putting others down. He quickly forgot about the favors that others, like John, had done for him. His short memory for John's charity showed its ugly self when Tony eagerly and ruthlessly joined a few fellow servers who were disparaging John's appearance and personality.

The trio didn't see John exiting the cooler as they engaged in their undeserved ridicule and trash talk. Although John expected as much from the other two, he was surprised and deeply hurt by what Tony had said. His knee-jerk reaction was understandable. Later that evening, John met with Tony at the end of his shift and fired him. It was a rash decision, but, completely understandable.

Tony crashed and crashed hard. This time was different from the last. He found it far more difficult to land on his feet and get a new job, despite his recent success.

Given John's influence, he could easily have blackballed Tony, but to what end? John figured that Tony's life was hard enough as it was; he wasn't about to allow his personal disappointment in Tony to cause more negativity and trouble for the guy. He remained unremorseful about firing Tony, but left it at that.

John's willingness to forget about it didn't stop Tony's former coworkers from gossiping about his firing. The story spread quickly through Toronto's restaurant scene. With negative rumors flying around and without a positive reference letter from John, Tony didn't get so much as a nibble.

Negativity and trouble did follow. It took only three weeks for all of Tony's progress and self-confidence to fade away. Fortunately, though, he had a glimpse of what life could be. He remembered how great he felt before he got cocky. Perhaps John's work wasn't all for not?

Tony came to the conclusion that he had no choice but to shift his job search away from the insular world of culinary hospitality. For the first time in years, he accessed his internet connection for a purpose other than playing games. He began researching different types of occupations and taking dozens of self-assessment tests. He learned more about himself—his personality, his skills and his motivations—than he had ever realized. Tony also took responsibility for his situation in life; one of many 'firsts' to come.

Through the process of self-inquiry and by considering alternatives that would shape his future in different ways, the adult boy started to mature. What he once viewed as closed doors were suddenly open; roads to nowhere were now potentially viable paths. He was no longer afraid to open his mouth or to meet someone new.

He realized the cocoon that he thought had protected him, instead, was suffocating him and preventing him from taking advantage of opportunities. But one of Tony's greatest breakthroughs was in his acceptance that he was actually deserving of those opportunities.

The boy was dead. Anthony held a mental memorial service and said goodbye to the limiting identity that was his former self. During the next three years, Anthony reinvented himself, pursued a career that was a far better fit and did something else that boy Tony's self-doubt previously prohibited; Anthony started dating.

* * *

He didn't want to open his eyes, but Anthony's phone alarm pried them open anyway. He rolled over and sat on the edge of his bed for a few moments before looking back at his wife, Amilee. He thought about how fortunate he was to have a wife so beautiful, kind and loving.

Amilee opened her eyes and smiled at Anthony. She said with a sleepy voice, "Good morning birthday boy!"

"No boy left in this body!" he replied.

"Hey, you don't look anywhere near your forty-four years, my handsome man!"

Anthony leaned over and kissed Amilee on her forehead. He said, "Thanks, gorgeous!"

He rolled out of bed and pulled-up the window shade. It was mid-October and the weather had begun to turn autumn-like. He didn't exactly like the feeling of being forty-four, but by the same token, he felt pretty good about his life.

Anthony glanced again at Amilee, then turned to the window and took in the beauty of the natural forest surrounding their large and modern suburban home. His mind flashed back to the dismal, prison-like view from his apartment window. He had forgotten about the concrete jungle surrounding his former Toronto dwelling. He thought about how far he had come since that dull time in his life.

A single leaf interrupted Anthony's musing. It appeared suddenly, drifting directly in front of his gaze. For a moment, it was suspended in the air, dancing in the gentle, cool breeze. He recalled seeing the same thing a long time ago. He wondered if it had a special meaning or if it was even the same leaf?

"Honey, you look like you're deep in thought..."

"I am, Amilee. It's a beautiful day!"

"Hey, I just remembered something. I hate to interrupt your birthday meditation, but I got a call from Aiden's guidance counselor yesterday after school. He said something about recognizing potential that Aiden seems to be obvious to and he's going to meet with him next week to talk about it."

Anthony said, somewhat mechanically, "We're really fortunate that Aidan has such great teachers! They obviously really care about him. You know, I could never do that job. Teachers don't get proper credit for all they do..."

The dancing leaf suddenly made sense.

Anthony remembered that there were two people from much earlier in his life who believed in him even when he couldn't believe in himself; Mr. Robbin, who put his neck on the line for him and never gave-up and John, his former boss, who gave him the rare gift of confidence. Anthony then recalled how terribly he treated both of them. He disrespected Mr. Robbin by failing to invest adequate effort after he had opened doors for him. He had also met John's kindness and support with ridicule and contempt.

Anthony had repressed his failure to treat these two supporters with the respect and effort they both deserved, but was suddenly reminded of it. He was filled with remorse and embarrassment. It wasn't how he had planned to start his birthday. He stood there silently, motionless for the longest time.

"So, honey, you did clear your schedule for the day, like I asked you?"

"Um, ah, what was that?" Anthony was deep in thought; he hadn't heard a word of what Amilee had just said.

"My goodness!" Amilee interjected, "where are you right now? You look a million miles away. It's your birthday, honey. Are you alright?" Amilee's bright expression turned to one of concern.

Anthony turned from the window and faced Amilee, who was still lying in bed. He was suddenly overtaken by her natural beauty. He smiled at Amilee, but she could see that something was obviously on his mind. She got out of bed and stood next to him. She looked out at the magnificent woodland landscape and turned to him. He reached out and took both of her hands in his.

"Honey, are you okay? You just got so quiet looking out the window. Is it because of your birthday?"

"No, sweetheart, I'm fine...I'm good."

"Well, part of you is here, but another part of you is somewhere else. What is it? *Is it us?*"

"No, no, no!" exclaimed Anthony, "we're good...we're better than good; we're amazing! I...I...was just thinking about my past and, you know, about how, sometimes, people can make a bigger difference in our lives than they realize."

"That's true, I guess. So, you've cleared your day, right? I've got some fun things planned for your special day, starting with a reservation for lunch in the city!"

"I can't wait, my love! I just need an hour or two before you get the ball rolling. There are a couple of very special people who've been waiting way too long—in fact, over twenty years—to hear from me."

Stephen J. Kristof

SAUVIGNON BLANC
SHE SAID, HE SAID

You probably know that May 5th is Cinco de Mayo, Mexico's popular cultural and historical day of victory and celebration. But did you know that the first Friday in May is known as International Sauvignon Blanc Day?

Although that may not mean a whole lot to most folks, it's a very important day for countless people around the world who grow Sauvignon Blanc grapes and for those who ferment those grapes into delicious white wine. Sauvignon Blanc is about as ubiquitous as it gets when it comes to white wine. The grapes are grown successfully pretty much everywhere wine grapes grow and vintners from all over export their particular versions of Sauvignon Blanc to thirsty wine drinkers around the globe.

Okay, but is it a popular wine? Has it found a comfy place in most white wine drinkers' hearts? Well, the answer really depends on who you ask! In New Zealand, a country where a LOT of Sauvignon Blanc wine is made, locals have for long joked about the varietal tasting something like cat's urine on a gooseberry bush. Umm, well, that doesn't exactly sound very appealing! In fact, in an example of self-effacing wine humor, one Kiwi wine producer has gone so far as to adopt that amusing, if not off-putting, description as a name for their own offering of Sauvignon Blanc!

Common tasting notes associated with Sauvignon Blanc wines often include descriptions such as grass, vegetable, citrus, mineral, green pepper and, yes you guessed it, gooseberry. Whether or not these flavors and aromas resonate with your own palate is a very personal thing. Some people love the wine and drink it liberally, while others avoid it like the plague!

That's one thing, at least, that most wine drinkers can agree on when it comes to Sauvignon Blanc. People either like it or dislike it; there aren't many wine drinkers who are on the fence.

If you enjoy drinking white wine and have never tasted Sauvignon Blanc, you owe it to yourself to give it a try. It may become your new 'go-to' quaff. If not, you'll at least educate yourself about a varietal that isn't your cup of...wine.

Just like Sauvignon Blanc, there are countless on-stage performers who have as many dedicated fans as they do detractors. When you think about it, there are so many different ways that people make a living on a stage!

There are live musicians; the talented ones who make obscene amounts of money and then all of the others who are even more talented, but who will never be discovered. Then you have stunningly sexy singers; some of whom have voices of velvet and others that can't actually carry a single note. Of course, there are stand-up comics; those who are sidesplittingly funny and others who are, merely, shockingly vulgar. Don't forget live theatre actors; some of whom are compelling in any role and others who can only play themselves. TV evangelists also make money on a stage; some of them truly instill faith and inspire their followers to be better human beings, while others are only interested in duping their dewy-eyed disciples out of their hard-earned cash. The list also contains inspirational speakers; those who encourage profound conversions and those who merely repeat popular cheerleading clichés.

Pammy Pickerpott was an on-stage performer. She was a motivational speaker who, after doing ten years of circuit tours on the road, started sounding more and more like a TV evangelist. She regularly performed in front of throngs of adoring devotees in several different countries. Her fans enthusiastically paid between fifty to over two hundred dollars per ticket in exchange for transfusions of fleeting hope and synthetic gusto.

Pammy knew human nature. Remarkably, even as a child, she loved observing people in various settings. She studied people's reactions to various stimuli, their emotions, their relationships and their traits. Pammy enjoyed predicting how different people would react differently to the same provocation and she was almost always correct. She was an emotional psychic of sorts.

The name Pammy was a parental pet name that stuck through her youth and into her professional years. She liked being called Pammy, because she thought it sounded fun and innocent. She also liked her name's uniqueness; she couldn't think of any other professional who went by such a childish name.

Whether or not her name sounded childish, Pammy was years ahead of people far older than she, even as a young teenager. Her parents were the quintessential social butterflies, frequently entertaining and throwing lavish dinner parties for other couples and small groups.

While her friends tried to escape the torture of being introduced to their parents' guests as they arrived for a party, Pammy couldn't wait to interact with her own parents' adult friends. She seemed quiet and polite—as model children were expected to behave in the 1950s and 1960s—but the reality of it was that she was observing carefully and soaking it all in.

Following the pleasantries between herself and her parents' guests, Pammy knew precisely when to graciously excuse herself to let the grown-ups have their time together. She would often plunk herself down on the den floor, just out of eyeshot of her parents and their guests; far away enough to make a quick escape, but close enough to hear everything that was said.

She got an early education when it came to mature subject matter and lewd jokes, but she never revealed that to her parents.

In any case, she really didn't care about that stuff. What was most interesting to her was connecting her initial impressions of the guests—her assessments—with their behaviors. And, oh my, were her expectations accurate!

Pammy knew far better than the adults, which ones would be offended, surprised, titillated or overly enamored with a joke. She could predict the direction toward which conversation would veer and how it would end. She was also unusually adept at discerning which guests had crushes on one another and which ones were secretly and lustfully doing something about it.

It was no surprise that Pammy chose to study psychology when she attempted to earn an undergraduate degree. She was such a natural at it. She aced her exams throughout her first three years, merely by attending and listening to lectures. She really didn't need to read or study the textbooks. However, Pammy left college after her three-year stint. It wasn't because she couldn't hack it; she was a brilliant student who was well-liked and respected by all of her professors. She left without earning that degree because she was simply bored.

She would have made an exceptional psychologist, but she wanted something else out of life. For such a quiet young woman, it was surprising that she was so comfortable with the idea of being a performer, but that was the path she chose. Pammy knew what she had to do to prepare herself for a life as a motivational speaker. She got a job as a waitress at a local roadhouse; a position she stuck with for about a month, before becoming a bartender at the same place.

Perhaps it sounds a bit disconnected with respect to a career path, but Pammy knew that she needed three things in order to move forward. First, she had to force herself to become more comfortable with talking to strangers and learning how to loosen-up in large social environments. Second, she needed stories—lots of stories—and bartending was an easy way to gather a large repertoire of stories. Third, Pammy needed to earn a lot of money. With her ability to read and manipulate others, bartending proved to be a very lucrative interim occupation in terms of her capacity to earn unusually generous tips.

During her four years mixing cocktails, listening to sob stories and providing remarkably insightful advice, Pammy kept a detailed journal of her interactions with her patrons, and of their many different struggles and stories; some of which were terribly worrisome. At the same time, she also began writing a book; the pages of which were filled with her anonymous patrons' stories and her advice to them.

It was a self-help book titled, "A Bartender's Guide to Human Problems" by Pammy Pickerpott. It was an instant hit, climbing to the top spot on several national best seller lists within just a month of its initial release. Before she knew it, Pammy's first book tour transitioned into a series of speaking engagements that continued to draw larger and larger audiences.

Four years and two more books later, Pammy Pickerpott was one the main draws for fans in major markets looking to buy tickets to motivational and inspirational speaking shows. At twenty-nine years old, Pammy was more successful than she had ever imagined. Talk about having the world by the tail! She was living the dream and loving every minute of it.

Right out of the gate, Pammy's audiences found her to be charismatic and captivating. She was a superstar at making personal connections with audience members by learning about the cities where she spoke. Pammy would routinely research the culture, history, recreation options and popular restaurants in the area in order to weave those local tidbits into her shows. Attendees at her shows lapped it up, which made them even more receptive to her messages.

She was also the consummate improviser! Talk about flying by the seat of her pants, Pammy often ad-libbed an entire two-hour show from a tiny kernel of an idea that popped into her head just a minute before she jumped on stage. Only her road crew knew that she had, once again, strayed from her script.

Even when she followed the script, she changed her performance, just enough each time to give viewers the impression that they were watching a distinct performance. Pammy was that good. She also knew her audience; she sensed it while on stage.

She knew what to say, how to contort her face and body, how quickly or slowly she needed to pace her speech and when to vacillate her vocal timbre in order to best captivate her audience. She easily had them wrapped around her little finger. Once there, she twisted and manipulated their emotions at will. Watching her in person was truly an inspiring and poignant experience.

For the first ten years of Pammy's road shows, her topics generally focused on emotional first-aid and personal growth. However, bit-by-bit, her themes took on a more spiritual tone. Her self-help performances drifted in and out of spirituality, but over the years, she swapped their priority. Titles of her road shows changed as well. Early show titles like, "Master the Real You" and "Define Your Own Success; Not Theirs" were replaced with more spiritual titles like "God's Plan for Your Success" and "You Deserve Multiple Blessings."

Eventually, she became known as a religious speaker; an evangelist of sorts. She wasn't even aware of her shift until a few years after she had moved in that direction, but by that time, her feet were planted firmly in sacred soil.

To her adoring fans, she became known as, "Pammy Pickerpott, Inspirational Speaker Who Invokes God's Goodness." For many, she was a quasi-priestess and for others, she was a preacher with a special connection to God. Some even believed that she was a modern-day prophet.

Pammy didn't think of herself in these ways. But it didn't matter to her devotees. She was more persuasive and energizing to them than she had ever been in the past, because of her perceived connection to our Creator.

Unlike popular TV evangelists' shows, Pammy's weren't considered to be revivals and show attendees were never asked to bear witness or accept Jesus Christ as their personal savior. Oh, and one more thing. Collection plates were never passed around. Then again, at fifty to two hundred and fifty dollars per ticket, there was no reason for her to be greedy and ask for even more!

But there was something untoward about the turn that Pammy's shows had taken shortly after her forty-seventh birthday. Maybe it had something to do with her unexpected marital breakup. Her divorce a year earlier was primarily due to her husband's wandering eyes and, more importantly, his wandering penis.

Pammy's health started to catch-up to her age and she began to experience medical issues that, although relatively minor, were terribly upsetting to her. She also began to feel increasingly fatigued. This was something she had never experienced before. In the past she had always had so much excess energy and drive that she found it difficult to turn off and relax. Being tired and unmotivated was an entirely new experience for Pammy; she couldn't understand why the dime store psychological advice that she regularly prescribed to her fans had no restorative impact on her own malaise.

Her shift in subject matter may have also been influenced by a tax audit that led to a conviction for criminal evasion of taxes. That felony was the result of undeclared income from fan swag merchandising sales and the attempted use of fake corporate expenses to offset that revenue. Pammy was able to work out a deal with the taxman and avoided incarceration. However, she paid an undisclosed, but, massive penalty; a forfeiture that was far greater than the money that the scheme was designed to save.

Unfortunately for Pammy, her reputation was scarred by the fiasco, even though she tried to shift blame to her accounting team. She lost a chunk of her fan base due to her dishonesty, but still managed to retain a good number of supporters who blindly followed her and kept attending her shows. However, in order to replace the lost portion of her flock with new followers, she had to try harder and become shrewder.

Pammy became increasingly provocative in what she said on stage. Her personal version of God mixed with a healthy dose of optimism, hope and success was no longer enough.

Pammy's religious angle became more extreme and unfounded. She simply made-up stuff and was creating an image of God that was distorted and dangerous. As the months passed, Pammy developed a new show that included a conspicuously political tone. She had always kept her political views to herself, but that was no longer the case.

Not only did she become vocal about her political leanings and beliefs, she twisted them and attached herself to the extreme. In doing so, Pammy managed to attract a new fanbase, but its members were very, very different from her traditional fans. Audiences at her shows became more vocal and aggressive. She even began to feel that she might lose control of her own shows.

Houston, Texas, 8:02 p.m., Saturday, April 2, 2022. Two minutes after the house lights dimmed, Pammy's audience was still enthusiastically chanting her name. The drawn-out and haunting sound of, "Paaameee, Paaameee, Paaameee..." echoed as the mantra ricocheted off the large arena's steel and cement walls.

Pammy did her usual prep. She was backstage, standing just a few feet inside the left curtain, but still out of sight from the audience. She exercised her jaw, mouth and tongue as though she was doing a workout. She contorted her mouth and shifted her chin from side to side.

A nearby stagehand observed her and smiled; she looked like a lion gruesomely digging-into its next live meal. Pammy then then whispered repetitive "f" consonant sounds while exhaling. Hearing her utter, "f-f-f-f-f-f-f..." made him chuckle out loud. Pammy noticed him and felt momentarily embarrassed.

The spotlight came on and Pammy walked briskly, almost dancing, to her position on stage, mustering as much pep to her step as she could. Her fans rose to their feet, cheering and clapping as soon as she emerged.

"Thank you...thank you! Thank you so much for coming out tonight!"

The arena erupted into an avalanche of even louder cheering. She smiled, pointed randomly at different fans and waved as though she knew them. After ten seconds, she motioned for her fans to have a seat so she could begin.

Most people in the audience started to sit down and the din hushed. A small minority of fans continued standing and began chanting her name. Others loudly recited some of Pammy's well-known short quotes. Based on the audience's behavior, she felt more like a famous actor or sports hero than an inspirational speaker, evangelist or political influencer; whichever she felt like she was. Boisterous screams with the phrases, "Live the Reality, Not the Dream," and "Love Yourself Before Your Neighbor" filled the arena.

That night was the first of a series of new shows based on Pammy's latest book, titled, "How to Get Others to Make You Rich." It was an unapologetically, appallingly, selfish manifesto about how to screw others out of their own share in order to get more than your own. Of course, it was an instant hit as soon as it hit the bookshelves, because it pandered to the lowest of human motivations; greed and power.

The degree to which Pammy's philosophies had shifted toward the negative was astounding. Each of her last three books and their respective road shows increasingly embraced the themes of avarice, winning at all costs and exploiting others. Her new approach was in shocking contrast to the noble values of self-sacrifice, charity and integrity that her early books and shows had once encouraged.

The most disgraceful part of Pammy's new credo was her repugnant endorsement of dangerously destructive quasi-political ideologies that openly endorsed fascism, racism and corporatism. These ideas emboldened her fans to feel good about being selfish at the expense of others.

Sensing the energy in the arena and feeling that she had the throng in the palm of her hands, Pammy was eager to start her show. After the last fan shouted some incoherent babble, everyone calmed down and the venue was pin-drop silent. Pammy reached under the front of her shirt and pulled out a US $1,000 bill from under her bra. Pulling-out money that was touching her breast was provocative enough, but a genuine thousand-dollar bill? That really got the audience revved-up.

Pammy had acquired the bill several years before at an antique shop. It was printed in 1945; the last year the US Mint printed large denomination currency. Whether or not the audience realized it, the bill wasn't a replica. She had paid a $7,000 premium for it on top of its legal tender value. It was a rather expensive little prop.

"This is a genuine, legal-tender one-thousand-dollar bill, people! The government hasn't printed these in nearly eighty years. You've got to ask yourself *why* these were in people's hands so long ago, but the government won't even make them today?"

The audience became restless and angry. Pammy had only been on the stage for less than a few minutes and she had already whipped her fans into a frenzy.

"Could it be that they don't WANT you to have that kind of money anymore? You know, they used to call it 'disposable income' which meant that most people had more money than they needed after paying their bills. Now, the government word twisters tell us that it's 'discretionary income,' which basically tells me that they're happy with us having less to spend!"

"Boo! Shame! Fuckers!" The chants were angry and rowdy.

Then Pammy dropped the boom. She roared, "But you know...you don't *have* to play their game! You can play by your *own* rules! You can make your own rules and get RICH! This is a free country, dammit!"

She sounded so passionate she seemed to actually believe the lies and negativity spewing from her mouth. Her audience lapped it up and wanted more.

"This dishonest administration in Washington... in OUR Washington... is trying to make us poor! They *want* us to have less money and influence, because it's easier to control us that way. Do you really think that inflation just happened because of things happening elsewhere in the world? Do you *really* believe that Washington is trying to curb inflation?"

Pammy's old core part of the audience—those who stuck with her despite the bad press and her change in philosophy—appeared to be collectively frightened by the atmosphere in the arena. Some were texting and posting to social media that they felt threatened by the new and growing part of her fan base. The arena became an unstable and angry place; this was something far different from the uplifting and encouraging mood at Pammy's older shows.

"Those do-nothing fat cats in Washington are responsible for inflation and everything they do is designed to make it even worse. As everything becomes more expensive—food, basic necessities, fuel, heating and cooling our homes—we become servants to the people in power! Think about it!"

Pammy suddenly stopped and intentionally injected an awkward pause in order to fix her viewers' attention on the next thing she had to say. She closed her eyes, tilted her head to face the floor and stood statue-still for a few seconds. Her audience silently and excitedly anticipated her next volley.

Slowly lifting her head and opening her eyes, she said very calmly and directly, "The very best thing we can do... The SMARTEST thing we can do... Is to get wealthy enough that their inflated prices don't matter anymore!"

Predictably, the audience cheered wildly. Pammy smiled and soaked-up the adulation and affirmation. She fed-off her fans' collective energy and became supercharged. She felt so high; it was a far more intense and pleasurable feeling than any drug or alcohol could ever produce.

Being the first night of this new show, Pammy was still using the teleprompter to cue and remind her about her next line. It read, "Do you want to WIN? (*look serious and long pause.*) People who play along with the government's losing plan are LOSERS! (*wait for applause*) And you are JUSTIFIED in using the losers to achieve your necessary goals! (*repeat it again with a very firm and loud voice*) GOD WANTS YOU TO BE A SUCCESSFUL WINNER! YOU ARE JUSTIFIED TO USE THE LOSERS TO ACHIEVE YOUR GOALS! IT'S THE ONLY WAY TO SURVIVE! GOD WANTS YOU TO WIN...AGAIN, I ASK YOU, DO YOU WANT TO WIN?"

Pammy took a deep breath and digested what the teleprompter showed would be her next verbal salvo. However, what came out of her mouth next was far different from what was shown on the teleprompter. She said, "And the only way we can win—you, me, everyone—is to have a more giving mindset and to watch out for each other!"

At first, she didn't even hear what she had just said. It was as if she heard herself saying what she read on the teleprompter. Her inner ear heard that instead of what actually came from her lips. Then she noticed the stunned looks on her fans' faces; they were staring at her in confusion. Their silence was also unnerving. It sounded as though everyone had left the arena at once, yet they were all still there.

"What the...?"

Pammy's spoken words caught-up to her racing mind. She then realized that the words she had spoken were not hers. She had difficulty processing what was happening. Reality didn't make sense.

"Pull yourself together," Pammy said to herself. She convinced herself that her imagination had run amok and shrugged it off. She started again.

"This garbage about using other people for your own personal gain is embarrassing! You all have a conscience. We *ALL* know that it's just not right!"

This time, she heard the words in real time as they left her mouth. Pammy was at a complete loss for what was going on. She was trying to form the words that she read on the teleprompter, but they came out differently; they weren't at all what she was trying to say.

Pammy remained silent for fifteen agonizing seconds; a fleeting moment that felt to her like an eternity. Audience members close to the stage and those whose eyes were fixed on the massive screens flanking each side of the stage couldn't help but notice that the color had drained from Pammy's face.

This was truly one of the most terrifying moments of her life. She initially thought she was having a stroke. What followed was a mini panic attack. She became light-headed and her world felt like it was spinning. She took two steps toward the podium; a speaker's fixture that she generally avoided standing behind. Pammy grabbed the podium with both hands, holding-on for dear life, as she felt like she was about to do a face plant in front of thousands of her adoring fans.

Her audience was confused. Some in attendance believed that she was playing a game; like she was trying to grab their attention by saying the opposite of what they expected her to say. However, her eyes revealed genuine panic and fear.

As she stood there feeling more vulnerable and exposed than she had ever felt on stage, she wondered if it was just a dream. "Yes, absolutely, this is a nightmare," she said to herself.

But clearly, it was not a dream. Pammy realized that she was very much in a conscious state and was very much in trouble. It's human nature to search for a logical explanation when the bizarre or inexplicable occurs. The more bizarre the occurrence, the more likely we are to accept preposterous explanations. Pammy was no exception to that way of thinking. She began to wonder if it was possible that somebody or something had hijacked her ability to speak. As implausible as that seemed, the explanation was the only one that she could conceive.

Pammy tried a third time to verbalize the words that she intended to say. She studied the teleprompter, quickly memorizing what she had *wanted* to say moments earlier and opened her mouth. She tried with all of her core to push the desired words out of her mouth. She focused like never before on pursing her lips and moving her tongue very deliberately in order to produce the sounds and words she wanted to say.

She pushed those words out of her mouth with tremendous vigor. Yet, what happened on this third attempt was devastating. She heard herself speaking the desired words, yet they seemed to transform instantly as they escaped her mouth.

"We can only truly win when everyone wins! Greed has no place in success!"

One of the most astonishing things was that the harder she tried to stick to her script and control her words, the more emotional and convincing she sounded. Almost half of Pammy's followers got up and walked out of the arena. These newer recruits were the ones who were drawn to the new Pammy who preached about the virtues of greed, selfishness and exploitation. Many of the ones who remained were her original fans who stuck with her over the years.

When you're in front of tens of thousands of people who are suddenly judging your every word and something has gone terribly awry with your plan, you have to think on your feet and make a very quick decision. Pammy decided to finish her show.

However, she quickly realized that it was not hers to decide. She wanted to say that the show was over. She wanted to walk off the stage. Both of these actions were impossible.

About an hour into her show, Pammy actually became somewhat less agitated with whatever it was that was happening to her. She stopped fighting the unfamiliar script that was flowing so easily from her mouth. She more or less yielded to it and let it happen. Really, she had no choice.

The ticket-holders that remained in the arena loved what Pammy (or whoever or whatever she was) had to say. This was the Pammy they knew and loved; the Pammy they were initially drawn to. Understandably, she finished her show early that night and made a quick exit. Her manager and handlers had no idea what was going on, but they whisked her off to a limo that was waiting near the arena's loading docks.

Pammy had planned to stay overnight at the poshest of all hotels in the show's host city. When she and her personal manager entered the hotel lobby, the hotel manager greeted her and handed her an envelope. She told Pammy that somebody left it for her in advance of her check-in.

"More useless fan mail," she thought, tossing the envelope into her leather messenger bag, where it nestled between her tablet and another envelope containing that thousand-dollar bill. Within minutes, she was safely ensconced in her hotel room, wearing her comfy pj's and trying to digest what had happened.

There was no getting around it. What happened to her that night was huge. It was a significant turning point in her life, one she would never forget and never want to relive. It wasn't the type of thing that she could just open-up about and share with someone...anyone. She couldn't just ask a friend—even her best friend—to join her for a coffee and say, "By the way, my performance last night was hijacked by some paranormal force. Everything I said was twisted into different words that I didn't intend to say."

Pammy was concerned about what the press would say. She thought it was highly unlikely that her major change of perspective would elude the media. But she had no idea how to tackle the hard questions that would surely come. A thousand things were going through her mind, keeping sleep at bay until morning arrived.

Pammy feared that her career was officially kaput. Trying to climb her way out of a pit after her conviction for tax evasion was hell. She wondered if this verbal hijack humiliation would throw her into an abyss that she ultimately could not climb out of. The prospect of it happening again was terrifying! If she had no control over the words coming from her mouth, she could say some truly scandalous things that she didn't mean. But the biggie, the huge question that was hanging over her head like a sledgehammer, was the mystery of *what* was happening to her.

Time away from the stage—away from everyone—was crucial. She needed to try and figure things out. To that end, Pammy instructed her manager to postpone her next four weekend shows. She needed a month, at a minimum, to calm her anxiety and to—hopefully, eventually—get a handle on what was happening to her. Figuring out her next steps was far too much in the future to even consider.

Home was too familiar a place to provide any relaxation or clarity. A few weeks at an ultra-private resort in the Turks and Caicos was more like what she had in mind. The exorbitant cost wasn't a deterrent; Pammy hadn't even given it a second thought. It goes with the territory when you have her kind of new worth. Furthermore, the offensive price guaranteed seclusion, which was precisely what she needed. Pammy had stayed there once before just to be pampered while soaking-up the tropical sun, but this time it was critical to her sanity. Or so she thought...

After spending a few days trying to decompress on the beach, Pammy came to the disheartening realization that no amount of sun, sand, margaritas, massages, hot stone spa treatments or plush bedding would make things seem right. She knew that she needed to deal with the elephant in the room.

She had her manager upload the digital file from the recording of her last performance. Pammy had all of her shows recorded, going back several years. She often watched the new ones in order to improve on any weaknesses they may have revealed. Of course, watching this particular show had nothing to do with tweaking her performance. Perhaps, she thought, it might provide some clues as to what had happened to her.

Obviously agitated, Pammy sat on the edge of her bed, clenching her tablet so hard that she left thumb and finger impressions in its leather case. Her eyes were glued to the screen. She watched every little detail. Nothing looked out of the ordinary from the moment she stepped on stage up until just before the first of the unintentional words left her mouth.

However, when her intended words were hijacked for the first time, she noticed something unusual. She kept playing that short clip over and over again in slow motion. She was astonished at what she saw. Just as her mouth began to open, her eyes rolled back partially under her eyelids for a tiny fraction of a second. It was such a short time, nobody in the audience would have noticed it. But it *did* happen. Pammy didn't know what it meant, but it definitely occurred and clearly had something to do with the event that followed.

The recording then revealed something else; something just as peculiar. As her mouth formed what she knew were someone else's words, Pammy noticed that she stared at one point slightly toward her left and didn't take her eyes off that spot until she stopped talking.

The recording also confirmed Pammy's worst fears about her appearance. She watched in dismay as her video-self stumbled toward the podium and took hold of it. Tiny beads of perspiration fell from her forehead and her right hand was shaking. She believed that everyone attending the show could tell she was disoriented, dizzy and panicked.

Pammy felt sick to her stomach as she re-lived the awful experience. It was just too much for her to bear. For a fleeting moment, Pammy thought about her ex-husband and craved his comforting embrace. She wanted to cry and feel his warmth as he cradled her; something he had often done when they were together. She longed to hear him tell her that everything would be okay. She missed *who he used to be* so much at that moment. Despite his infidelity, she couldn't deny her longing. However, she was also ashamed for having those feelings, because he had caused her so much hurt and anger. She didn't understand why she still missed the louse.

Pammy dabbed her tears and hesitated. She didn't want to look at the recording anymore. It was too painful to relive. She was terribly embarrassed for herself to have performed so unprofessionally in front of such a large audience. However, she knew that she had to get to the bottom of what happened.

As difficult as it was, she continued to watch the show. She noticed a pattern. Each time she began speaking words that she had not intended it was the same routine; the rolling eyes for a millisecond, followed by the stone-like gaze in the same spot.

Was she in some sort of trance? Had she been possessed? Or was it nothing more than a cruel joke played by some mysterious universal force? The questions kept coming, but there were no answers.

It was getting late in the day and Pammy hadn't eaten dinner. She decided to venture out of her villa and visit the pool bar, where she hoped to nibble on whatever happy hour appetizers were available. Of course, that meant washing them down with copious amounts of wine.

The bar wrapped around one of the four curved corners of the larger of two resort pools. Bar stools lined the patron side of the bar. The serving side of the bar was sunken. The bar extended into the pool, where plastered guests often sat with their bottoms under the water.

Pammy made it a rule to never sit on those submerged seats nor to venture very close to anyone occupying them when she took a dip in the pool. She noticed that, despite sipping endless streams of rum drinks and frothy beers, nobody ever left the pool to pee.

By the time Pammy arrived at the bar, most of the resort guests were dining either in their private villas or in the trendy and tropical open-air restaurant on the property. It was a sprawling resort with limited accommodations. Being so exclusive and luxurious, the resort had few guests.

Despite that, Pammy recognized five people during her first few days there. They were all celebrities of one sort or another. Three of them were well-known Hollywood film stars; two of whom were in what she figured was a very temporary relationship. Another guest was a rather corrupt and flamboyant politician and the remaining celebrity was a sports hero with a household name.

Pammy was pleased that none of those famous guests were at the bar. It was fairly secluded; just a bartender and three people she didn't recognize. A couple sat at the far end of the bar; they were too enamored with one another to notice anyone else. There was also a single man sitting on one of those underwater barstools. His boiled lobster complexion suggested he had been sitting there in the sun for most of the day. He was far too sloshed to start-up or carry a conversation with anyone.

There's an unspoken rule at resorts like this. You will likely recognize others and they may recognize you, but social distance and discretion is expected unless you already have an existing relationship with each other.

Pammy ordered a glass of Sauvignon Blanc, her wine of choice. She drank it quickly, ordering her second glass only ten minutes later. Eldon obliged and asked if she would like to see a bar menu. It was past happy hour and the appetizers were long gone. Pammy was already feeling a bit woozy from the first glass, so she thought it would be a good idea to eat something sooner than later.

She ordered a bowl of black truffle potato soup and, for her entrée, grilled grouper on a bed of asparagus and balsamic-drizzled orzo. By the time a waiter emerged from the restaurant with her soup, Pammy was already working on her third glass of wine.

Her soup was delicious and she finished it quickly. Eldon was the consummate bartender. He saw the job as a true profession and was at the top of his class. In this respect, he was much like Pammy when she was a bartender far earlier in her career. Eldon saw and heard *everything* and never missed a beat.

Seeing that she was coming to the end of her soup, Eldon stealthily texted the kitchen to let them know. Shortly thereafter, the same waiter brought Pammy's grouper to the bar. Eldon sensed that she was ready for conversation.

"May I ask you something, Miss?" Eldon's deep, beautiful, round voice was so soothing. She didn't recognize his sing-song accent, but she thought it had a Caribbean influence.

"Of course."

"If you don't mind my saying, Miss, it seems like you're carrying the weight of the world on your shoulders."

Pammy thought she had concealed her emotions, but obviously not nearly well enough. She understood the bartender-patron relationship better than any other guest at the resort and trusted in Eldon's instinct and his discretion.

"You're very perceptive. I thought I hid it sufficiently."

"Sometimes, Miss, hiding our feelings achieves the opposite of what our heart and soul need. It's like putting a banana leaf on a deep machete wound. Nobody else sees it, but the wound just festers anyway."

"Call me Pammy. Please."

Eldon recognized her openness as a signal that Pammy was okay to talk about whatever was bothering her. He established a greater level of trust by revealing something more personal to her. He said, "Okay, Pammy. My name is Jeh, you know, like the letter 'J'."

"Jeh? But your nametag says Eldon."

"Ahh, Pammy, sometimes a nametag is just a starting point."

"How so?"

"It's my bartender name. My given name is Jeh."

"So, why don't you go by Jeh?"

"Fair question. For me, the name Jeh is very personal. It's a powerful name that I don't share with just anyone. And I don't believe that you are just *anyone*, Miss Pammy. There's nobody else like you!"

"You can drop the 'Miss' part, Eldon, just call me Pammy..."

Eldon interrupted her with a similar clarification. He pointed to his chest and said, "Jeh. Please."

"Okay, Jeh, so, why do you think that I'm more than, 'just anyone,' as you say?"

"Don't you believe that you're special?"

"I guess so, but you don't really know me."

"I know you well enough. I'm guessing that you were a bartender in another life. Am I correct?"

"How could you know that?" Pammy was a bit concerned. She wondered how he could have had such accurate insight into her early career. She thought it had to have been more than a lucky guess.

Eldon laughed heartily and said, "Miss Pammy, I am just that good a bartender. You know what I mean. We bartenders see a lot more than other people."

"Again, with the 'Miss Pammy'. You're not going to drop the Miss part, are you?"

"No, Miss Pammy."

"So, you actually sensed that I had been a bartender in my younger years? What gave it away?"

Eldon leaned forward and whispered, "I didn't really sense it at all, Miss Pammy. I know who you are. I know who most people are that can afford to stay here!"

He then pulled his smartphone from his back pocket and flashed the screen in her direction. It showed the results of a search for Pammy's career timeline.

"See, it's right here! Your bio says that you were a bartender before you started your career as a professional speaker."

Pammy began clapping. The couple at the end of the bar that had been getting far too intimate for a public place were momentarily distracted. They both looked in Pammy's direction and, disinterested, quickly returned to their physical exploration.

"Well bravo for you, Jeh! You found me out. Thank you, at least, for being honest. You could have led me on about being so perceptive."

"That wouldn't have been truthful, Miss Pammy. So, back to my initial question. Why is this most beautiful and successful woman sitting in front of me so troubled and lost?"

"Something happened to me during my last show. Something inexplicable and scary. I just started my new tour on my latest book and my first stop was in Houston. I still don't know what to make of it."

"What happened?

"Well, I don't know how to even explain what happened. It was, like, supernatural or something. Shortly after I began my show, I thought I was having a stroke."

"Are you okay now? I mean, you didn't have a stroke, right?"

"No, but it sure seemed like it at first. The crowd was super charged and, like I've never felt that much energy at one of my shows. But it was a different kind of energy than before. Like, kind of on the cusp of being out of control. I hate to say it, but maybe even dangerous."

Eldon maintained a poker face. He was clearly interested and invested in what Pammy had to say, but his expression revealed nothing in terms of how he felt about what she was saying.

Pammy didn't understand why she felt so comfortable opening-up with such authenticity to a virtual stranger. This was one of the most terrifying and private things that she had ever experienced, and here she was, about to spill her guts to a bartender who she hadn't even known an hour before.

She began to feel vulnerable. Looking for reassurance that it was safe for her to be so open, she drew herself closer to him and whispered, "I don't know if I should be sharing this with you. I haven't shared this with anyone else, except for my manager."

"Look, Miss Pammy, deep in your soul, you know you can trust me. You may not realize it right now, but *you* came to *me*. And I'm happy you did. So, tell me, what happened?"

His words resonated with Pammy and gave her the reassurance that she sought, However, there was something more. Something indefinable, incorporeal, emanated from this man. Whatever it was, it filled her heart with peace and trust. She felt calmer and more hopeful than she had felt in years.

"You were saying that the crowd was feeling out of control?"

"Yes, it was strange. They began chanting my name and yelling phrases from my new book. It felt great and scary at the same time!"

"What felt great about it?"

"Well, you probably won't understand this, because, well, um, I don't want to sound condescending…I…you know, I better just keep my mouth shut."

"No, please, I have very thick skin! Please, tell me what you're thinking!"

"This is going to sound rude, but, look, you're a bartender. You've never been in my position, so I don't think you can really relate to this. I…I don't mean to sound haughty by saying that, but, when you're on a stage with fifty-thousand adoring fans listening to your every word, there's no high like it! Seeing and hearing them go nuts to every word I say is incredibly energizing…it's like being superhuman."

"I've not been on a stage like that, but I think I can imagine a little bit of what that must be like. So that's the great part of it. What about the scary part?"

"It's scary when you feel like your audience is in a frenzy and you've lost control over them. But there's more. I now realize something else."

"What's that?"

"So, it's been less than a week since this happened, but I've done a lot of thinking about things during this time. I don't know how it happened or even when, but sometime during the last ten years or so, my message changed. I now realize that I migrated from a motivational speaker to an inspirational and sort-of weird spiritual speaker. I'm too embarrassed to admit the rest. Seriously."

"Okay. I don't want to press and make you feel uncomfortable, Miss Pammy. You're here to relax and feel better, right?"

Pammy considered just leaving it at that and returning to her villa. But that didn't feel right. She realized that doing so would merely catapult her back into the desperate and depressed state she was in before she started talking with him.

"Listen, Eldon..."

Eldon interrupted, saying, "Jeh, please."

"Okay. Jeh, my embarrassment is about what and who I've become. I'm ashamed at what my books promote and I'm mortified at the thought of the harm that I've caused."

"Explain it to me. Please, I'm not sure I follow. You've done a lot of good through your career, Miss Pammy, I'm sure of that."

"I *DID* some good, for sure. But lately, I've encouraged my readers and fans to embrace greed, anger, self-interest and...and...um," Pammy froze. She looked down at what was left in her wine glass and exhaled deeply.

Eldon could have expressed disapproval, but instead, remained silent and smiled gently.

"...and I actually told my fans that it was not only okay, but was admirable to exploit the weak. I see this now. I didn't before, but I understand how terribly far off I strayed."

"That sounds dreadful! I'm so sorry that you experienced this aspect of humanity. It's unsettling to see how easily people can be led to some pretty dark places. Why do you think your fans did that?

"What? I don't understand. How would *I* know?" Pammy looked confused.

"Look, Miss Pammy, sometimes people are led astray. They end-up going in the wrong direction and visit places that cause bigger problems. Other times, they go to those places willingly. Either way, it's unfortunate, and I feel disappointed when that happens."

"That makes sense. So, remind me, what did you just ask?"

"Why were your fans so gullible? Why did they embrace such negative messages so willingly?

The encouragement that Pammy had felt in talking with the bartender vanished. Her face showed it. She said, sheepishly, "I think they fell for it because I made it okay in God's eyes. I basically fed them a bullshit line that God wants us to be powerful and rich, and..."

Her voice became weak. She regained her composure and said, slowly and quietly, "I've been saying that, in God's eyes, it's justified if we step on people to get what we want, because He has given everyone the same opportunities. I told my fans that it's just too bad if some people won't take advantage of those opportunities."

Eldon said, "Ohhh, I get it. Kind of like leading a horse to water, but not being able to force it to drink?"

"Sort of. But I failed to recognize that for many of those horses, the watering hole is dry. There's *no* water to drink. And that's because I encouraged people to take, not only their own share, but to basically steal others' shares as well."

Eldon's eyes began to tear-up. He said nothing and allowed Pammy to continue unloading.

"Prey on the vulnerable; that was basically my message. If others aren't quick enough, smart enough or privileged enough, take whatever little they have." She closed her eyes and shook her head from side to side, then said, "I'm so embarrassed. I've really screwed-up."

Jey held out his hand to comfort Pammy. She grasped his hand and squeezed it tightly. She felt as though she was transfused with new life. An indescribably intense sensation of love and hope filled her heart.

He poured some more wine into Pammy's glass and changed the subject. They talked about the beauty of the landscape and ocean, the stars in the sky and the very best aspects of human nature. Pammy forgot all about her voice hijacking incident and eventually returned to her villa, where she had a more restful sleep than she had experienced in years.

When she awoke the next morning, Pammy realized that, somehow, she never got around to sharing her frightening on-stage incident with the bartender. She recalled how, the night before, she had begun to tell the bartender about it, but, somehow, their conversation swerved in a different direction. Nevertheless, she didn't know why, but she was no longer concerned about it happening again.

Pammy stretched her body and focused for a few minutes on how comfortable the bed felt. She allowed herself to sleep-in a bit longer. The second time she awoke, she noticed how lovely the air smelled; the gentle breeze wafting through the window screen carried heady scents of seawater and tropical flora, which she found intoxicating!

It was already past nine-thirty and she was hungry. Breakfast service would be over soon, so she took a quick shower. Something was different. Living felt different; it was somehow richer and sharper than she ever remembered it being. As she showered, she concentrated on the wonderful sensation of warm water stroking her eyelids.

She threw on some knee-length shorts and a comfortable top. She felt lighter than usual. Just as she was about to leave for breakfast, Pammy noticed that she had left her tablet on the nightstand, so she went to lock it in the room safe.

As she picked up the tablet from the table, an envelope fell onto the carpet. It was the envelope containing that vintage thousand-dollar bill. Something didn't make sense; she had previously put that envelope in the safe. She wondered how it had become stuck to the bottom of her tablet.

She bent over to retrieve it. As she turned the envelope over, she realized that it wasn't the money envelope at all. It was a different envelope with an ivory hue; one that she didn't recognize. Her name was written in pen on the front.

Pammy walked it back in her memory and remembered that on the night of the disastrous show, the Houston hotel manager handed her an envelope just like it. She was so frazzled, she never did open it and immediately forgot that it ever existed.

Pammy sat down and opened the envelope. Inside was a single page of thick cottony paper. The writing matched the same lovely penmanship that was on the envelope.

> *"My dear Pamela, thank you so much for seeking me out and talking with me at the pool bar last night. It was truly a highlight of my day!*
>
> *I know that this must be very confusing to you, but please realize that I love you beyond your comprehension and have always loved you! You are a truly beautiful person.*
>
> *Please keep sharing my true message throughout the world, using the special talents that have been entrusted to you.*

I am ecstatic that you found your own beautiful voice again.

Love Jeh"

Pammy was absolutely overwhelmed. She was instantly flooded with emotion and began crying happy tears as she read Jeh's sentiment. She didn't fully comprehend its meaning, but it was like a seed that was beginning to sprout in her. Her first instinct was to rush to the poolside bar to find Jeh and talk with him.

Sun worshipping guests were already taking an early swim and splashing in the pool, while several hard-living partiers had already knocked back their third and fourth drinks at the swim-up bar. Pammy looked for Jeh, but he wasn't there.

She approached one of the two bartenders and asked when Jeh would be starting his shift. The man looked puzzled and said there was no bartender named 'Jeh' working there. She realized her mistake, and corrected it, remembering that Jeh's bartender name was Eldon.

The man just shrugged and said that there had only been three bartenders working at the resort in the past four years; he and the woman to his left, and the nighttime bartender named Jameison. He then explained that Jameison had taken ill a few days prior and that's why the pool bar was closed the night before.

Pammy insisted that she had been at the bar the previous evening and that she stayed until the bartender, Eldon, closed it. She maintained that she had talked with Eldon for a long time and then described his appearance. The bartender apologized and said that nobody looking like that ever worked there. He didn't want to be rude, but drink orders were beginning to pile-up, so he moved-on to tend to other guests' endless thirsts.

On her way back to the villa, it dawned on Pammy that she had been handed the envelope containing Jeh's note several days before she even met him. It was handed to her well before she even got on the plane that took her to the islands. She didn't understand how Jeh's note foretold the future; how he wrote about their time together before it even happened.

She picked-up her pace and raced back to her villa. She couldn't wait to read Jeh's note again. She mentally retraced her steps and saw herself placing the note on the nightstand, the envelope on top of it, then securing them both in place with her phone.

Pammy tapped her key-card several times to unlock the villa's door, but it wasn't working. She was so flustered she wasn't paying attention to what she was doing and tapped the wrong spot. She tried again, this time more deliberately, and tapped the contact just above the door handle. The electronic lock made a subtle ding sound and its indicator glowed green. She opened the door and went directly to the bedside table.

Her phone was there, but the note and envelope had vanished. In their place was a Bible, left open as if someone had carelessly thrown it there. She initially felt violated, assuming that someone had broken into her room. She looked through her personal items in the drawers and examined the contents of the safe, in the process, realizing that nothing had been taken.

She wondered who could have wandered-off with Jeh's note and why they would have even taken it in the first place? She started to feel anxious, but the sensation left before it even had a chance to bother her. The fact that she no longer felt the angst and dread that she felt when she arrived at the resort really began to sink in. Her systemic anxiety brought-on by the recent on-stage incident—her reason for coming to the resort—was gone. But it was far more than just that. She felt exceptionally calm and her heart was at peace.

Pammy did nothing in that moment, except to allow the feeling of serenity caress and envelop her; it felt to her like a cozy warm blanket. She couldn't remember how long it had been since she felt that way. She also experienced a sense of assurance, in that she only needed to be herself. It wasn't self-assurance as such. It was as if a powerful external force was telling her that she was perfect the way she was; that she need only listen to her heart and express what was there to others.

Suddenly, Pammy sensed that a veil had been lifted from her consciousness; she was able to understand things that had eluded her for years.

Although Jeh's note had disappeared, she could remember every word of it. Parts that were previously cryptic were suddenly clear. A vital clue was contained in the sentence about Jeh being ecstatic that Pammy had found her own voice. Although Pammy previously perceived the on-stage episode—when she spoke unintentionally—as a horrific moment in her life, she now saw it as a point of salvation!

At once, Pammy understood that the truthful and virtuous words that *did* come out of her mouth when she was on stage in Houston *were* her own words! She thought about Jeh, once again, and connected him to some sort of divine guidance that helped her find her true words.

Pammy continued to stand there silent and motionless as it all sunk in. Through her process of enlightenment, Pammy was given a vision. The vision was difficult to watch. The warm feelings of peace and love took leave momentarily as she experienced this revelation.

She saw her beautiful soul being covered by a mountain of deceitful and greedy garbage. That heap of garbage took years to grow as she became a corrupt servant to the worship of money and power. Her soul eventually become fully obscured as though one was trying to look through a filthy window. The film covering that window became thicker and darker. Out of that darkness, Pammy saw words swirling around like a swarm of stinging hornets. The hornets were in the form of words from her most recent books; words that she spoke to her fans.

As much as she didn't want to see any more of this dread, she was unable to look away. Pammy then saw herself dishonoring her own core values, believing her own lies and spreading them to fans. As the vision ended, she gasped when she saw that the hornets were flying from her mouth, stinging and inoculating her fans. Those fans produced even more powerful hornets that they, too, began spreading to others.

The horrific vision disappeared in an instant. Pammy had no idea how long she had been standing there seeing it. She just knew that she, once again, felt the calm, loving embrace that she experienced just before the vision began.

You would presume that such a vision would make one feel ashamed. Not at all. Pammy was overjoyed! She was flooded with gratitude, realizing that she had been gifted with a life conversion. She understood that early in her process of conversion, her voice was never hijacked at all; rather, it was merely foretelling of what was to come.

Pammy was consumed by a desire to make-up for lost years and to make things right as quickly as she could. She gathered her personal items and began packing her bags. As she carefully folded and packed her clothing and other belongings, she thought of an idea for her next book and came-up with a tentative title. She would name it, "The Power of Truth and Love." She hadn't felt so excited about her career in several years!

Just before she left the room to check out, Pammy sat on the sofa to process everything that she had just seen and the range of emotions she felt. She thought about Jeh and how he seemed to be some sort of catalyst for her conversion. She wondered who he really was.

Was he an angel sent by God? Was he a long-departed relative who had come to visit her in a different form? Or was Jeh even there at all? Was *he* merely a vision? After all, she thought, earlier that morning, the poolside bartender said that nobody bearing his description ever worked there and that the bar had been closed the previous evening when she spoke with him.

Whoever or whatever Jeh was, whether he was real or not, none of that mattered. She felt drawn to Jeh and missed him.

She rose from the sofa and, just before grabbing her luggage, once again noticed the Bible that someone had left on the nightstand. She walked over to it and took a second look at the open pages. Although she was brought-up in the Christian faith and attended church in her youth, she had never considered herself a 'churchie' kind of person. Other than recalling certain readings from church services, she couldn't recite much else from the Bible. In fact, she had never actually *read* the Bible, beyond scanning some of its Psalms while sitting in a church pew.

As she stared at the Bible, her eyes were drawn to a passage in the Book of the Prophet Isaiah, Chapter 12. She read it aloud and was mesmerized by the depth of its meaning and by how much it touched her heart.

> ***"AND in that day, thou shalt say, 'Oh Lord, I will praise thee: for though you were angry with me, thine anger is turned away and thou comforted me.' Behold, God is my salvation; I will trust and not be afraid: for the Lord JEHOVAH is my strength and my salvation!"***

She read it three times, each time more slowly and consciously than the last. The third time, she stopped after reading the name

"JEHOVAH" and, suddenly, made the connection between the biblical Jehovah and her mysterious bartender Jeh.

Not fully understanding the passage or the origins of the name Jehovah, Pammy quickly searched for it on her phone. She was not prepared for what she was about to read.

She was entirely taken aback as she read the search results.

> *"Jehovah is the principal figure, God, in the Hebrew Bible, the Old Testament; He is the Creator of all things. In modern day Christian Bibles, he is known by the names Yahweh, God and Lord."*

* * *

It was just another flight home. Pammy had been on so many flights to and from her performances, special appearances and book signings, that she lost count of them decades earlier. However, despite having flown on so many different planes from here to nowhere and back, she was never a fan of air travel; she was always apprehensive about safety and never felt comfortable until she was back on terra firma.

Pammy watched the flight tracker on the video screen in the back of the seat in front of her. She was happy to see her jet crossing from over the ocean to dry land. As she sipped her coffee and poked at a particularly bland in-flight meal, Pammy realized that she had never been so relaxed on a plane and had never before looked forward to *returning* from a vacation!

She thought about Jeh, how intensely she felt drawn to him and his transformative impact on her. She was humbled and deeply appreciative for the gifts that Jeh gave her; the gift of forgiveness, grace to be granted a second chance and joy to experience the purest love she had ever known.

CABERNET FRANC
EASILY OVERLOOKED

If a glass of Cabernet Franc were to be placed in front of a random group of red wine drinkers, most of them would have no idea what type of wine they just tasted. Once shown the bottle, fewer, still, would know how to pronounce its name. Of course, the "Cabernet" part is easy, but people often butcher the second part. Common mispronunciations often sound like "Frank," "France" or "Fronce." To be frank (*awful pun*), that's not how the French pronounce it and they know best, since this varietal originated in France!

For those who care to know, add a hard "k" to the end of the word "Frawhn." If you're doing it right, it should rhyme with the word "honk."

Even though you may not have been aware of it, you've likely swigged Cabernet Franc before. It's one of the oldest grape varieties on this planet, thriving in countries such as France, Italy, Chile, Argentina, United States and even Canada. It's the parent grape of both Cabernet Sauvignon and Merlot, and it's used today both as a single varietal and to blend in a wide variety of red wines.

It's a wonderfully versatile varietal, both in terms of how it ends up in the bottle as well as in how it adapts to different climates. In cooler regions, such as the Loire Valley in France, Upper New York State in the U.S. and the Lake Erie North Shore area in Ontario, Canada, it's vinified into wines that have moderate body, higher acidity and cherry-raspberry flavors. However, in warmer regions, such as southern areas of France, Tuscany in Italy, California in the U.S. or the warmer central valleys of Chile, it reveals more body, bolder fruit flavors and higher tannins.

Cabernet Franc is found in some of the most average wines around...as well as in some of the most expensive and complex wines in the world, such as many first growth French Bordeaux and "Super Tuscan" Italian wines.

If you've been reading this book from the beginning, you are likely expecting a short story to begin peeking out from under the covers. Well, you won't be disappointed! Everyone likes a story they can relate to; this one may feel distinctly familiar. But, just like an ordinary dessert, it becomes far more special when served with a little cherry on top.

This story has something to do with one of the prime traits of Cabernet Franc; that of *versatility*. Goodness, there's no arguing that versatility—or flexibility—as it's often called, is such an important characteristic in our world; particularly in the world of work. However, sometimes people become stuck on the career ladder because they are so good at such a wide variety of tasks, that they become too valuable to promote.

The main character of our story, Franck *(of course, pronounced the same way as our aforementioned wine),* works for a pulp and paper goods manufacturing company headquartered in Colorado. The company has branch offices across the country, along with satellite offices in the U.K., Canada, Germany and France. They also have manufacturing facilities in multiple domestic and international locations that are in heavily forested areas that support the paper pulp industry. For most people, it's pretty boring stuff.

Franck's surname begins with the letter "B". You really don't need to know his entire last name, because, frankly, Franck is a nobody. Like hundreds of millions or even billions of people who work on this planet, Franck isn't particularly notable, memorable or celebrated when it comes to his job.

Collectively, Franck and his millions or billions of versatile counterpart workers *are* absolutely invaluable...however, they would never know it based on how they're treated by their superiors. And as invaluable as they may be, they are also highly replaceable. As individuals, Franck and the rest of the Francks out there are, well, somewhat disposable.

Truth is, while Franck is an extremely important "cog in the wheel" of a huge and impersonal organization, there are many more Franck-like cogs out there who can replace Franck at a moment's notice. They, too, are versatile workers who do a good job at a variety of tasks.

Speaking of replacing other cogs, Franck has also replaced his share of other workers who retired, quit or were unceremoniously shown the door by security. Along the way, Franck also replaced a few people who were groomed and promoted. That means that he was neither groomed nor promoted. Get it? It's just the way these things work.

What if Franck *wasn't* all that flexible? What if he was more of a unique individual? Well, without that ability to adapt, multitask and perform different tasks successfully, chances are, he wouldn't be working for the pulp and paper company that provides that almighty paycheck. Perhaps he wouldn't be working very successfully anywhere at all.

Scour any open job board or online job bank and take a close look at what the successful candidate needs to bring to the table. Yes, there are specific academic qualifications, certifications, years of experience doing this or that and a host of other requirements. And then there are the personal characteristics that any employer needs. Among those, the person being hired must almost always be *flexible*.

There's that word again. Flexible. If you think about it, the work world has become a far more demanding place in the last four or five decades, in terms of the need for flexibility. It's ubiquitous these days. There was a time when employers needed and truly valued specialists; trained professionals, tradespersons and everyone in-between. In other words, people who excelled in their respective fortes.

Franck didn't have the opportunity to excel at anything; just be flexible and get the job done. It's not a great recipe for employee morale or job satisfaction.

After a particularly difficult day, Franck decided to do something wildly uncharacteristic on his way home. Frustrated with his inability to climb the company ladder and feeling unappreciated, Franck decided to make a pit-stop at a local bar before continuing on to his home to have dinner with his wife, Margie.

Feeling a bit uncomfortable as this was way out of his normal routine, Franck plopped himself onto a barstool and ordered a double bourbon with a single cube of ice. The bartender went to grab a bottle of well bourbon, but Franck insisted on a more expensive and far better brand that was sitting on the shelf above. That was also uncharacteristic. Under normal circumstances, Franck would never have spoken-up; he would rather just take the inferior booze and say nothing more.

The bar was mostly empty, except for a few guys playing pool in the corner and a couple sitting at a darkened booth. Frank noticed that they were both wearing wedding rings, but were clearly not married to each other. The novelty of whatever kind of relationship they shared was evident, as was the fact that they were anxious to be physical with one another.

Franck shook his head, disappointed with their dishonesty and dishonor. He could tell that the bartender was also fully aware of what was going on. Judging from the bartender's expression, Franck could tell that he also didn't approve.

"Can you believe that? That couple over there? Pretty pathetic, when you think about it, huh?"

"Hey buddy, it's nothing new. I see it all the time. I've never seen this particular couple before, but they're all the fuckin' same, just different bodies and faces."

"Doesn't it get to you? I mean, the cheating. The dishonesty. Like, I'd never do that to my wife. Don't get me wrong. Things aren't perfect between us and we've got our struggles like anyone, but one thing that we do have is trust in each other."

"Yup," the bartender concurred, "that's something those cheaters will never know. Yah. Now you. I've never seen you in here before...what's on your mind?"

"Just feeling down in my work. To be painfully honest, I've never been given an opportunity to really shine." Franck looked up as though he just remembered something. "Hmph, well, actually, a few years back I was given a new portfolio and I really kicked ass. Completely nailed it."

"And, so what was the upshot of that?"

"They removed me from that job and moved me along to something far less challenging. It was like they were uncomfortable with the improvements I was making. Bizarre."

"Not at all," the bartender said. "I see it all the time, guys like you. The guys at the top don't really want progress. Today, that kind of thinking is passe. As industry touts its own progress with excellence in all phases of operations, the truth is that anyone who can remember life and work, say, thirty or forty years ago, knows it's a bunch of hogwash."

Franck was surprised by the bartender's unusually coherent grasp on the subject, but then felt guilty for pre-judging him based on his occupation. Trying his best not to sound condescending,

Franck said, "You've got a good head on your shoulders. Most people can't see beyond the obvious or what they've been told."

"Not bad for a bartender, eh?" The bartender smiled slyly. Although it sounded like self-deprecation, what he said was actually intended to underscore the fact that he did have a superior intellect.

"What's your name?"

"Franck. What's yours?"

"Tom." He reached out and shook Franck's hand and said, "Good to meet you."

"To me, Tom, it's like our world's gotten so much more complex. Technology is through the roof, but I'm not convinced that it's contributed to humanity in any meaningful way...certainly not in the workplace."

"Fuckin' right about that. Has your life really gotten any easier? Has the *quality* of your life or of your work life gotten any better?"

Franck held his chin high and shook his head. He shifted his gaze back at Tom and said, "No. Things used to be far easier and were way more enjoyable. And nowadays, the workplace is fascinated with multitasking and centralization. It just makes people feel like damn machines."

Tom nodded in agreement. "I'm going to tell you something else I've also noticed. Nobody talks about it, but it's happened all around us. Every company, every workplace, every job..." Tom's voice grew louder and more serious. He may not have realized it, but he began thumping his closed fist on the bar counter. "There used to be employees with unique skills; people who were *really* good at their jobs. Today they call anyone a 'Specialist', even though they don't know shit."

"You're *so* right! I look around work and all I see any more, are all-in-one wonders of mediocrity who can do anything, but who can't do anything exceptionally well. Now, everything is consistent, but nothing is very good."

"Frank..."

Franck interrupted Tom. He respectfully clarified how to pronounce his name. "It's Franck."

"Yah, sorry, Franck. Here's the thing. Everyone in the world has lower expectations now. I think it's been purposely cooked into the system. Efficiency, uniformity, profit. It has nothing to do with what people really want, but we completely accept the bullshit. We even expect it."

"What do you mean?"

"Well, like even here at this bar. When you asked for a bourbon, I automatically reached for the crap stuff. Most people don't care. It's like they've been trained not to complain about poor service, poor anything, and are genuinely surprised when they get anything better than poor or average."

"Whoa! Tom. You're speaking my language. I waited on the phone today, on a single call, for forty-eight minutes, just waiting to speak with a real human. There I am following-up on an overdue account...like WAY overdue and a HUGE balance...and instead of that client going out of their way to call me and try to make arrangements to pay, I'm expected to hunt them down and then wait on hold for forty-eight fucking minutes just to be turned-around by a centralized dipshit who couldn't understand who I needed to speak with and then who cut me off!"

"Tell me you didn't call back and wait another forty-eight minutes?"

"No. I'll probably do that again tomorrow. Unbelievable!"

"I'm telling you, Franck, it's everywhere. My wife and I got booted off a flight a few months ago. My dad had been rushed to the hospital and they said he could go either way. Of course, I booked a flight...paid full price on the earliest flight to Philly.

When we got to the gate, the clerk called me over to the desk and said the flight was overbooked and we'd have to take a later flight. I...I was livid! I even paid extra for the actual seat assignments so we could sit together...what the fuck did I actually pay for?"

Tom grew increasingly agitated.

"That's unforgiveable. What did you do?"

"Couldn't do much. I basically bent over and asked for more. Yah, sure, they ended-up paying for the flight and we got a voucher, but so what? I could care less about the money. Too little, too late."

"When did you finally fly out?"

"We didn't get to Philly until way later. Took a red-eye and by the time we got to the hospital, my dad was unconscious, He never came back. I never had the opportunity to tell him what I really needed to."

Sharing the story clearly knocked the wind from Tom's sails. His eyes welled-up and he looked defeated.

"I'm so sorry about your dad, Tom. I can't imagine how difficult that must have been, dealing with the airline on top of everything else."

"Stuff like that happens all the time these days."

They continued to chat for another ten more minutes, then Franck got a notification on his phone. It was a text from his wife, who was wondering when he would be home. He returned the text promptly, letting her know that he was on his way. Franck shook Tom's hand and thanked him for the conversation.

He took his wallet from his back pocket and Tom told him to put it away, saying that the drink was on the house. Franck was appreciative of the gesture. What really buoyed his spirits, though, was the opportunity to share his broad frustrations about the workplace and to hear Tom's own insights and experiences.

Over the course of the following evening and for most of the next day at work, Franck couldn't help but continue to reflect on the idea of the forced mediocrity of his own career. He became increasingly angry with the lack of recognition for his own workplace contributions, frustrated with the lack of opportunity to accomplish anything of true value and, most importantly, regretful of the precious time he had wasted there.

It happened to be the last day of his twenty-fifth year working for the same pulp and paper company. It was four-thirty and he planned to be on his way home in a half an hour. He glanced at the stack of business cards on his desk. The imprint read, "Frank B., Supervisor, Accounts Receivable, Home Office...blah, blah, blah, Colorado."

Franck began to reflect on his time with the company. He had been in the Accounts Receivable department for a year and a half. For him the work was very tedious, uninspired and unfulfilling. Over the years, Franck had been the recipient (or victim) of countless lateral moves. Prior to his current role, Franck was in yet another lower management position in Asset Management and before that, he was plunked into a special "hybrid" low rung managerial role in Strategic Initiatives and Programs.

That particular role was his favorite of all the different positions he held since he started working for the company, because he felt as though he was actually making a difference. And he was! Customer care surveys indicated a significant uptick in everything from product quality to customer retention in ways that directly stemmed from Franck's initiatives.

He was warned just before moving into that position that upper management didn't really want anyone who would make waves, change things very much or actually try to improve anything. Franck didn't listen to the good advice and that's why he lasted only a few years in that position; long enough for his superior's superiors to see that his tendency to deliver change and results could be problematic.

At 4:43 p.m., Franck glanced at the molded resin clock on his desk. The tiny timepiece featured a 3-D dolphin jumping through a wave that curled around the clock's dial. It was a kitsch little souvenir that his then five-year-old son, Brandon, wanted to give him. Frank and his family had been vacationing that summer in Myrtle Beach, South Carolina. Twelve years had passed since that summer, but it might as well had been fifty. Franck spent the remaining seventeen minutes of his day reminiscing about that trip and thinking about life in general.

Franck's mouth curled up in a bittersweet smile as he remembered how happy he and his family were on that vacation. He glanced at the few family photos on his desk. In one of the pictures, Franck, his wife and their two kids were building sandcastles on the beach.

He then picked-up a ceramic dish that his daughter, Melissa, made for him as a classroom project when she was in grade four. The little dish was decorated with flowers and was inscribed with a handwritten note that read, "I love you, Daddy." Now twenty years old, Melissa had just started working as a hairstylist for a nearby salon.

"How time flies," Franck thought wistfully.

He shook his head while thinking about how much simpler times were back then. He also couldn't let go of the nagging feeling that he had wasted twenty-five years of his career. During the last five of those years, Franck had grown increasingly bothered by the notion that he had been plugged into different roles that, ultimately, didn't allow him to make much of a difference. They didn't even begin to nibble at his true potential. However, he was flexible and obedient.

He couldn't shake the unnerving feeling that, if only he hadn't been so darned flexible, he would have made more of himself. He made it easy for his superiors to pluck him out of a round hole and plug him into a square one, just to be reassigned to an oval one after that. "Maybe, just maybe," Franck thought, "I would have shone brightly as someone who was tremendously valued and appreciated for the special talents that I actually have...had I just tried to shine more as an individual.

His son Brandon, was working in an HVAC job with a local contractor. He was a year away from completing his apprenticeship and was already making decent money. Franck thought about both of his kids and wondered if they could have done more, only if *he* had done more? He questioned if his own example to the kids played a part in limiting their own career paths?

Without considering his children's own part in choosing their respective career paths and his important role in supporting those choices, Franck fell deeper into an emotional pit of self-blame and worthlessness. He disregarded the fact that both of his children were, ultimately, interested in and happy with what they were doing.

Clicking his fingernails rhythmically on the desk while waiting out the last few minutes until five, Franck stared at his screen. He was looking at an email from his supervisor's boss, Finn Clarus, Vice President, Central Operations. Mr. Clarus wanted to see him in his office at the end of the day.

Franck hated the uncertainty that preceded such meetings. They were never scheduled in the middle of the work day. This type of meeting request was intimidating and was intended to show power. The email would come near the end of the workday, requesting a meeting the next morning. Alternatively, the message was sent first thing in the morning, requesting a meeting at the end of the day. Either way, there was never a mention of what the meeting was about and there would always be several hours to stew and agonize about it beforehand.

What did Mr. Clarus want? He didn't like the guy and sensed that the feeling was mutual.

He hated the fact that this senior executive insisted on being addressed by the formal salutation 'Mr.' "How pretentious," Franck thought!

His own boss didn't say much about Mr. Clarus, but she was just watching out for her own ass, which is something most people learn they have to do to survive in a large corporation.

Outside of occasionally seeing him in the elevator or on one of his rare walks through the department, Mr. Clarus was pretty invisible. Franck didn't have a lot of contact with him, but when he did, it was often uncomfortable and Clarus never went out of his way to make it less so. He was one of those guys that enjoyed the distance between himself and employees like Franck. His so-called "open-door policy" only existed on his own top floor. For workers like Franck, it was not only a closed-door office, but a closed-door elevator. There was no reason for an average employee to press that top button; doing so would produce an awkward and unnerving result.

What was it going to be this time? Would he be transferred to a new department? He hoped that wouldn't be the case. As much as he disliked where he was and what he was doing, it's the old "Devil you know" kind of deal. With every transfer, Franck had to learn how to navigate new systems and procedures, new policies, new coworkers and new bosses.

As his anxiety mounted, Franck's fingernail clicking became faster and more rhythmic. He began to play-out different scenarios in his mind.

He thought, "Is this some sort of passive-aggressive bullshit? That seems to be Clarus' style. Dangle a carrot on a stick, but beware of being whacked by that same stick."

He was partially correct in pegging Mr. Clarus as a sadistic son of a bitch. If Clarus ever doled-out an extra helping of anything, it was generally nasty. Franck imagined it this way, "The carrot on the stick is shriveled and rotten to begin with. Don't do it exactly his way and he berates me in front of others. Make him look bad and he rams the fucking carrot up my nose."

The alternative to a lateral transfer or passive-aggressive new assignment was far worse. Until that moment, Franck hadn't come to terms with it on a conscious level, but the possibility had been floating around in his subconscious mind all day. He felt angst about this meeting; he dreaded it through the day without realizing why. The resin dolphin clock continued to tick away through those last few minutes; each tick dragging-on more slowly than the last. Just before five o'clock, the thought percolated into his consciousness. "What if I'm being fired?"

He had just turned fifty-five. A few other employees around his age and at the same pay grade had recently been sacked for no apparent reason, other than what appeared to be purely age discrimination. He knew them personally; super flexible supervisory or lower management company men and women who became dissatisfied with the status-quo and futility of their jobs.

Those people became too dangerous to shift around anymore. They could infect other, more naïve and compliant employees with that kind of thinking. Because of the very culture of flexibility and mediocrity, they were easily replaced. The process was formulaic; the fired employee would retain legal counsel. A wrongful dismissal suit would customarily be settled out of court and life goes on. The cost of settling the civil suit was already baked-into the budget required to eject a potentially dangerous employee from the corporation.

Sad...so sad. Could this be Franck's last trip up the elevator? He wasn't prepared for this. Suddenly, it dawned on him how difficult it would be to find another job with comparable pay at his age.

He became angry. "You've got to be kidding me! I've got 10 years of work left in me, 15 years left on our mortgage, a way-too-underfunded 401K and...I...I could be out on my ass tonight!"

The elevator door closed. As he pushed the button for the 15th floor, Franck's eardrum began twitching and he could hear his heartbeat. He tried to catch a glimpse of himself. He bounced his head back and forth, trying to see his reflection in the stainless-steel plate that housed the elevator controls. His face was flushed and his eyes looked tired.

As the elevator door opened, Franck saw a group of senior executives huddled in front of one of the offices. They were all laughing. One of them was laughing so enthusiastically, he was bent-over with his hands on his knees. Frank thought whatever they were laughing at must have been quite the joke. "Maybe it's me," Franck said to himself. "Maybe I'm the big joke."

One of the executives noticed Franck getting off the elevator and motioned toward him. That's when he noticed that Clarus was part of the group.

Clarus looked at Franck and, at once, his smile dissolved into a scowl. The executive's change of disposition made Franck feel as if he wasn't senior enough or important enough to be worthy of the smiles and the jovial tone that the group of executives had just enjoyed. He wasn't one of them. He didn't belong. Hell, he didn't even belong on the floor. It was an exclusive club that he would *never* be part of.

"Franck, glad you didn't forget to come see me. I have some important news to share with you. Come on into my office and we'll go over this." Clarus' tone was not encouraging.

"Okay." Franck's voice was subdued. He tried to appear calm, but was a ball of nerves.

Clarus led Franck through the heavy wooden door and closed it behind him. Clarus was a good five inches taller than him, but to Franck, he seemed even taller than that. He motioned for Franck to have a seat and then turned his back on him. Clarus then walked over to the window and stood silently, just looking at the city beneath him for what seemed like an eternity. It was clear to Franck that Clarus was trying to make him squirm. He was correct in his assessment.

"So, let's get this over with." Clarus sat down and continued, saying, "This meeting has two parts. I'm starting the first part now."

Franck said nothing and took a labored breath. He could hear the air drawing into his own lungs in staccato spurts.

Reaching into his top right desk drawer, Clarus retrieved an envelope and handed it to Franck. With monotone delivery, Clarus said, "Five o'clock today marked your twenty-fifth year of employment with this corporation. On behalf of the C.E.O., I'm extending our heartfelt congratulations for reaching this milestone and for your dedicated service to the company."

Franck thought, "Heartfelt? Heartfelt, my ass!" Clarus' delivery was devoid of any joy or sincerity. Franck opened the envelope. Inside was a congratulatory form letter that was very impersonally auto-signed by the C.E.O., along with a $500 gift card to a high-end local restaurant.

"Thank you." Franck said nothing further, based on the negative dynamics of the situation.

"Sure thing. Treat your beautiful wife, Margie, and your children, Melissa and Brandon, to one of the finest dinners money can buy around here."

Franck was shocked that Clarus remembered, let alone, even *knew* his wife's and kids' names. Then he realized that Clarus was reading from what looked like a script on his phone.

A very awkward silence followed this clumsy first part of the meeting. Franck was waiting for the other shoe to drop. He had just experienced Clarus' passive side. He prepared himself to be struck by the wrath of Clarus' aggressive side.

"I said this meeting had two parts, so let's move onto the next part. As you well know, the pulp and paper industry has been hit hard by changing times and the overall shift to digital. Everywhere around the world, newspapers are either shutting down their print editions or have closed completely. People don't print anything anymore; they just click and send."

Franck's eyes grew wider. He could feel it coming. Still, he tried hard not to show his concern and remained poker-faced.

"The only product we sell that's managed not to lose money is toilet paper and even those sales are pretty shitty." Clarus didn't smile at his own little pun.

"Let me cut to the chase, Franck. Eyes and ears are everywhere in this organization. I know you're dissatisfied with your work and I think it's beneath your dignity to carry-on doing something that you feel is so far less than your potential."

There it was. He dangled the gift card like a carrot and was about to beat the hell out of him with the stick. Either that or shove the carrot up his nose, as predicted. Franck felt something well-up inside of himself; something he hadn't felt in a long time. He thought he had lost his self-respect, but just realized that it was merely dormant.

Franck shouted angrily, "Beneath my potential!? Give me a break! You may have temporarily beaten-down my dignity, but you never gave me a chance to even come close to my potential!"

Clarus was visibly shocked. He didn't expect Franck to respond with such force. His plan was not going the way he had expected. He apologized, saying, "I'm sorry. Poor choice of words."

"No, it wasn't a poor choice of words at all! You're absolutely right! Ever since I made actual progress... ever since I showed just a hint of my true potential as the Strategic Initiatives and Programs Manager, you saw fit to bury me...to make sure I couldn't make much noise or progress."

Franck was livid. Even *he* was stunned by the vigor in his own voice and in the words he chose.

Clarus glared at him and said nothing for the longest time. To say one could cut the tension with a knife was a huge understatement. Even a machete wouldn't have done the trick.

Clarus rose from his plush leather chair and, for the second time, walked toward the floor-to-ceiling window. He just stood there, silent and unwavering.

Franck couldn't read what was happening, but he started to regret very deeply his earlier outburst. His expression was at that point stoic. He didn't know whether or not to say anything; whether to apologize or to double-down.

Clarus turned half-way toward Franck. He squeezed his nose between his thumb and the side of his forefinger. He inhaled deeply and exhaled loudly. His tall frame looked so imposing against the window. He shook his head. It was a *tell*, but Franck couldn't discern what it told.

He returned to his desk and sat down. He bounced his flat hand on the desk four times and took a deep breath. He said, "I think you already know why I wanted to see you in person today. I made a decision. It was my decision and only my decision, but.."

Franck did his best to put on a brave face, interrupting Clarus, saying, "...but what?"

"...but I've changed my mind, Franck. Anybody in my position would be stupid to let you go. You're right. I did bury you. I never saw you as a threat, but you were getting in the way and it was far easier to just make you go away in the least painful way I knew. It happens all the time, but to be honest, you made it easier for me to do."

Franck, angry at Clarus' admission, said, "Don't put that on me. It may be hard for you to understand in your own privileged world, but with my modest salary and a family to look after, a mortgage that's like a chain around my neck and no special clout to pull out of my ass, it just seems like the responsible thing to do. Take the damned hits and shut my fucking mouth!"

"That's not how it was supposed to be," said Clarus, looking sheepish. "I should have supported and taken advantage of what you were offering. Instead, I smothered it. That had to be hard to take."

"Wait a second. Am I reading this right?" Franck wondered. Had he just witnessed a complete and total conversion of human spirit? It happened so rapidly, even Clarus hadn't seen it coming. But it was too big to ignore. Both men paused, as if in suspended animation. Time stood still for a moment as the men tried to process what was happening.

Franck pulled it together and said, "Yes, you did smother it. I'm sorry, but it had to be said, My potential, my enthusiasm, my special talents; basically wasted. It was very difficult to take and it still is. So, where do we go from here, Mr. Clarus?"

"Well, first of all, I owe you an apology. And it's Finn, not Mr. Clarus. I've been an asshole to you and I can't begin to even understand why I thought that was okay. Seriously, that wasn't right. Maybe someday I'll understand why I thought it was acceptable to treat you and so many other people so terribly. I don't expect you to accept my apology; I really don't deserve it."

Franck felt his anger and frustration begin to fade. For the first time since he started working for the company, he began to see Clarus as a person rather than as an uncaring, self-centered nemesis. Mind you, a person with tremendous faults, but, still, a person.

"Franck, I'd like to offer you the position of Director of Operations for our entire Western Division. I know it doesn't make-up for how I've treated you in the past, but maybe it's a start."

"I...I don't know what to say. I didn't expect this." Franck was confused. It was so far from what he was expecting.

"Say you'll take it," said Finn. "I wouldn't offer the position if I didn't truly believe that you're the best person for it. Tony dropped a bomb on us earlier today. He accepted a new position with our primary competitor. He was escorted out of the building just a few hours ago and...uh...we want to keep this as low profile as possible. I have the power, er, the choice, to get a headhunter involved or to make a decision and promote from within. And I just chose you."

"Yes. Absolutely, yes!" In his shock and enthusiasm, Franck felt like his entire world had just flipped upside-down. But it wasn't upside-down at all; it was how his world *should* have been all along.

Franck's head was anywhere but on the road during his drive home. He replayed the highlights of his meeting with Clarus over and over again in his head, but as much as he loved how the meeting ended, he couldn't comprehend that it actually did.

"Why," he wondered, "did Clarus pivot one hundred and eighty degrees? I'm sure I'm not the first person who spoke-up for themselves and gave the douchebag a dressing-down."

As he thought about it, Franck remembered other coworkers who once stood-up to Clarus. Each one had their asses handed back to them along with their walking papers. Why was it different for him? Clarus started off their meeting being the same son-of-a-bitch he had always been.

Franck was right to question it. People don't just go and instantly change who they are after having been cruel and arrogant excuses for skin for most of their lives. Franck realized that personal epiphanies are rare in the first place and are even rarer based on the little bit of resistance he gave Clarus.

It was the last time Franck would ever think about it. Whatever was behind Clarus' conversion was none of Franck's business and it didn't really matter. He turned his focus, instead, to the reality that *he* would be riding that elevator to the top floor, that his value was finally being recognized properly and that he had greater control over his path moving forward than he had ever had before.

Franck pulled into his driveway. Up until that moment, his home had been his refuge from work. It still felt comforting to come home to his family, but he no longer felt like he needed a protective sanctuary from the negativity of work. A new flame had been lit.

Margie thought Franck looked different when he walked through the front door. She chalked it up to the golden sun of dusk that was beginning to set behind him, but he really *did* look younger, taller and more vital. She asked, "How was your day, honey?"

Before Franck could answer, Margie interrupted her own question. As she gave Franck a once-over, she smiled playfully and said, "...and, don't get a big head, but you look damned handsome!"

Franck kissed her cheek and said, "It was uneventful for most of the day. Oh, but I did learn some news just before I left."

PINOT NOIR
A DISTINGUISHED GENTLEMAN

Its fruit is thin-skinned, it's a notoriously finnicky grape to grow and winemakers find it particularly challenging to turn into a consistently good wine from one vintage to the next. Of course, we're talking about Pinot Noir, one of the more storied varietals in the world of wine!

While Cabernet Sauvignon is a red wine varietal that's often referred to as the King of Wines, Pinot Noir wine grapes have been around for more than a thousand years longer than the "King." Pronounced "Pee-No-No-Are," its wines may not be as universally popular as Cabernet, but wines made from Pinot Noir grapes still tend to fetch higher prices on average than do wines made from Cab grapes.

Yes, there are a lot of Pinot Noir fanatics that are willing to pay a virtual ransom for well made Pinot's! The fact that the wines can vary so greatly from vintage-to-vintage despite being grown on the same land and made by the same vintner, only adds to their legendary allure.

Pinot Noir wines tend to be fruit-forward with a medium body. Although fine examples of it usually have soft, round tannins (the stuff that makes some wines puckery and occasionally even bitter) this grape can deliver powerfully rough tannins if not tamed properly in the growth and winemaking phases.

In France, Burgundy wines are synonymous with Pinot Noir, however, the grape is grown and fermented into red wine all over the world! Now, if you're wondering if this varietal has any connection to the other Pinots—Pinot Grigio, Pinot Blanc and Pinot Gris—those lighter colored white wine grapes are all genetically related to the darker red wine grape Pinot Noir.

While there are scores of stories about famous winemakers, and their particular triumphs and disappointments working with Pinot Noir, there is *one* story that really stands out among them. Meet Lang Wodrowe.

Lang wanted to be seen as a highly esteemed individual in all of his endeavors. He wanted the world to know that he had superior intelligence and proficiency, and squandered a great deal of time and energy trying to convince others that he was a very distinguished gentleman.

Despite his ardent efforts to establish such a veneer, he was nevertheless known by others as an arrogant and egotistical little man.

Lang Wodrowe, that is, Dr. Langdon Malachi Wodrowe, was a tenured university professor who, after divorcing his third wife in just eleven years, finally came to a conclusion. He thought it was extremely unlikely that he would ever find a partner who could live up to his high ideals or who was worthy of his magnificence.

The truth? He was exceptionally difficult to live with. His standards were unattainable and often ridiculous. To make matters worse, the professor wasn't particularly fond of others. He had little interest in anyone else and, therefore, had little use for them.

Shortly after his third divorce was finalized, a date that coincided with his 46th birthday, Dr. Wodrowe decided to live a single life. He dated occasionally, although nothing ever stuck and he was fine with that.

During these occasional dates, the professor would typically fill any void in conversation with his own thick stream of strong opinions, tidbits of mostly useless knowledge and self-indulgent chatter. There wasn't much room for his date to join in the conversation and he rarely asked them anything about themselves.

Self-absorbed might be one adjective that aptly described the professor. Boorish might be another. But there were so many more that were needed to provide an adequate picture of who Dr. Wodrowe really was.

The professor insisted that others address him as his doctorate endowed; *never* as "Langdon," *not* as "Mr. Wodrowe," *only occasionally* as "Professor Wodrowe," and *almost always* as "Dr. Wodrowe."

His physical appearance was quintessentially professorial. He looked ten years older than he actually was. His disheveled salt and pepper hair was fashioned in a comb-over that covered a receding hairline; a hairline that was, annoyingly, moving northward with vigor. The hair that remained was more silver than black and he seemed to be losing that particular marathon as well.

He had a classic professorial mustache and goatee, and wore rectangular glasses that rested far too low beneath the bridge of his nose. Truth of the matter is that wearing glasses so far down the nose makes one look pretentious or too cheap to purchase modern progressive lenses. In Dr. Wodrowe's case, it was part of his show.

He almost always wore a brown tweed jacket—he had five that looked almost identical—along with drab long sleeved button-down shirts that had unremarkable crosshatch patterns. The professor didn't care for ties and wore them reluctantly when required at convocations and similar formal occasions.

He lived in a 150-year-old Brownstone not far from the main campus where he taught. He liked that he lived in a building that looked as distinguished as he saw himself.

Dr. Wodrowe had few fans and many detractors. He was oblivious to that fact and convinced himself, instead, that it was the other way around.

Among his small group of admirers, there were those who didn't actually like him or even respect him, but rather, had personalities which were similar to his. Other 'friends' had achieved less in life than he had and fed their own bloated egos by association with his tenure and apparent brilliance. The remainder was a small cadre of suck-ups and codependents who thrived on his approval.

His detractors? Everyone else. Counted among them were, chiefly, most of his current and former students, along with many of his colleagues and personal acquaintances. Ex-wives, girlfriends and failed dates had a special status among his growing squad of detractors.

In short, he was not a well-liked individual. Sad, really, when you think about the potential that a single human life has to positively impact so many others. Such a waste of opportunity and endowment.

Dr. Wodrowe's disconnection with others wasn't due to a singular trait; it was more of a combination of things. More about that in a bit.

However, you should know that the professor was blissfully ignorant of his lack of fans and even more unaware of the distasteful chatter about him that had gone on behind his back for decades.

A few months after turning forty-six, the professor decided to take-on a new adventure outside of academia, which eventually led him to believe that he was a successful winemaker. It started with 'making wine' at one of those bottling shops that rapidly ferment bags of pasteurized grape juice concentrate for their customers. Those customers, like the professor, merely bottle and cork the fermented product that store staff actually make for them.

A positive thing about his new 'hobby' was that it gave the professor the winemaking bug; it was, at least, something new and different in his life. That bug continued to pester him until he took the next step and eventually began fermenting and vinifying his own wine at his own home from crates of real California grapes. However, it wouldn't be an exaggeration to say that his wine was—in a word—awful! Regrettably, his attempts resulted in wines that were sour, bitter or fizzy, often imparting unusual, funky bouquets and flavors that didn't belong in any wine.

He was quite generous with his dreadful wine, gifting bottles of it at Christmas to faculty secretaries who helped him far more than he recognized. Of course, his mostly awful wine was a poor substitute for the much preferred and customary fifty-dollar gift cards that his fellow professors gave.

Interestingly, Dr. Wodrowe was as woefully ignorant of what others thought about his homemade wine as he was with what they thought about his teaching style and his likeability as a human being.

It's easy to be unaware of our personal shortcomings when nobody will dare share them with us. Others' reluctance to be honest and critical was due to his terribly thin skin. This was not unlike the thin skin of his favorite wine grape; Pinot Noir. Even when squeezed ever so gently, that grape often breaches and falls apart, leaving the handler disappointed with the mess that's left over. In a similar fashion, Dr. Wodrowe's reaction to criticism or even to a gently challenging question was predictable. He would routinely go on the offensive, lashing out at and ripping apart anyone who dared utter the words. It would always result in a messy and uncomfortable scenario.

That's exactly why nobody had the nerve tell him that his wine's best virtue was that it made decent cooking vinegar. Lacking the proper perspective about his own limitations as a winemaker, at forty-eight years of age, Dr. Wodrowe dove in with both feet and purchased a small working winery. It was a six-acre plot of land that had already been planted with Pinot Noir vines by a previous landowner who had failed miserably at her own attempt to become a successful winemaker.

Whatever made the professor think that *he* could be successful at it where she was not, was anyone's clue. However, people who knew him best presumed that his arrogance was the real reason. Nevertheless, he did purchase the land, which included 4 acres under vine, meaning that he, alone, would be responsible for tending to around 4,000 ten-year-old vines. The property included a pre-fab metal building that housed fermentation and bottling equipment, and a sprawling old stone farmhouse with a large basement that had been converted into a huge wine cellar.

To be honest, the property had everything that a very hard-working and expert grower/winemaker would need to produce, ferment and age award-winning boutique-style Pinot Noir wines. Unfortunately for Dr. Wodrowe, who wanted to operate his winery as a part-time venture, he had neither the time nor the expertise to come anywhere close to seeing the property's potential.

From a financial standpoint, when he was just a young man, he inherited a huge wad of old family money. That made it possible for him to purchase the small winery. He could never have even dreamt of such a thing based solely on his academic salary. Even after purchasing the winery, there was a lot of cash remaining. Unfortunately, that money created a comfortable cushion, rather than the burning fire under his butt that was needed to motivate him into taking his new venture far more seriously.

There was so much money left over, that he could easily have lived a very relaxed and contented life without ever having worked at all. His path as a professor with a doctorate was chosen as a means to feed his voracious ego, because it really wasn't needed to feed his bank account.

Irrespective of his balance sheet, Dr. Wodrowe quickly came to realize how greatly he underestimated the time and effort that his new venture would demand. Even without taking it very seriously, the new venture was taking more and more of his free time; so much, in fact, that rather than returning to his brownstone, he often worked late and slept at the farmhouse overnight. This became such a common practice that more and more of his personal belongings were ending-up at the farmhouse.

He temporarily sublet his brownstone to a fellow professor while he tried to catch-up at the winery. At some point along his journey, Dr. Wodrowe finally came to the conclusion that his new endeavor was demanding far more time than his profession allowed. He therefore took a sabbatical to study viticulture and oenology; topics entirely unrelated to his academic specialty of American History.

During the ensuing year, Dr. Wodrowe never once picked-up a book, took a course or even surfed the web for anything related to grape growing or winemaking. Of course, he knew everything. So, he went about pruning, spraying, harvesting, crushing, fermenting and cellaring his pinot noir, based merely on ideas he had about those very precise and scientific processes.

After his first harvest, he returned to teaching, but reduced his courseload by half to try and accommodate the two bosses in his life; academia and winemaking. He continued to live at the farmhouse and, as the months passed, became increasingly comfortable with the prospect of living out the rest of his existence there and not ever returning to his cherished brownstone.

Something new took root in his brain, not unlike the new vines he had planted on a previously unworked area of his land.

While his first harvest of Pinot Noir began the long process of aging in oak barrels under his new home, Dr. Wodrowe became increasingly excited about bottling and selling cases of his debut offering. Despite having something new in his life—something fresh to look forward to—he continued to be the self-centered son of a bitch that he had always been. Consequently, students and colleagues continued to mutter, "Asshole," under their breath whenever he was around. Some things never change.

However, at some point along the way, as the wine was *trying* to mature, Dr. Wodrowe began to experience a bit of his own maturation. He started identifying with the simple nickname, "Lang." He used the name in his own self-talk and in introductions to those whom he hadn't met before. Astonishingly, he dropped the "Doctor" prefix altogether.

After aging his "elixir" in barrels for a full year, Lang decided it was time to put it on wine store shelves. He spent what seemed to him to be an eternity bottling and labeling hundreds of cases of that first fateful batch. Lang was content with the result, although there was no surprise, because he had been drawing samples from barrels to taste every few weeks during the aging process.

His four acres of grapes produced nearly a thousand cases of wine. To be more precise, Lang had to sterilize, fill, seal and label 11,528 bottles. That is a particularly arduous and lengthy process when you're the only one doing it!

He eventually completed that bottling process just before his fiftieth birthday and celebrated his special milestone the very next day. The entrée for his birthday dinner was a single Filet Mignon wrapped in bacon. He grilled it over charcoal along with a red skinned baked potato. Lang poured a glass for himself from the very first of his labeled bottles. Without a dinner companion to share clinks, he raised a glass to himself and exclaimed out loud, "Happy Birthday Lang, Old Boy!"

In his estimation, the wine was as delicious as his entrée, but he knew that the hard work of marketing and distributing cases of it would prove challenging.

As he blew out the candles on his birthday cake; a cake he ordered for himself to eat by himself, Lang's fiftieth birthday came and went. After wiping the last cake crumb from his dry, cracked lips, it suddenly dawned on him that he was far happier working the vineyard and making wine than he had ever been as a professor. He unexpectedly found that the ego massage he got by playing professor was no longer nearly as satisfying as it had been in the past. Of course, he didn't frame it that way, but that's precisely why his university life became increasingly unfulfilling.

He named his winery "Sweet Creek Estates Winery," a name he figured would create a bucolic image, even though there wasn't a creek or stream within several miles of his property. Since all of his grapes were of the Pinot Noir varietal, he had only one offering to bottle. He named the wine, "Velvet From Heaven," which he thought was quite a cultured tag.

It was awful. Not just the kitsch moniker, but the wine itself. It had never occurred to Lang that the name was so tacky. He also didn't grasp the irony; his sour, thin and funky tasting wine really deserved funky name like that!

Lang's arrogance and bloated ego influenced his assessment of the wine rather than what should have been a job for his tongue and nose. Convinced that he and his wine were the next big thing in the winemaking world, he took to the road for half a year to flog his horrible concoction to independent wine and spirits store owners, supermarket managers and buyers for major wine and spirits chains.

Alas, true change is difficult. Although his character was beginning to improve, people could sense that Lang didn't take well to criticism. Wine buyers—prospective clients—didn't dare reveal their true assessments of his wine.

What he *did* hear was, basically, a litany of lies spun by merchants and buyers who didn't have the guts to put him or his wine down and who wanted him out their doors as quickly as possible. And, seriously, why *would* they have told him the truth? After just one sip of his foul-tasting product, it was clear to all of his prospects that the man had to be delusional to believe that he could actually sell it to anyone! If he was *that* crazy, they wouldn't dare insult him; God knows how he would react! It was that bad.

He believed their lies and excuses…

* * *

"I don't think this has the flavor profile that we're looking for right now. Thanks for the tasting, but we're moving in a different direction at this point."

* * *

"This is fine wine, no doubt about it, but we're overbought on contracts for the next few years. Come back then and we'll give it another taste and see where we're at."

* * *

"Nothing wrong with your wine, Lang, but I'm just not feeling that it offers anything unique or complimentary to what we already offer."

* * *

"Good wine, especially for your first vintage! But we can't take this on, because you can't deliver the minimum quantities that we need in order to make a contract with you. Good luck with the smaller guys – I'm sure they will want to sell your product!"

* * *

For Lang, it made no sense. It was such a good wine; buyers even said so. He couldn't understand why was he was unable to sell any of it. Not even a single case!

Following six months of disappointment, frustration and anger, Lang questioned his decision to buy the winery and was ready to throw in the towel. His last-ditch effort was to sell his wine by the glass at a local annual outdoor food and wine festival. He thought, "Surely, when average people taste my wine, it'll create a buzz. This is exactly what I need! If enough people visit my kiosk, it could be the turning-point I've been looking for!"

Acceptance as a vendor to this event wasn't automatic. Not every restaurant and drink vendor who applied to be part of it was accepted. The stars must have been aligned when Lang was approved. When he called the event hotline to inquire, an inexperienced new organizer picked up the phone. She misheard Lang's winery name and, thinking that it was a far more established—and good—producer, she spontaneously approved him and emailed the paperwork to make it official.

It was at this festival that Lang finally got an earful about his beloved, albeit, shockingly bad wine. Initially, bottles were emptying quickly as a flood of festival patrons queued up to buy a glass of his vino. However, as the afternoon turned to evening and fewer people entered the festival gates, the flood of customers attending his tent dwindled to just a trickle.

Most of the other wineries at the festival were so busy they had to bring in extra staff to keep up with the brisk demand for their offerings. Seeing this all but dashed Lang's remaining hope for a turnaround. After sitting at his table without a single patron for over a half an hour, Lang decided to take a walk. He put up a sign that read, "**Back in 10 Minutes**." Dusk had arrived; it was just before eight in the evening and the sun was beginning to set.

The event was very well attended; the crowd was thick and difficult to navigate. Spirits were high as couples and larger groups ate, drank and socialized. The sound of live music wafted through the warm evening air, mingling with the ambience of happy chatter and profuse laughter. Gentle humid breezes aroused the nose with an exotic and alluring marriage of charcoal smoke, wine, aged cheeses and spicy foods. Despite their range, the aromas complimented one another. It was a memorable and beautiful evening that delighted all of the senses!

As he began to wander the festival grounds, Lang soaked it all in and took note of the mood. He was more accustomed to the stodgy environments and subdued conversations that were so common to academic gatherings. He loved the celebratory atmosphere, but was particularly struck with the fact that so many people were genuinely enjoying themselves. He also realized that he had never before seen so much wine being consumed in one place!

His stroll first brought him to another winery's kiosk that wasn't visible from his own tent. He purchased a glass of their Pinot Noir. Lang studied the label and noticed that the winery's name was simply the owner's name. The name of the wine itself was, plainly, "Pinot Noir," along with the vintage date. For the first time, Lang began to question his own choices for his winery and first wine release.

Swirling the wine in the plastic goblet, Lang then raised it to his nose and was surprised at how alluring the bouquet was. He felt as though he was being seduced. He actually wondered, just for a split second, why his own wine didn't have this effect. Bringing the red wine to his lips, Lang drew the wine into his mouth and was pleasantly surprised by how well the seduction kept its promise.

The wine was far smoother, more full-bodied and more approachable than he expected. The flavor was hard to describe; it was complex and had many layers, although there was no denying that it was delicious.

Still standing under the vendor's tent, Lang decided to strike-up a conversation with the boutique winery's owner. Lang was an unknown entity in the local winemakers' community. He kept a low profile, partly, because of his lack of self-confidence; he didn't see himself as a part of their community. His general lack of interest in other people was the other reason.

Suddenly, Lang found himself wanting to know more.

> ***Whatever took root in his brain over a year earlier was starting to put out new shoots.***

Lang didn't realize it yet, but those new shoots stimulated in him an insatiable desire to get to know other people. Lang's insular little world was about to get much bigger.

"Are you the winemaker?" Lang asked.

"More like winemaker, owner, chief cook and bottle washer, quite literally!"

"I've got to tell you; your Pinot Noir is excellent! My mouth is very happy right now!"

The owner thanked him and was about to return to his duties, but Lang pulled him back into conversation. This was something the former Dr. Wodrowe would *never* have done.

Extending his hand toward the winemaker, Lang said, "My Name is Lang Wodrowe. I'm the owner and winemaker of a little winery in the area called Sweet Creek Estates."

"I'm Drew Donohue. Good to meet you."

After shaking hands, Lang pointed to the right and said, "My tent is around the corner and back that way."

"Lang, you said?"

"Yeah, Lang. Short for Langdon."

"I'm aware of who you are. Glad I finally got to meet you. So, you bought Sheila's winery, huh?"

"Yes. The jury's still out on whether or not that was a good life decision. But I'll be honest, based on the last 6 months of failure trying to get my inaugural wine on store shelves and judging from today's dismal flop, I'm leaning toward the, 'Not such a great decision' perspective."

They were Lang's own words, but he couldn't believe he was being so open, honest and even self-deprecating with a stranger. It was the first time in a very long while that he could remember admitting to failure or poor decision making.

> **The vines that were growing in his head were beginning to flower. They would soon produce fruit.**

Drew's expression became more serious. He asked, "Lang, do you have a few minutes to talk? I have to share something with you and I really feel that if I don't, it would be a terrible disservice to you."

"Yes, yes of course," Lang answered. "I put up a sign at my tent, but I don't think I'll be missing any business anyway."

They walked through Drew's small vendor tent and out to the rear area behind it. The music and ambience were still loud enough to drown-out their conversation, offering privacy.

Drew said, "Lang, I don't know how else to tell you this, but I have to be honest, because I have the feeling that nobody else has been."

Lang looked perplexed. And scared. Deep down, he knew what Drew was about to say.

"Your wine is..." Drew stopped mid-sentence and pursed his lips. He raised his left hand, waving it back and forth, as though he was trying to grab a better word. "Terrible. I...I'm...sorry. I said it. But it had to be said and, and, you need to be aware of it."

Drew expected Lang to appear dejected and disheartened. That didn't happen. Instead, his expression actually lifted a bit, as though a huge burden had been removed.

"You realize you're the first person who's told me that?"

"I suspected. But, Lang, please understand, it's not the end. It's only a first step toward better outcomes."

"Thank you for being honest, Drew. I appreciate it. I'm not just saying that. I...I... ignored what should have been painfully obvious and, well, I attribute that to my own damned arrogance rather than ignorance." Lang threw his hands up and took a breath, adding, "Actually, I've obviously got more than my share of ignorance as well!"

The first of the flowers had just set fruit.

"Listen, we have a pretty close-knit group in this county, us winemakers. Most of us have small properties like your own. There are a few big boys in the mix, but we work *with* each other to support and bring as much success to each other as possible. And, uh, I'd really like for you to join us. I know that the others would share the same warm welcome."

Lang was speechless. He could sense that Drew's invitation was heartfelt and genuine. He never expected such kindheartedness and sincerity from a stranger, let alone a competitor. Lang's veneer was worn down, his pretentiousness all but dissolved. He began to make a connection between his newfound humility and the stranger's kindness.

Lang thought about the offer for a few moments. He initially said nothing. He realized that, if his wine was truly as awful as Drew said—and it obviously *was* that bad—it would likely be difficult for him to fit-in. This group of successful winemakers were so far ahead of him and he was so very far behind. Frankly, Lang was feeling embarrassed.

Drew could sense Lang's humiliation and attempted to assuage his discomfort.

"Listen, I get it. But we've all been there. Do you really think that my first or even my third vintage was good? When I think back, I'm mortified that I actually sold some of my earlier wines, but it's all part of the process. Lang, you just came out of the gate, and from what people around here have been able to gather, you haven't had any help at all, let alone professional assistance."

Unlike the old Lang, he listened—*actually listened*—to what Drew had to say.

Drew continued, "Forget the first wine itself. Think about the experience of growing and vinifying. Have you enjoyed it?"

"Yes. YES! I've discovered something new in my life and I have to admit that I've gotten more personal satisfaction from this little patch of land than I have in my other professional life."

"Word's out that you're also a university professor. Is that true?"

"I'm seriously thinking that it may soon be a former life. People reinvent themselves all the time. Maybe my time to reinvent myself is past due."

The two talked for an hour, after which Drew took Lang on a personal meet and greet, visiting the other wine tents and introducing Lang to the area's fellow winemakers.

Later that evening, when Lang returned to his winery, he sat down and opened a bottle of his own wine. For the very first time, he actually smelled his wine with his nose and tasted it with his tongue. He was flummoxed at how dreadful it was. However, his experience now made sense and he was ready to move beyond his initial stage of failure.

The fruit was growing and would soon mature.

His fellow winemakers left him with a great deal of encouragement in reinforcing that his patch of land was one of the best in the county to grow not only Pinot Noir, but also to introduce other varietals. They also offered help in terms of advice and assistance. With genuine humility and gratitude, Lang accepted their offer to formally join their collective and to attend the monthly meetings.

One of the best things that came out Lang's new membership in the local winemakers' group was an introduction to Lainey Upcott. Lainey was a hotshot winery consultant who had made quite a name for herself transforming failing wineries into stellar success stories in parts of California and Oregon.

Lainey had just completed a three-year contract with one of Lang's neighboring winemakers and was looking for a new challenge. Was it fate? Hard to know, but it seemed like more than just mere coincidence that she would become available and show-up in Lang's life at the precise moment that he had decided to turn-over a new leaf.

The now mature fruit was harvested and the vine sprouted new leaves.

No doubt, this was a new Lang. He had put the old Dr. Wodrowe to rest for good and was, for the first time in his life, really excited about starting on a new path that brought challenge and satisfaction without stroking his ego. Lang had just finished marking finals for his half-load of courses and had tendered his intention to enter early retirement from his professorial post.

His colleagues at the university were dumbfounded when they heard the news. Not so much because he decided to retire far earlier than expected, but rather, because they sensed the new person that Lang had become. For once, they felt connected to him as partners in this thing we call humanity. Lang took the time and displayed the sensitivity to connect individually with each of his close coworkers to let them know about his decision. That, in itself, was something that the old Dr. Wodrowe would never have bothered to do!

During these farewell encounters, Lang actually asked his colleagues questions about themselves and was genuinely interested in what they had to say. He was not only sympathetic about their difficulties, but was genuinely empathetic.

Above all, the one thing that floored everyone who knew Lang was his honesty and openness about his own weaknesses and failures. Hearing him talk about his dreadful first wine, his disastrous sales attempts and his personal concerns about the future of his winery was something no one ever expected.

Over many years, those who knew Lang developed tough callouses in the part of their hearts that prevented them from feeling any sympathy or compassion for him. Sensing Lang's unexpected personal conversion allowed those callouses to soften; for once, Lang's colleagues saw him as a person who was worthy of their support and friendship. Lang's conversion not only benefitted himself, but took root in others to make them better people as well.

Some of the old wood of the vine was replanted in new soil, where it developed roots and generated new life.

With the academic segment of Lang's career fully completed, he was able to focus his effort and attention on rebuilding his brand and on the quality of the wine itself. More notably, on a human level, he was also able to focus on rebuilding his soul; a goal in which he was becoming increasingly successful. Lang's perspective on the gift of life and on his place in the world had expanded vastly, compared to when he first bought the winery.

This occurred so rapidly that he was struck by the swiftness of his personal transformation. He was also embarrassed when he reflected on the person he was and the time that he wasted. It had been a whirlwind of a month since he first met fellow winemaker Drew at the festival!

Lang followed destiny's unexpected invitation and made the decision to offer Lainey Upcott, the wine consultant, a position with his winery. Lainey ignored her many misgivings and became a full-time employee at the newly named, "Lang Wodrowe Estate Winery." She got straight to work educating Lang in even the most fundamental of winemaking concepts. She was astonished at his lack of overall knowledge of wine, especially, considering what he paid for the property and the fact that he had just thrown-in the towel on the only profession he had held for his entire working life.

She negotiated an initial three-year contract that gave Lang the right of first renewal for her services at the completion of that contract. Lainey made a lot of progress through the first year of her employment. During that year, she managed to modernize much of the agricultural, fermentation and bottling equipment, using her experience and contacts to do so in the most effective, yet, economical way. She also acquired new rootstock and oversaw the clearing of two acres of land, upon which the new varietals were then planted.

During this initial year of rebuilding, reshaping and rebranding, Lang and Lainey became close friends. They shared a connection that was far warmer than would be expected in an employer-employee relationship.

The vineyard grew in size and became increasingly productive.

Lainey had a personal policy about keeping work relationships professional. She managed to avoid fraternizing with the winemakers who hired her, beyond what was necessary for business and product success. However, this time was different. Lang was different. She wasn't even aware of it at first, but she increasingly allowed herself to be drawn-into Lang's personality, his thoughts and his dreams.

While tending to various winemaking responsibilities, they would have long and deep conversations about countless topics that had nothing to do with the tasks at hand. Lang felt the connection and did nothing to stop it from growing deeper. His heart was more open than it had been since he was a child and, although he was careful not to verbalize it, he was hopeful that something more would develop between them. He felt the spark and wanted it to ignite a flame.

Lang's newfound emotional maturity was matched by a sense of selflessness and a remarkable concern for Lainey's wellbeing. Although she had never met the old Lang—Dr. Wodrowe—she got an occasional earful about him from others who knew or worked with him during previous times in his life. She appeared not to care much for the "crusty old gossip," as she called it and openly shared *some* of the less hurtful tidbits that she heard with Lang. When she did, Lang was clearly ashamed, but fully admitted to being a jerk in what he called, "a former life."

Others could see that his humility only made Lainey more enamored with Lang. Hours spent together far exceeded contractual hours and, more often than not, the two would dine together at the farmhouse. Lang turned-out to be quite the chef and got much satisfaction from trying-out adventurous new entrées with an employee who had become more like his best friend.

The seasonal agricultural workers just assumed that the two were either married or attached. It was that obvious. Wine consultants rarely spend so many hours at the winery; some split their services simultaneously between different wineries. Lainey was an exclusive and constant fixture at Lang's winery. Lang realized how unusual this was and was quite happy about it.

Lainey decided to release the new winery's first offering, simply named "Pinot Noir," but did so only when she was fully confident that this was the very best wine that could possibly be produced from the terroir (the land), the weather, her own expertise, and her influence in the growing and vinification process. The newer varietals would have to wait until those newly planted vines were mature enough to produce grapes capable of producing respectable wines.

The new vines were pruned and trained in order to produce finer, sweeter, more concentrated fruit in the coming years.

Lang realized just how important this first release was for the new brand. It would be judged with great scrutiny; not just the wine, but the winery itself. Even though a new brand had been created, local and regional winemakers and, more importantly, buyers, knew that it was a re-brand and that Lang was the same owner responsible for the previous dreadful offering. Everything was at stake; the future of the winery and the suitability of Lang's decision to put all of his proverbial eggs into this one basket of wine.

Lainey timed the release to coincide with the annual autumn winetasting event sponsored by the local winemakers' association. This was a huge deal for everyone in that tightknit community. It was *the* evening during which members would parade their latest releases from previous years' vintages to be tasted and judged by all in attendance.

It was not only an important evening of potential celebration, it was also a very daunting and even frightening evening, because of the fickle nature of the tasters and critics who were present. Of course, the event drew participating winemakers, staff and families, but also dangled the carrot of free admission to institutional wine buyers who held the keys needed for a winery to enter the crucial realm of actually selling their wines.

The widely recognized wine writers and critics at the event were, ultimately, a group of make-or-break royalty who could only be handled with the softest of kid gloves. A winemaker's only hope was that the critics' palates would be kind and generous!

Lainey showed-up at Lang's residence a few hours before the winetasting event was to begin. She no longer considered the place to be the "farmhouse" or the "winery house," but rather, Lang's home. She let herself in with her own key and went straight to the spare bedroom. She used the ensuite bathroom to begin doing her makeup and hair. She had a few large bags filled with cosmetics, brushes, hairspray, an evening gown, shoes and everything else she needed.

She lived close enough to have gotten ready before arriving at Lang's, but told him earlier that day, that she wanted to get ready at the winery just before leaving for the event, so that she would be as fresh as possible. Lang was far too smart not to see through her explanation, but kept it to himself anyway.

Lang didn't at all mind her using the extra bedroom and privately wished she would actually use it to sleep over every once in a while...if not in his own bedroom. It's something he never mentioned and, as close as they had become, he tried to keep their relationship professional. Nevertheless, Lang knew how deeply he wanted their relationship to be more than it was; much more. He also sensed Lainey's fondness for him, but had convinced himself that *if* they were to take things to the next level, he would have to wait until fate's timeline was right.

Lang's physical appearance had changed dramatically since buying the winery and retiring from academics. Former colleagues and students would often fail to recognize him during chance meetings while shopping or out at a restaurant. They were surprised to learn his identity when he approached them to say, "Hello."

Of course, he wasn't any taller, but appeared to be so. Perhaps it was due to the fact that he was no longer walking around with a gloomy slouch. He was far more fit, having taken on a great deal of physical work in the vineyards. He killed that awful rodent of a comb-over on his head, and trimmed his goatee and mustache so it was presentable. He had finally learned to smile and his hardness of expression had been replaced by one of warmth and approachability. Lang somehow took ten years off his old self. Hiding beneath that mountain of physical and emotional baggage was a very attractive man, and he was finally revealed.

Lainey called out to Lang from the guest room to help with her gown and necklace. Lang, who had just put on a new shirt and necktie, knocked on the door and entered. Lainey was taken aback at how handsome he looked and, with a mildly mischievous smile, said, "Hey, stranger, you clean-up nice!"

Lang could hardly speak. He was in awe of Lainey's beauty. He knew she was beautiful, but he was mesmerized seeing her dressed-up, with her hair and makeup done. He paused, took both of her hands into his, looked deeply into her eyes and said, "My God. I'm speechless. You are truly beautiful."

Neither Lang nor Lainey wanted to let go of each other's hands. They paused long enough for the warmth and tingle of each other's touch to create a desire that was impossible to ignore. Lainey blushed and, stumbling over her own words, finally managed to ask Lang to help her with the zipper on the back of her dress and to close the clasp on her necklace. Her dress was simple but elegant; a form-fitting black, sleeveless, mid-length dress that emphasized her figure. Her petite frame had a well-toned and softly feminine physique. For a necklace, she wore a sophisticated, braided gold chain with a dazzling pendant—a huge pear-shaped, blue-purple tanzanite stone surrounded by inlaid baguettes of jade.

Lainey brought along a very expensive bottle of Napa Cabernet with which to share an early toast before they left for the big evening. She had spent the last year and a half introducing Lang to a wide variety of wines—many exemplary and some seriously lacking—to expand his palate and perspective. Tonight's wine was far more special than a mere tasting example.

About a half hour remained until their ride would arrive. Lang and Lainey went to the rustic kitchen, where she opened and poured the wine. She raised her glass and said, "Here's to whatever tonight brings. I really hope we have a good response to our first wine, but let's humbly accept what shall be."

Lang was about to jump-in and say something about their relationship before they toasted, but Lainey continued.

"More important, though, than tonight's event, may our relationship continue to be the most precious part of this venture."

God blessed the vineyard and it began to produce superior new fruit with abundance.

Lang was stunned. Did she just say that? It was what he wanted to say, but he was afraid of the gamble. He clinked his glass with hers and, after having a sip, they both put down their glasses and embraced. Where was this going? Did she want more than friendship? Was she ready?

So many unanswered questions. He wanted to show Lainey how much he was on the same page with her, but without pushing harder than her comfort level. Above all, he didn't want to scare her away. He wondered if it was possible that she was more focused on mere friendship? Then again, he thought, "If she's ready to be more than just friends, then what?"

He didn't want to blow the opportunity and leave her out in the cold, feeling as though her advance was unreciprocated. Lang suddenly had a vision of himself standing on the ledge of a tall building, his arms spread apart, letting the wind take him where he was destined to go.

"Lainey, I have to share something with you. You've become far more than just an employee to me; I think you already know that. You've been with the winery for over a year now, but...the months have flown by and I...well, I can't think of anyone else I'd rather have shared that time with."

Lainey's eyes began to tear-up and her lower lip started to quiver.

"I find myself thinking about you all of the time," Laing continued, "and I miss you when you're not here." His voice was trembling. He paused, then took a huge leap of faith, saying, "I think I'm fa..."

DING-DONG

The doorbell rang. The driver hadn't received a response to his texts, so he came to the door to let Lang and Lanie know he was waiting.

Lang stopped his eloquent soliloquy in mid-sentence and wondered whether he was either saved by the bell or if it interrupted something he should have kept saying. He left it to fate and they quickly got in the car.

It was a glitzy affair, to be sure. Live jazz echoed gently off the distant hills as guests milled about the outdoor pavilion. Waitstaff in crisply pressed white and black uniforms roamed the venue with platters of upscale hors d'oeuvres, their glittery red bowties shining like beacons. Guests wore a variety of lovely gowns, and handsome suits and tuxedos. Many of the women and some of the men appeared to be vying for either status or attention with their showy jewelry. The dinner proved to be equally fancy, with six delicious courses, each one more exceptional than the last.

Other than the wine critics and buyers, the majority of guests were somehow connected to one of thirty different wineries that were being featured at the event.

To say this annual tasting event was a success for Lang and Lainey would be an understatement. From the moment they arrived, they were treated with respect and honor.

Somehow, word had gotten out in advance of the tastings; likely leaked by an official who, as part of his remuneration for planning the event, received a couple of bottles of each wine under review that evening. Everybody knew that this was common practice, but in the past, officials had been far more discreet about their personal private tastings in the lead-up to the big night. Regardless, the gossip was definitely in favor of Lang and Lainey's Pinot Noir, and the couple had no intention of complaining about any breach of protocol!

Dinner was simply lavish. Each course included two different, perfectly matched wines. Everything was served at well-timed intervals; service was like a rehearsed ballet. Unlike regular blind wine tastings which do not feature food, there was no cuspidor to be found on any table. It would have been both disgusting and unsanitary for any guest to be spitting their wine into containers while others were trying to enjoy their fine food.

Lang Wodrowe Estate Winery's Pinot Noir was the second wine of the evening, paired with a Charcuterie Board that was overflowing with sweet dark figs, a variety of sharp old cheeses, mandarin segments, grapes (of course), smoked dry sausages, pickled artichokes and Sicilian style Mission olives from California. A board of fresh baked mini bread loaves was flanked by soft herbed butters, extra-old balsamic vinegars and extra virgin single estate olive oil.

The pairing was simply divine. The wine itself was already proving to be something that could easily stand up to even the far more expensive and storied wines that were being featured that evening. Lang and Lainey couldn't ignore the happy banter bouncing around the pavilion as their wine was poured and tasted from one table to the next.

As the evening came to an end, the couple grew weary of the salvo of congratulatory greetings. Even many of the world-renowned wine critics in attendance—who are known to keep their assessments private until publication—were effusive in their praise.

When Lang and Lainey's ride returned to the winery, the driver asked if she would be completing the trip to her home as originally arranged. She looked at Lang, almost as if for approval. Lang quickly suggested that it would be a terrible waste of fuel to continue on, since her other clothes were already at his home.

Whether they were a bit tipsy from all of the wine or from the success of the evening didn't matter. They didn't have to talk about it or question each other's expectations. They had just savored a taste of the future and couldn't resist inviting it to become the present.

Lainey went to the guest bedroom to change. She returned to the study, wearing a comfortable nightshirt and loosely-fitting light cotton shorts. Lang was already waiting for her. He had changed into a fresh pair of track pants and an old 1970s rock band

T-shirt that clung to his torso, revealing his now trim and muscular chest.

He had arranged the bottle of Napa Cabernet and glasses on the coffee table; the same wine they started to toast with before leaving for the event. Referring to Lang's interrupted toast just before their ride arrived, Lainey asked, "So, you were saying?"

Lang smiled softly and reached out to grasp Lainey's hand. They sat silently, eyes fixed together, for what seemed like a beautiful eternity. At precisely the perfect moment, Lang reached out with his other hand and caressed the back of Lainey's head and the left side of her face. He brought his head closer to hers. They could no longer ignore the feelings building within, and kissed deeply.

As night turned to morning, the couple continued to explore each other's bodies and made passionate love. Lang professed his true feelings for Lainey and she reciprocated.

Lainey's contract was soon replaced by a contract of marriage; a marriage that would be Lang's last and Lainey's only. They became full partners in the winery, which enjoyed decades of success. Their love, friendship and respect for one another only grew as the years went by. This was well-known throughout their community, as was their generosity in sharing their monetary success with those in need.

Different parts of the vineyard shall become harmonious; the winemakers shall generously share their abundant yield.

Decades passed and Lainey wanted to throw a huge 75th birthday party to celebrate Lang's life and success. He was initially reluctant to accept the offer of a party; this was partly because he didn't feel worthy of all of the adulation and partly because he would rather that the party honor Lainey. He believed that she was far more deserving of such a celebration.

Lang eventually accepted Lainey's offer to have the party, which led him to reflect on his journey in life and to take stock of his accomplishments. On the evening of the party, Lang became flooded with emotion. He couldn't help but remember the self-centered, solitary man that he had been and the judgmental, selfish existence that defined who he was for over half of his life.

Lang toasted his guests and then expressed his profuse gratitude for all that Lainey had done for him, truly enabling him to live a life that was legitimately productive and full of love. He said that, because of her, he was able to yield a far greater harvest in life than had he stayed on his previous lonely, selfish and arrogant course in life.

He then professed his true love for Lainey, and the crowd erupted in cheers and clinking glasses.

For her own part, Lainey expressed her own love for him, exclaiming, "You know, years ago you confided to me that, way back when you were teaching, you thought of yourself as a "distinguished gentleman". You said you were ashamed of that notion, because it was a pompous and narcissistic idea."

The guests were silent, waiting anxiously to hear what she would say next. She paused and added, "Lang, it's not a pompous or narcissistic idea when it's true. I have to tell you that you *are* truly one of the most distinguished gentlemen I have ever met. You have earned that designation and I am so fortunate that you are *my* distinguished gentleman!"

The couple was blessed with many more years of good health and love. They continued to nurture their shared passion for making excellent wine and always celebrated the gift of each other.

Stephen J. Kristof

A new root emerged that continued to grow and sustain abundance far beyond the scope of mere mortals.

ABOUT THE AUTHOR

STEPHEN KRISTOF is an author of both fiction and non-fiction books, who has enjoyed an extensive and exciting career.

His keen insights into people and situations developed during his 35 years in roles spanning media, education, management, advertising, professional consulting and creative arts. His academic background includes university degrees in Media Communications and Teacher Education, along with additional certifications and studies at the Graduate level.

As an author, his vivid imagination comes to life with fascinating stories, richly-developed characters and captivating scenarios. Whether it's romance, adventure, fantasy, mystery, crime, passion, paranormal or feel-good nostalgia, Stephen loves spinning tales that keep his readers engaged and wanting more!

When he's not writing, he loves creative photography, gardening, and celebrating life with family and friends. He also has an unquenchable appetite for sandy beaches and warm, salty breezes!

 StephenKristof.com

 facebook.com/StephenKristofAuthor

 youtube.com/@stephen-kristof-author

Next Book Volume 2:

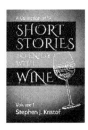  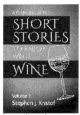

Coming in 2024

Manufactured by Amazon.ca
Bolton, ON